P9-BBU-240

Mobilizing Technology for World Development

Edited by Jairam Ramesh and Charles Weiss

Published for the
International Institute for Environment and Development
and the Overseas Development Council

PRAEGER

PRAEGER SPECIAL STUDIES • PRAEGER SCIENTIFIC

The views expressed in this publication are those of the authors and do not necessarily represent those of the International Institute for Environment and Development or the Overseas Development Council, or of their directors, officers, or staff.

Domestic Copublications

Published in 1979 by Praeger Publishers
A Division of Holt, Rinehart and Winston/CBS, Inc.
383 Madison Avenue, New York, New York 10017 U.S.A.

© 1979 by the Overseas Development Council
All rights reserved

9 056 987654321
Library of Congress Card Catalog No.: 79-53493
Printed in the United States of America

Mobilizing Technology for World Development

Acknowledgments

The International Institute for Environment and Development gratefully acknowledges the financial assistance provided for convening the Jamaica Symposium and for preparing this publication by the World Bank, the International Development Research Centre of Canada, Appropriate Technology International, the Norwegian Ministry of Foreign Affairs, the Danish Ministry of Foreign Affairs, and the Australian Development Assistance Bureau.

The publication of this volume in time for the August 1979 United Nations Conference on Science and Technology for Development was made possible by the Overseas Development Council and several individuals to whom the IIED and the editors wish to extend special thanks. Valeriana Kallab of the Overseas Development Council arranged IIED's and ODC's joint publication venture with Praeger Publishers and organized the publication phase of the project. Phillip Sawicki and Virpi Kairinen edited and prepared the manuscript for publication. The cover, format, and composition of the book were designed by Paddy McLaughlin of Designing Women Advertising, and executed by her in collaboration with Scott Photographics, Inc.

The IIED also wishes to thank the publishers and organizations cited in the credits appearing in individual chapters for granting the authors permission to use material which they wished to excerpt and revise from their earlier presentations on the issues addressed in this volume.

Contents

As the 1980s begin, one fact about our world economy is coming to be more and more widely recognized. It is not working really well for anybody. Few developed nations have overcome the combination of high inflation and high unemployment which, touched off by a general boom running into the oil and grain price explosions of the early 1970s, has been carried grimly on by the strength of internal pressure groups — conglomerates, unions — and by the overlap of competitive manufacturing capacity in sluggish world markets. The poorest communities have been the worst hit by rising fuel prices and by low economic activity among the rich. Newly industrialized economies, with their exuberant "export-led growth" of the 1960s, find overseas markets no longer growing to match what they have to offer. Many also carry an alarming load of debt. Even the oil states have experienced gluts and shortages and cannot avoid all the consequences of "stagflation" among their rich trading partners.

Behind all these separate dislocations lies a wider risk which, if not sure, is at least a possibility. Have the first hundred years or so of industrialism creamed off so much of the world's unrenewable resources (while launching an unprecedented acceleration of population growth) that the results — irreversible inflation, inadequate markets, increasing trends toward protectionism, and a general breakdown of economic stability — may now lie fatefully and unavoidably ahead? At the end of the 19th century and again in the 1930s, years of instability, increasing competition, and protective national reactions thrust the world on to the ultimate disaster: general war. Is this the history we have failed to learn and are destined to repeat?

The short answer is, of course, that nations are not the necessary victims of ineluctable catastrophe. World conditions in 1946 were in complete disruption after five years of war. It would have been easy indeed to forecast continuing and unavoidable disaster. But in a unique act of statesmanship, the Americans launched the Marshall Plan — giving away for half a decade 2 per cent of their gross national product each year to restore the economies of both allies and enemies

Foreword
Barbara Ward

—and in doing so laid the basis for their own prosperity and for the twenty-five years of world economic expansion which followed. The essence of the difference between historical inevitability leading to collapse and historical decision leading to success was that the United States government had the wisdom to see that *mutual* interests were involved in restoring the world economic system and that not only generosity but an enlightened view of national purpose and survival demanded a positive response.

There is thus vital historical relevance and urgency in the questions whether such common interests can be perceived today on the wider scale of a vastly expanded world economy and whether the rich countries—all of them wealthier on a per capita basis than the United States in 1947 — have the combination of vision and enlightened self-interest to perceive these interests, and to take the kind of action that will at once hold steady and expand their own economies, restore dynamic markets for the middle-income countries, and lay the foundations of sustained — and sustainable — growth among the billion people who have today barely entered the world market at all and live on its desperate fringes in unemployment, illiteracy, and hunger.

It is easy enough to draw a pessimistic conclusion. For over half a decade, the rich and the poor nations have been engaged in a dialogue —the so-called North-South dialogue—to discover whether common interests, mutual needs, and a convergence of policies can be discerned or whether confrontation, disillusion, and deepening hostility lie ahead. The choice between 1931 and 1947 has not been taken yet, but the dragging on of the discussions about that choice seems, as year follows year, to point increasingly to the possibility of breakdown. But before one opts, in despondency and foreboding, for a disastrous outcome, some factors must be given a new weight on the other side.

The first is, quite simply, the disarray of the rich. If all were going well for them while half of humanity confronted deepening trouble, one would unhappily have to admit that their interest might not be much aroused. But the very uneasiness which tends to protective and shortsighted action can also be the root of deeper questioning and a readiness to consider new possibilities. To give only the most obvious example, the growth of competitive manufacturing capacity both among the rich and among such newly industrialized states as Brazil and South Korea demands a corresponding widening of the world's markets. This, in turn, is possible only if the millions now excluded by total poverty are drawn into the system by becoming productive themselves. Only thus can they emerge as new consumers. It follows that a sustained strategy by the rich nations—over, say, two decades—to double the income of the poorest, to enlarge the market for basic needs, such as clothing, textiles, fuel, and foodstuffs, and to keep this newly expanding system open to all competitive producers would serve a double purpose. Obviously it would meet elementary standards of justice and stability. Who can foresee future social peace in a world where, to quote the old and familiar but unchanging figures, 80 per cent of the wealth, 90 per cent of the industry, and nearly 100 per cent of all research capacities are controlled by a mere quarter of the population? But it would also serve direct material interests. To name only the most obvious, it would ease protective strains among the rich by widening the world market. It would bring down unemployment as new demand expanded and also stand a chance of lessening inflation as cheaper goods became available in a number of consumer sectors.

This is not "pollyanna" optimism. It is what happened after 1947. It is even what happened between 1963 and 1973, when, according to the latest figures published by GATT, world output of manufactures doubled while trade in them trebled. Between industrialized countries, the growth was fivefold. Repeat the essential preliminary—the creation of fresh capacity where, at present, poverty imposes non-consumption—and a similar surge of growth could recur. It would take longer, but the direction is not in doubt. After all, even today, both the United States and the European Economic Community depend upon Third World markets to absorb over 30 per cent of their manufactured exports. To overlook or underplay mutuality of interest here requires a really formidable degree of dedicated ignorance.

Ah, say the pessimists at this point, but when you talk in this complacent jargon of "new growth," you forget the second range of constraints: the growing shortage of materials, shrinking oil supplies just as minerals that require more energy for transformation have to replace higher grade ores, and fears for basic food supplies as soil and forests — and hence reliable water — all come under pressure. The "Marshall" solution of restimulating growth by massive investment belongs to the days of oil at a dollar a barrel. A worldwide expansion of manufacturing capacity and higher consumer standards, even if it did — as in the North — help to stabilize population, would still be large enough to spell a not-too-distant exhaustion of planetary supplies.

Yet this risk, too, need not point to inevitable confrontation. On the contrary, the very risk has within it wholly new concepts and possibilities of planetary cooperation. It is, after all, only in the 1970s that nations have even begun to realize the extent of their inescapable biospheric interdependence. Northern pesticides turning up in Antarctic penguins, fish catches which exhaust whole species, forest-felling that imperils climate, pressure on farmland which irreversibly erodes the soil, chemical emissions that take acid rain and carcinogens across all our petty political boundaries drawn over indivisible continents and oceans — these are the new facts of humanity's imperilled environment; and since they are rooted in sheer, brute physical fact, they cannot be evaded or shrugged off. Once again, the realization of *mutual* interests is not simply a philosopher's dream. It is beginning to look like a realist's necessity.

And fortunately for our future hopes, this necessity already includes a growing, practical, technological content. The big reserves for rising food production lie in the Third World, where few nations have reached the high and stable yields of a Japan or a Korea. The kind of crisis which in 1973/74 tripled world food prices—for rich and poor alike — can be avoided given a sustained strategy to bring under-cultivated lands up to the best and safest standards of cultivation. Or take energy: again, not only are most of the undiscovered and undeveloped oil reserves in the Third World but, as the Brazilian experiment in adding alcohol to gasoline has shown, the abundance of vegetable growth in the damp tropics could create large, renewable alcohol reserves to lengthen and finally replace dependence upon dwindling petroleum.

And this energy substitution can be carried on jointly and constructively by North and South for a further reason. Within a couple of decades, research and development are likely to have covered the cost and storage problems of solar cells, which may become one of the bases of safe and renewable energy for modernization in the South and for the creation there of new and expanding manufactures and markets. The vast tropical sunbelt may suddenly wake up to new "comparative advantage."

Here, too, the opportunities are only beginning to leave the drawing boards. But many of the materials used now in Northern industry—in particular, feedstocks derived from petroleum and other chemical sources—can be replaced by materials from quick-growing trees and plants, scientifically farmed to avoid any soil depletion, transformed into basic industrial inputs, and then used both for local manufacture and for export. The advances possible in the rubber industry are described later. But sugar, cassava, sisal, pine, eucalyptus—the list is endless — can become the basis of industrial supplies which are not only renewable but carry none of the health hazards that seem to lurk in too many of industry's carbon-chlorine compounds. By joint efforts in this whole area, with greater Third World research and the building up of the sunbelt's skills and capabilities, South and North together could come nearer to the vision of safe and sustainable growth. To give one not too fanciful possibility, if Europe's sugar-beet farmers were providing the alcohol to be substituted increasingly for petroleum — the "gasohol" breakthrough — and if cane sugar were grown and

processed where climate and soil and humidity create prime productivity—it would be difficult indeed to decide whether North or South
would have done better out of the switch. The chances are that *both*
would gain — and have a better environment thrown in for good
measure.

In short, the potential gains for both rich and poor countries so
clearly implicit in a new, joint, far-reaching and sophisticated program for world research, investment, management, and expansion of
renewable supplies and mutual trade make up the fundamental argument for moving the North-South dialogue out of its present stage
of uneasy confrontation. That such a mood should exist is historically
inevitable. You cannot undo four hundred years of colonial experience in a couple of decades. You cannot unconcernedly concentrate
all but 7 per cent of the world's industry in the already developed
lands. You cannot dispel protectionist fears without providing alternatives for markets and employment. Above all, you cannot leave the
majority of mankind on the margins of indigence and despair and
expect "a calm world and a long peace." But surely the hopeful point
about deliberations such as those of the Jamaica Symposium is the
degree to which, after the complacency of the 1960s and the confu-
sions of the 1970s, the signs are beginning to appear that in both North
and South, mutual interests are recognized, common goals are conceivable, and the notion of a shared responsibility can rouse a positive
and rational response.

If this proves to be the trend of the 1980s, our planet can hope to
survive and prosper. The agreements outlined in the pages that follow
are remarkable not simply because they do recognize a possible trend
toward the realization of mutual interest. They also show what diversity of background and breadth of interest in both North and South—
from high officials in multinational firms to ministers in radical
governments — can be mobilized behind that recognition. Our divisions are not rooted in inescapable material limitations or ineluctable
historical destiny. They are the remnants of an outdated age. If we
learn in time that wisdom and interest can be partners, we may see
these divisions overtaken by the emerging facts of shared interest and
a creative human future.

Mobilizing Technology for World Development

Three decades of international discussion of the role of technology and science in the economic development of the world's underdeveloped countries have given rise to an atmosphere of confrontation between sharply polarized views. Some of these conflicts can be broadly categorized as being between:

(a) Advocates of policies designed to master the advanced technologies of modern industrial states and proponents of policies directed at meeting the basic needs of the poor;

(b) Advocates of policies that call for national self-reliance, and proponents of policies based on greater integration of developing countries into the world economic system;

(c) Those who perceive the current emphasis of bilateral and multilateral assistance agencies on "appropriate technology" as a diversion from the goals of building political and economic strength, and those who see "appropriate technology" as the basis of international cooperation;

(d) Advocates of a laisser-faire, or pragmatic, approach to transnational enterprises (TNEs), and proponents of greater regulation of TNE behavior.

In an attempt to reconcile these seemingly disparate points of view, the International Institute for Environment and Development (IIED) convened the Symposium on "Mobilizing Technology for Development" in Ocho Rios, Jamaica, January 7-11, 1979. The main objective of the Symposium was to seek common ground between the developed and the developing countries that would permit mutually beneficial technological cooperation.

This introductory chapter discusses in detail the background of the Jamaica Symposium. Specifically, it argues that there are a great many long-term objectives which are shared by the developing and the developed countries. To attain these objectives, it is in the long-term common interest that the world technological system meet the needs of developing countries and that developing countries learn to mobilize and master technology, whatever its source. The chapter

Introduction: A New Approach to the North-South Technological Agenda

Charles Weiss, Jr., and Jairam Ramesh

suggests additional elements of the North-South technological agenda that deserve a place in the discussions on technology transfer now taking place in the United Nations Conference on Trade and Development (UNCTAD) and other forums.

The Narrow Focus of Past Debate on Technology

Almost all the North-South issues — food, energy, natural resources, geographical distribution of industrial capacity, to name a few — have critical technological elements that should be at the center of the international debate on technology. This debate, however, has for some time concentrated on narrower issues: greater regulation and control over transnational corporations (e.g., through a Code of Conduct), terms of trade in technology more favorable to the developing countries, reform of the patent system, and greater expenditures by the industrialized countries for research and development activities on problems specific to the developing countries (often expressed as a target percentage of their total research and development budget).

These issues are important, but as an agenda for action they are deficient on three counts. First, they do not encourage nations to seek out areas where North-South cooperation in mobilizing technology could further common long-term goals, such as the reduction of poverty, stable trade in raw materials, and greater use of renewable sources of energy.

Second, they do not adequately take into account the complex interplay between national and international actors in mobilizing and applying technology to broader development goals. The process is not simply a matter of technology transfer, on the one hand, or the development of indigenous capability, on the other. It is affected by the objectives, attitudes, policies, capabilities, and practices of a plethora of institutions in both the developed and the developing countries — including finance ministries, banks, tariff authorities, and tax agencies — for whom technological development is not a high-priority objective.

9

Third, these issues relate chiefly to the sophisticated technological needs of modern industry rather than to the more elementary needs of the masses of poor urban inhabitants, landless laborers, and small farmers, whose emphasis may have to be on upgrading simple or traditional technologies. A number of developing countries have developed integrated national policies to build local technological capability in industrial sectors which they deem critical to their development — e.g. steel, aircraft, petro-chemicals, electronics, and energy. These policies define sectoral goals from which are derived approaches to the mobilization and mastery of technology, as well as approaches to the scientific and technological research needed to keep that technology up to date. In contrast, few developing countries have a development strategy which attacks poverty directly and mobilizes technology capable of providing for the needs of poor people with available resources and in a manner suitable to local conditions.

The introduction of high-yielding varieties of wheat and rice into the nations of south Asia has shown clearly that the application of science and technology to agriculture often has ramifications that extend far beyond technology policy to issues not usually considered in discussions of the subject at the national, let alone the international, level. For example, it often requires substantial reforms in land tenure, and in the policies and practices of financial institutions and those rendering other essential services, such as water, education, health, and energy. The use of science and technology also compels attention to needs of the so-called "informal sector," with which formal technological institutions generally have little contact. Moreover, the people affected by development must themselves be involved in critical decisions affecting their welfare, a fact which may necessitate important changes in patterns of decisionmaking.

Interdependence and the Nation-State

A deeper problem in the North-South debate on technology arises from the fact that both traditional and emerging interest alignments are between and among nation-states, which are accepted as the only genuinely concerned or efficient units. Common interest groups that transcend national frontiers have rarely been mobilized to increase the bargaining power of the developing countries. As Paul Streeten observes, "multinational and transnational producing firms and consumer associations are important advocates and pressure groups of better market access in the industrial countries."[1] Although they are political realities, national governments sometimes hinder progress by importing technology which is unsuitable or by applying technology where it is far removed from its proper localized context. Perhaps the most serious limitation of current international discussions of technology is the absence of a long-term perspective. Because technological issues normally have a lifespan which is longer than the lifetime of governments, most governments tend to focus not on the underlying issues but on the need to "score points" for domestic political purposes or diplomatic ends.

Developed countries have reacted to global technology issues by expressing concern over the prospect of losing jobs and stressing the need to acknowledge and take advantage of the inescapably interdependent nature of the world economy. They have professed their inability and in many cases their unwillingness to interfere with the operations of private business enterprises, while calling for global cooperation.

In the case of technology, too, interdependence implies both conflict and cooperation — both self-reliance and willingness to accept resources from abroad. The step from acceptance of interdependence to the institution of measures to further international cooperation is a big one; interdependence does not always imply that cooperation will be of mutual benefit, and the dynamics of international diplomacy lead to efforts to "grease the squeaky wheel"—to deal with areas of present conflict rather than areas of potential cooperation. The potential benefits of global cooperation in the solution of shared problems and the management of global resources are too numerous and important to be lost because of confrontations over other issues.

Moreover, the industries whose production has shifted to the developing countries are often technological laggards in the present industrialized world. It is reasonable to believe that these industries can become technological leaders, first by mastering the technology they imported to establish production, then by making improvements in the technology and maintaining the technological edge thus achieved. In fact, important advances in steelmaking and mineral processing have originated in developing countries, and "world premiere" pilot demonstrations of new processes for the manufacture of cement and high-protein cottonseed meal are taking place in developing countries with the full participation of local technologists. Individual developing countries have become technological leaders in aquaculture, arid zone agriculture, and such "software" areas as very low-cost urban housing and urban traffic control.

The international debate on the technological aspects of development has been both furthered and hindered by such terms as "appropriate technology" and "basic needs." These terms are now a rallying cry for critics of the traditional development strategy, which involves the use of technology to build a modern industrial sector in the developing countries.

The international response to this criticism of the traditional development strategy is made difficult by the fact that poverty—despite its seriousness—is an extraordinarily awkward and sensitive subject. No country is eager to air its most distressing social problems or to embarrass its friends by forcing them to do so.

Moreover, developing countries differ among themselves over whether the needs of poor people are best addressed by direct action or by taking steps to enable them to benefit from economic growth and modernization. Some suspect that an emphasis on simple technology is a device to deny the developing countries the latest and best technology. Our understanding of technology's role in development is incomplete enough to allow ample room for honest disagreement.

Preconceptions concerning the suitability of broad classes of technology — "advanced," "intermediate," "traditional," "indigenous," or "imported" — have blurred the vision of decisionmakers seeking the best technological approach to a particular situation and have often prevented the use of technology which was well-suited to a particular objective. In many parts of the world, regulations and institutions make it difficult for traditional technologies to survive, even when they result in socially needed products and provide productive employment. In other cases, unrealistically high standards (e.g., for roads, housing, or public services) have resulted in expenditures well in excess of those needed to satisfy real needs in both developed and developing countries.

Another source of inappropriate technology is the universal human tendency to treat scarce resources as "free goods." Pricing policies and institutional practices in both the developed and the developing countries have led to the wasteful use of resources which are in limited supply, locally or globally. In developed countries this tendency is most dramatically displayed in the profligate use of energy; in the developing countries, on the other hand, it is capital that is too often spent as if it were plentiful instead of scarce. Both developed and developing countries underprice and hence fail to make careful use of irrigation water, urban street space, and other limited resources. In both developed and developing countries, neglect of all the costs of environmental degradation has led to the use of technology which causes avoidable pollution and other environmental harm.

The long-term consequences of such policies can be observed in both developed and developing countries and extend to almost every phase of life—urban sprawl and traffic congestion, inefficient use of energy and water, air and water pollution and other forms of environmental degradation, unnecessary unemployment due to failure to consider labor-intensive alternatives, and unnecessarily elaborate and expensive projects. In this sense, "appropriate technology" is a worldwide problem, not one peculiar to the developing or the developed countries.

The True Meaning of Self-Reliance

There is no question that, by any measure, nearly all of the technological capacity of the world is located in the developed countries. They have a vast preponderance of the world's technically qualified manpower, research and development facilities, patents and commercially licensable technologies, design and manufacturing capacity, organized engineering and management capability, universities, information industries, and computers. As a consequence, technology is, by and large, developed in the developed countries, predominantly with their immediate needs in mind. This technology is subsequently transferred intact to the developing countries, for the most part through commercial or government assistance (aid) channels.

Critics of this system have argued that the first task of the developing countries is to achieve technological self-reliance—in essence, to become masters in their own houses, capable of technological decisionmaking and mastery. Only in this way, they contend, can a technology evolve which is suited to local conditions and subject to local control.

While self-reliance is an important development objective, two caveats must be kept in mind. First, the objective of the developing countries is not—or in any case should not be—to acquire or generate technology for its own sake, but rather to use it to reach development objectives: to modernize, to grow, to meet social needs. For this reason, the focus should not be on indigenous technological capacity per se but on the pragmatic mobilization of all available technological resources to meet the needs of the user: the farmer, the processor of an agricultural commodity, the entrepreneur, the public works department, the consumer, the schoolchild, the sick person.

The central technological problem facing the developing countries is that locally suitable technology backed by a system of inputs, technical services, engineering, and research is not available at the point of use, and is not mastered and implemented by (or for the benefit of) the ultimate user. Few developing countries have effective research, extension, or technical assistance services. The great majority of developing-country farmers and entrepreneurs still lack the education, technological information, and financial resources to use non-traditional technology, or even to improve traditional technology to meet new needs and integrate it into a more modern system. Technologically sophisticated suppliers of credit, information, raw materials, and machinery are available only to larger and more sophisticated farmers and entrepreneurs. Even these have access primarily to technology which originates abroad, which was developed with other people's needs in mind, and which may not be adaptable to their particular requirements.

Secondly, self-reliance in and of itself does not guarantee that technology will contribute to the solution of the massive social and economic problems facing the developing countries. Agencies in the developing countries which concern themselves with the problems of the poor are too often accorded low political priority, and hence are underfunded, unmotivated, and poorly managed. They are often incapable of choosing or managing available technology and are frequently unreceptive to innovation.

Ultimately, however, each country must choose, through its own political processes, the objectives that it wishes to achieve through the application of science and technology. Different countries may desire a different balance between such worthwhile objectives as the development of advanced industrial capabilities and the achievement of social objectives. There is no necessary contradiction between these objectives. Depending on local circumstances, modernization may mean subways or bicycles, skyscrapers or low-cost shelters, mechanized plantations or small farms, hospitals for cardiac surgery or clinics for preventive health care, steel mills or cottage industries.

"Modern" and "traditional" technologies do and should exist side by side, complementing and supporting each other in different proportions, depending on local circumstances.

Technology in Relation to Broader Issues

A first step toward a more fruitful discussion of international policy issues concerning technology is to relate technological issues to the broader issues confronting the developed and the developing countries. This should make it easier to determine which issues are amenable to agreement and to refine the debate on those issues on which disagreements are more fundamental. It might also encourage nations to seek out areas where cooperation between North and South could help to mobilize technology to further long-term goals held in common, such as reducing poverty, hunger, disease, and ignorance in all countries; the achievement of expanding yet stable world trade in food and raw materials; the generation of productive and fulfilling employment for all who seek it; the use of non-renewable energy resources in a manner consistent with the principles of conservation; the application of non-conventional energy sources, especially in areas remote from power grids; maximum use (appropriate to the local situation) of sources of energy which neither carry with them the implicit threat of terrorism and weapons proliferation nor are available primarily from one part of the world; the reduction of the population growth rate to a point consistent with man's ability to provide resources adequate to assure a minimum standard of living for all; the rational management of global resources (the oceans, space, weather, and the radio-frequency spectrum); and the maintenance of global and local ecological sustainability — i.e., assuring that no unilateral actions harm the earth's complex but fragile ecosystem.

None of these goals can be reached by a "technological fix." Still, in areas where there is broad agreement in principle but practical political difficulty in implementing agreement in the short term, technology may provide a feasible, politically attractive approach to long-term cooperation. Such cooperation need not take the form of research. In most areas, the existing supply of knowledge is great enough for its application to begin today, even in the expectation that there will be better information tomorrow. In these areas, it is in the interests of both the developed and the developing countries for the developing countries to build the capacity to: define their own needs, plan and analyze alternative approaches, formulate and implement policies and projects, mobilize technology from any available source in order to reach their goals and set in motion the processes of evaluation of past experience, research and training, and education and institutional development so that future needs will be foreseen and met. This is the true meaning of self-reliance: not autarky but simply the capacity to mobilize and, if necessary, invent the technology best suited to the problem at hand.

Numerous common interests can be identified on which technological cooperation would be beneficial and feasible. It would be in the interests of producers and consumers all over the world to marshal the powers of modern technology and marketing to maintain the competitiveness of those natural commodities exported by developing countries which are in danger because of competition from synthetic or other materials. It is a global humanitarian objective to seek cures for tropical diseases and sustainable measures to control their vectors; to develop improved, low-cost technology applicable to nutrition, education, health, water supply, sanitation, and the mitigation of effects of natural disasters. It is a global ecological imperative and a prerequisite to stable and expanding trade in raw materials to provide the developing countries with the ability to implement and manage technology for the rational exploitation of natural resources, and to develop low-cost, ecologically sound technologies for the management of forests and marginal lands threatened with destruction.

It is in the interests of both the developing countries, with their severe and seemingly permanent crisis of unemployment and their recurrent foreign exchange difficulties, and of developed countries, seeking to cope with the social effects of massive population movements from the developing countries, to apply modern technological principles to the improvement of traditional agricultural and industrial skills and the development and diffusion of efficient, labor-intensive technology suited to local needs and capacities.

The certain prospect of technological development and increased competition from the Third World will compel the developed world to maintain a steady rate of innovation and R&D activity to find new areas of technologically based comparative advantage — a process which will provide the developing countries with a steady flow of new technology and will encourage the developed countries to develop new industries to replace those which shift to the developing countries.

Finally, it is the responsibility of the scientific community in the developed countries to help improve the capability of the developing countries for basic research and for education in science and technology. Scientists should encourage the scientific spirit throughout the world and ensure that local phenomena of global interest — coastal upwelling, tropical atmospheric circulation, astronomical and geophysical phenomena, unstudied or uncharacterized local plants, animals, and biological communities—are understood for the benefit of all and with the active and responsible participation of their colleagues in developing countries.

In all these areas, then, it is in the interests of both the developing and the developed countries to improve the effectiveness of the world technological system in meeting needs whose satisfaction is in the interest of all mankind, even though they are located primarily in the developing world. The achievement of self-reliance by the developing countries is not a subject for debate and confrontation but a goal which is clearly in the interests of everyone. Likewise, the execution of research by developed countries on problems of direct interest to developing countries is in everyone's interest when this approach is the one best suited to the resolution of a particular problem. Ironically, pragmatic cooperation in the pursuit of these goals is too often hindered by short-term political considerations, often reinforced by dogmatic attitudes.

Once tacit or explicit agreement on any of these long-term objectives is achieved, there remains the problem of organizing technological capabilities at the national and international levels, with the help, as appropriate, of United Nations agencies. The articulation of such a strategy involves careful consideration of the social, political, and institutional barriers to innovation, as well as the role of multinational corporations, purchased technology, scientific and technological research, human resource development, technology transfer, and the building of local capability — i.e., all the elements of the traditional agenda of North-South technological issues.

The Jamaica Symposium

A number of activities make the present time a good one for a better formulation of national and international technological issues and their relationship to the broader issues of the North-South dialogue. The United Nations Conference on Science and Technology for Development (UNCSTD) will provide an occasion for reexamination of the policy problems associated with the application of science and technology to economic development. The United Nations Development Programme coordinated a conference on technical cooperation among the developing countries in late 1978. The Independent Commission on International Development Issues — the "Brandt Commission"—is preparing to issue a report in October 1979 which is to be a statement of agreed-upon, politically feasible goals for North and South. The Special Session of the U.N. General Assembly on the goals for Development Decade III and beyond will take place in 1980.

The coincidence of these efforts provides a unique opportunity to arrive at a better formulation of the issues in mobilizing technology for development. A similar opportunity on a related set of issues arose and was seized in 1972, prior to the U.N. Conference on the Human Environment, in response to the controversy over whether the environmental carrying capacity of the earth limited possibilities for future economic expansion by the world, both North and South, or whether pollution and environmental degradation were solely problems of the industrialized countries that the developing countries could defer until they, too, had become developed. To prevent this controversy from causing the Environment Conference to dissipate its energies over the divisive aspects of this issue, its Secretary-General, Maurice Strong, then convened a meeting at Founex, Switzerland, consisting predominantly of leading development economists from both developed and developing countries. The Founex meeting concluded that both poverty and industrial pollution were major environmental problems all over the world and that they affected different countries in different proportions, but that there was no necessary contradiction between protecting the environment and furthering economic development. The meeting played an important role in defining the issue so as to minimize confrontation at the Environment Conference.

To meet the present challenge, IIED organized the Jamaica Symposium. The most remarkable feature of the Symposium was the diversity of the participating group, which included development economists, scientists, technologists, political and social leaders, bankers, business executives, and project managers for whom technology planning is a matter of daily activity and not a matter for theoretical or polemical debate. The viewpoints and interests represented covered a wide spectrum. One particular working group, for example, was composed partly of people who believed very strongly in international and national control and regulation of the operations of the transnational enterprises, partly of people who stressed the positive impact of transnational-enterprise operations while conceding that *voluntary* standards of behavior in *some* form are required, and some who actually managed and operated transnationals in developing countries and believed that their potential could be realized without control.

Despite this diversity, the discussions were remarkably free of acrimony. The participants, many of whom were newcomers to the international circuit and few of whom knew more than half of the others, recognized the unique combination of talents present, jelled quickly, and in many cases discovered that, despite their varied backgrounds, they had been thinking along similar lines. They readily recognized that there can be no simple ideological solutions to the problems of technological development, only intelligent choices in keeping with the multiplicity of development objectives and interest groups.

. The main purpose of the discussions was to find grounds for consensus without making any effort to mask conflict, and to arrive at an end product that would attract a broad base of support. The main message from the Jamaica Symposium—which has already generated a considerable amount of enthusiasm in the international community —may be summarized as a call for "strategic pragmatism," based on greater openmindedness and vision — *openmindedness* because there is much common ground between seemingly antagonistic and mutually exclusive positions that can be used for mutual advantage, and *vision* because the evolution of an indigenous technological capability is a painfully slow, costly, and risky experience for which there nevertheless is no substitute.

The papers in this volume are meant to further illustrate this concept of "strategic pragmatism," with their accent on practical actions that countries can take to solve national and global development problems through the mobilization of technology and science.

Notes

[1]Paul Streeten, "The Dynamics of the New Poor Power" in *A World Divided: The Less Developed Countries in the International Economy*, G.K. Helleiner, ed. (Cambridge University Press, 1976).

I. Mobilizing Technology for World Development: Report of the Jamaica Symposium

1. The Jamaica Symposium met in the midst of the major international debate on the ends of economic development and the extent to which the world technological system favors the interests of the industrial countries over those of the developing ones. Uncomfortable questions are being raised by past experience. Given the potential shortage of fossil fuels and the vast capital expenditures that would be needed for alternative energy supplies, is all-out economic growth a viable world goal? Should not countries search for alternative development styles oriented more to the basic needs of the poor and more conserving of resources and the environment? Should not development of technology be based on participation and self-help? Is there not an international responsibility to help this process? A certain unease pervaded the Symposium's deliberations despite the emergence of such questions about the relationship of technology to development at the international level. This mood of unease was prompted by yet another, underlying concern: To what extent is the present inter-national debate genuinely motivated by the goal of sound and equitable development, and to what extent is it concerned about retaining the levers of technological power in the hands of those who now control them?

2. The Symposium participants quickly agreed that the present world economic and technological systems are neither meeting the basic needs of millions of people nor adequately serving the interests of either the rich or the poor countries. They also agreed that appropriate technological choices and systems can result only from well-conceived and socially relevant development objectives at the national and the international level.

3. The Symposium recognized at the very outset of its deliberations that *technology ought to be only one tool for meeting socio-economic development objectives.* In fact, in the absence of clearly defined development goals, technology itself has frequently determined development priorities and patterns. The first question is not *"what technology?"* but "technology *for*

Summary and Conclusions
The Jamaica Symposium

what?" People-oriented development policies clearly require people-oriented technological strategies. Such a readjustment of perspective is urgently required at both the national and the international level.

4. The issues related to the mobilization of science and technology for meeting basic development objectives are often posed in mutually exclusive, conflict-ridden terms, but the Symposium concluded that they need not be. It pointed out that:

(a) *A country can support a development strategy that simultaneously alleviates poverty and promotes growth and industrialization.* Critical elements of such a strategy are increased emphasis on agricultural growth and agrarian reform, decentralization of industrial production, and rural industrialization. To accomplish these objectives, developing countries need to use all kinds of technology — the largest and the smallest, the most complex and the simplest, the most expensive and the cheapest, and the latest and the best as well as the tried and true. All are re-

quired, depending upon the socio-economic characteristics of the potential user and the particular milieu in which the technology is to be used. Therefore much of the debate over meeting basic needs versus economic growth and over "advanced" versus "appropriate" technology is artificial. A judicious mix of technologies is needed.

(b) *There is considerably more common ground than has usually been realized between transnational enterprises (TNEs) and the proponents of equity and self-reliance.* The transnational enterprises, through their dynamism, are a major creator of wealth. They also have important company-specific technological, managerial, and marketing capabilities which other economic actors and host countries frequently lack. As a result, the latter must seek the services of TNEs to meet certain key developmental objectives. For that purpose, a reduction in the uncertainty governing relations between host countries and TNEs could create conditions for more stable relations and provide important benefits for all parties. For example, more awareness and information on both sides about the activities pursued by the other side could help to produce mutually beneficial agreements. At the same time, however, the Symposium recognized that the business practices pursued by the TNEs often do little to reduce serious inequalities in real income or to influence other key economic and social concerns in the host economies. The resolution of conflicts between the creation of wealth and the correction of existing inequities is not automatic, but requires continuous awareness, explicit strategy, and cooperation of all parties involved.

5. The Symposium identified *three specific areas of convergence between the interests of the North and the South: First*, the North and the South share an interest in evolving effective international mechanisms for the integrated management of, and cooperative research on, the technological elements relating to global problems, such as food, energy, health, and raw materials; and those relating to global systems, such as weather and communications. *Second*, North and South share an interest in enhancing indigenous technological capabilities in the developing countries to enable them to participate fully in the identification, analysis, and management of global problems. And *third*, North and South share an interest in the development of improved capability on the part of developing countries to negotiate more effectively with transnational enterprises and to participate more

effectively in the implementation of agreements reached so that these become more equitable and, hence, more stable.

6. On the basis of its recognition of these mutual North-South interests, the Jamaica Symposium made several major recommendations:

(1) An ad hoc independent commission of non-governmental experts, consisting of both thinkers and doers, and representing all parts of the world, should be set up (a) to analyze present and future technological and scientific trends, and (b) to define and recommend priority areas for major new programs of North-South collaboration. For example, the commission might consider how to develop an integrated approach to the research, development, and promotion of non-food agricultural commodities whose export is vital to the developing countries and whose availability is important to the developed countries. The commission should also consider the advisability of creating, and the structure of, a permanent mechanism to carry out its functions. The recommendations of the commission should lead to major new programs of North-South technological collaboration based on mutual self-interest. This collaboration should take advantage of scientific and technological resources wherever they may be located — specifically including the developed countries — but it should be designed to

strengthen the capability of the developing countries and to give as much responsibility as feasible to developing-country participants.

(2) Research and development (R&D) expenditures in the developing world, which are only about 4 per cent of the worldwide total at present, should be greatly increased by the year 2000. More research needs to be directed to social needs, and R&D organizations should be kept relatively autonomous, with adequate financial support to sustain their long-term activity.

(3) External assistance agencies should use a larger part of their resources to support R&D and other innovative programs within the developing countries and should channel such support — preferably through relatively autonomous funding mechanisms — to groups capable of generating and disseminating technology. The International Development Research Centre of Canada, which is dedicated to the enhancement of research competence within the developing countries, is a good illustration of such support through bilateral channels. Some participants suggested that a certain proportion of current assistance should be set aside by the external agencies to be channeled through a specialized international organization (under genuine international control and with its own specialized knowledge and operational policy), created to

handle the complex issues of the technology market. The establishment of autonomous (including non-governmental) funding institutions in developing countries would facilitate a link between the development of local capability and programs of international cooperation on global problems.

(4) National scientific and technological capability in the developing countries needs to be greatly enhanced at all levels of society, specifically including training programs, natural resource surveys, common service organizations, and specialized financial institutions for the small farmer or entrepreneur. Although the group recognized that the task of building indigenous technological capacity is slow, arduous, and costly, it believed that the ability of the developing countries to define national development goals clearly, and then to choose and adapt the technologies needed to achieve them, is essential if the international system is to evolve into an equal partnership.

(5) International assistance agencies should invest a greater proportion of their resources in identifying and testing innovative approaches within the developing countries. The agencies should be more cautious about relying on "proven" technologies; such technologies have often been proven in different resource and other contexts than

those prevailing in the developing world.

(6) Improved mechanisms must be instituted to gather and disseminate information on technological alternatives. Sector-specific data banks at the national, the regional, and the international level need to be expanded.

(7) More frequent and improved cooperation among science and technology organizations, along the lines of those being supported by the Consultative Group on International Agricultural Research, are needed to facilitate the transfer of technology and of supporting scientific knowledge, both between the developing and the developed countries, and, in particular, among the developing countries themselves. Practical suggestions in this direction were made at the 1978 United Nations Conference on Technological Cooperation among Developing Countries.

(8) More effective institutional means and incentives need to be developed for the transfer of commercial technologies to the least-developed countries, particularly from the industrialized developing countries.

(9) Non-governmental organizations (foundations, universities, non-profit agencies, public volunteer organizations, etc.) have a proven capability in innovative, risk-taking, and people-oriented activities. More support, both internal and external, should be channeled to them.

(10) Educational and training institutions at all levels should be established in developing countries, and transnational enterprises should be encouraged to do more to train technical and managerial personnel.

(11) The ability of the developing countries to negotiate the acquisition of foreign technology should be greatly strengthened so as to increase the prospects for effective, stable agreements in the basic interest of all parties. Among measures toward this end, efforts to revise the Paris Convention on Patents and develop a code of conduct for the transfer of technology are most important.

(12) Higher priority in national policies (and in international forums) should be given to the need for more effective adjustment mechanisms and employment policies in the industrialized countries. The impact of technological and economic competition within the North on the nature of North-South technology flows needs to be carefully monitored.

7. The Symposium expressed the belief that these recommendations are consistent with and would contribute to a number of global and national development goals that are attracting increasing support. These goals are: (1) overcoming the worst aspects of poverty by the year 2000; (2) facilitation of a more effective and equitable international division of labor; (3) the more efficient management of global problems, particularly those relating

to natural resources; and (4) achievement of self-reliant, sustainable economic growth, including a doubling of per capita income and food production by the end of the century.

8. The group concluded that the political will required to sustain progress on any one of these four goals over the long run depends on simultaneous and coordinated action on one or more of the other goals. Overcoming the worst aspects of absolute poverty, for example, will depend on the amount of international cooperation that can be mobilized for advancing self-reliant growth and vice versa.

9. The Symposium invited the United Nations Conference on Science and Technology for Development, the Brandt Commission, the United Nations Conference for Trade and Development, and the 1980 Special Session of the U.N. General Assembly to take account of its conclusions and recommendations in their deliberations.

1. At the invitation of Barbara Ward, President of the International Institute for Environment and Development (IIED), twenty-five distinguished scientists, technologists, business executives, development economists, bankers and political and social leaders met in Ocho Rios, Jamaica, from January 7 to 11, 1979. They discussed the common interest of rich and poor countries in mobilizing science and technology for development. The Symposium was co-chaired by Mahbub ul Haq and Ivan Head. James Grant and Constantine Vaitsos coordinated the drafting of the final report.

2. The Symposium members quickly agreed that the present world economic and technological systems are neither meeting the basic needs of millions of people nor adequately serving the interests of either the rich or the poor countries. They also agreed that appropriate technological choices and systems can result only from well-conceived and socially relevant development objectives at the national and international levels.

3. The Symposium met in the midst of the major international debate on the ends of economic development and the extent to which the world technological system favors the interests of the industrial countries over those of the developing ones. Uncomfortable questions are being raised by past experience. Given the potential shortage of fossil fuels and the vast capital expenditures that would be needed for alternative energy supplies, is all-out economic growth a viable world goal? Should not countries search for alternative development styles oriented more to the basic needs of the poor and more conserving of resources and the environment? Should not development of technology be based on participation and self-help? Is there not an international responsibility to help this process? A certain unease pervaded the Symposium's deliberations despite the emergence of such questions about the relationship of technology to development at the international level. This mood of unease was prompted by yet another, underlying concern. To what extent is the present international debate genuinely motivated by the goal of sound and equitable

Report of the
Jamaica Symposium

development, and to what extent is it concerned about retaining the levers of technological power in the hands of those who now control them?

4. The Symposium's participants discussed these issues in an open and frank atmosphere. Although a large measure of agreement emerged, there was no attempt to minimize differences. The basic purposes of the Symposium were to clarify the perspectives from which technological choices have to be viewed, to seek areas of common interest, and to offer concrete proposals for action.

5. The six major sections of this report summarize the deliberations and the conclusions of the Symposium's plenary sessions as well as its three working groups. The three groups focused on (a) issues related to mobilizing technology for national needs, (b) the question of technology flows and transnational enterprises in the context of a new international order, and (c) the mobilization of technology for the management of global problems.

I. Toward Mobilizing Technology for Development: The Current Political and Economic Context

6. The Symposium was held at a time of active planning for a series of international conferences, including the United Nations Conference on Science and Technology for Development (UNCSTD), the United Nations Conference on Trade and Development V (UNCTAD), and the 1980 Special Session of the United Nations General Assembly on the international strategy for development cooperation in the Third U.N. Development Decade and beyond, which will convene in 1980. Together with the work of the Brandt Commission on International Development Issues, these meetings could significantly influence the course of events over the final two decades of this century. The Symposium also met at a time of growing consensus that important aspects of the international economic system are not working

adequately for either the developed or the developing countries. Among the chief problems are the following:

(a) The most basic needs of some 800 million people are not being met. This number is even larger in absolute terms (though smaller proportionally) than thirty years ago and could easily increase further in the absence of major policy changes. Some 400-500 million people remain hungry and malnourished at a time when the United States has returned to restraint on crop production and India finds itself with major market surpluses of grain.

(b) In both the developed and the developing countries, a large proportion of technological effort is devoted to military purposes. Of the remainder, little benefits the poor. Less than 1 per cent of the world's R&D expenditures on health, agriculture, housing, and industrial technology is spent on the needs of the poorest half of the world's population. The relatively small investment in R&D in the developing countries is devoted largely to defense and to the urban and industrial sectors.

(c) Most developing countries now face growing barriers to the flow of technology from, and the export of manufactures to, industrial countries as protectionist pressures in these countries increase.

(d) There is increasing technological differentiation among the developing countries themselves. Some countries of Asia and Latin America have achieved a relatively high degree of industrial and technological power. This brings into sharper focus the special problems of the less-developed countries that have slow growth and little bargaining power.

(e) The international economic system no longer seems to work adequately for the industrialized countries of the northern hemisphere. In the absence of major policy changes, the industrial democracies face the prospect of persistent inflation and slow growth in the 1980s and beyond. A consensus is emerging that a return to satisfactory economic conditions in the developed countries, including lower inflation, will require not only more effective domestic policies, but also much greater involvement of the developing countries of the South in the world economy and much greater North-South cooperation.

(f) In the continued absence of a clear approach by the industrial democracies to North-South issues and to international development cooperation, the dialogue launched so hopefully after the Seventh Special Session of the U.N. General Assembly in September, 1975, now seems headed for stalemate.

(g) Finally, there is a growing unease in both high- and low-income countries over the ends of development itself. A debate on this issue has been triggered both in the North, in part by analyses of the "limits to growth," and in the South, in part by the continued failure of patterns of growth modeled on the experience of the industrialized countries to meet the needs of large numbers of people.

II. Technology as an Element of Development Strategy in Historical Perspective

7. The driving force behind the 1975 General Assembly decision to convene the United Nations Conference on Science and Technology for Development (UNCSTD) in August, 1979, was the widespread conviction that the world technological system, like the broader economic system, is not working adequately or equitably for the developing countries or for the world's poor. Technological capacity — engineering, management, design and manufacturing capacity, patents and licensable technology, information, and research and development — is overwhelmingly concentrated in the developed countries. According to a University of Lund (Sweden) estimate, only 4 per cent of worldwide R&D takes place in the developing world. An even smaller percentage is devoted to meeting the basic needs of the poor majority.

8. Most developing countries are still well short of their goal of technological self-reliance. Self-reliance does not mean autarky, but it does include the ability to make autonomous national decisions on technology—to choose, implement, manage, and operate technology, and to innovate. Commercial technology transfers tend to be inequitable and expensive for the developing countries, frequently providing technology inappropriate to their needs, inhibiting the development of their own technological capabilities, and reinforcing their dependence on outside sources. Developing countries may thus feel themselves faced with a bitter choice: their integration into the present international technological system may only increase their technological and even cultural dependence, but disengagement may force them to forego the benefits of worldwide scientific and technological advances.

9. The Symposium recognized at the very outset that technology ought to be only one tool for meeting socio-economic development objectives. In fact, in the absence of clearly defined development goals, it has frequently operated to determine development priorities and patterns. The real question is not "what technology?" but "technology for what?" People-oriented development policies clearly require people-oriented technological strategies. Such a readjustment of perspective is urgently required at both the national and the international level.

10. In the 1950s, the primary goal of national economic development was to increase the gross national product (GNP), chiefly by creating a strong and largely urban industrial base. This policy assumed that technology consisted primarily of applied science, which required large investments in research and in scientific and technological manpower. It stressed the acquisition of capabilities that would reduce the economic gap that then existed between the industrialized countries and the newly independent nations.

11. The experiences of the 1960s and 1970s have demonstrated the limitations of this approach. In spite of impressive technological performances in certain sectors in the developing world, widespread poverty persists, in part because of past development and technological decisions. Attacking poverty will therefore require new development priorities, which in turn will require new technological strategies. Such strategies should pay explicit attention to the needs of small farms, small-scale rural industries, and the informal urban sector. They should aim at raising the productivity of the poor sufficiently to channel purchasing power to them directly.

12. Technological innovation results more from the "pull" of the marketplace than the "push" of laboratories or other generators of technology. Innovation is affected by all the factors that affect the market — patterns of income distribution, the economic climate, and government policies, as well as cultural, institutional, sociological, educational, and other factors. Technology is not simply the efficient application of scientific knowledge but rather an integration of social, economic, political, financial, managerial, institutional, and scientific elements.

13. Thus national development and technological strategies need to be clearly and explicitly articulated. Otherwise, entities not explicitly involved in technological development (e.g., financial institutions) may, in effect, create conflicting policies which make technological objectives impossible to achieve. An explicit strategy brings into focus the trade-offs involved in achieving different objectives and facilitates coordination of the different actors contributing to technological development.

14. Technological change must be viewed in the context of the social, institutional, cultural, and political milieu in which it is taking place. Whether technology is appropriate or inappropriate does not relate to qualities inherent in the technology as much as to the social and political realities at its specific point of application.

15. People affected by technology should be involved in the choice of technology. This will require important and fundamental changes in existing patterns of decisionmaking and implementation. In the absence of adequate capabilities, technology choices in many developing countries are being made by foreign aid agencies and transnational enterprises. Developing countries are, for the most part, deprived of the opportunity to make and implement their own choices.

16. Failure to define goals and strategies in national policy can lead to technology having unintended — and frequently undesired — results. This is seen clearly in the contrasting rural development policies of the developing countries. A few of these countries have implemented national strategies and created an appropriate technological infrastructure to increase rural productivity through labor-intensive means. In many others, however, emphasis has been

placed only on increasing output, with the result that capital-intensive agricultural technology imported from the North has often had the harmful effect of displacing or bypassing massive numbers of small farmers and landless laborers.

17. The ready availability of advanced technology, furthermore, may distract attention from its negative social ramifications. In extreme cases, the application of sophisticated, large-scale, capital-intensive technology may become an end in itself. Policy may be driven by an explicit technological vision of a future that must be reached even if the cost is high unemployment—a cost that too many countries in both the North and the South are now paying.

18. What is true of the effect of goals and strategies at the national level is equally true at the international level. The goal of the First U.N. Development Decade to increase national outputs annually by 5 per cent was achieved, yet global hunger and poverty rose over the same period.

III. Goals for the 1980s and 1990s: Priorities for Science and Technology

19. The Symposium identified four goals related to the mobilization of science and technology for development which it thought worthy of concerted international and national effort: (1) overcoming the worst aspects of poverty by the year 2000; (2) facilitation of a more effective and equitable international division of labor; (3) more efficient management of global problems, particularly those relating to natural resources; and (4) achievement of self-reliant, sustainable economic growth, including a doubling of per capita income and food production by the end of the century. These goals are complementary, and they interact with one another. The Symposium's participants agreed that, to be successful, technological strategies must be addressed to one, or preferably more than one, of these goals and that they should not operate to undercut any one of these goals.

20. *Overcoming the worst aspects of absolute poverty in all countries and seeking to halve the disparities in life expectancy, infant mortality, and literacy between the developed and the developing countries by the year 2000.* A number of developing countries with highly different political and economic systems have now achieved the level of life expectancy and infant mortality that prevailed in the United Kingdom and the United States in the 1930s. But they have done so, it should be noted, at income levels only as high as the income levels of the United Kingdom and the United States two centuries ago. This suggests that there is very real potential for overcoming the worst aspects of poverty in the developing world without a commensurate increase in prevailing income levels.

21. Several sources have suggested that "success" in achieving the goal would be the attainment of an average life expectancy of 65 (compared to the present average of 48 years in low-income countries); a literacy rate of at least 75 per cent (compared to 34 per cent today); an infant mortality rate of 50 or less per thousand births (compared to the present rate of 136 per thousand); and a birth rate of 25 or less per thousand population (compared to 40 per thousand today).

22. Halving these disparities in key social indicators by the year 2000 will require an annual average reduction of 3½ per cent of the differences between the developed and the developing countries by the end of the century. Achievement of these targets by all countries would mean some 10 million fewer deaths and 20 million fewer births a year than are now projected for the end of the century by the United Nations.

23. Although it is still difficult to set quantitative targets for social objectives — because the production function for each target cannot, with our current knowledge, be meticulously planned or controlled, and because countries cannot all make simultaneous progress in each social field — it was agreed that a substantial reduction in such social disparities should guide the formulation of future national and international development efforts.

24. Progress in meeting basic needs will require greatly increased research in the social and natural sciences of relevance to the world's poor majority. Thus, if scientists were able to develop grain seeds that would fix nitrogen the way soya beans and alfalfa do, this would lessen the need for costly chemicals to restore fertility to the soil. This, in turn, would lower the capital requirements and attendant risks which present such difficulties for small farmers. Important as such a breakthrough would be for small farmers, very little of the world's research budget is spent on their needs. Yet small farmers, and those who depend on them, make up about one half of humanity.

25. A similar situation has prevailed in health. Over one hundred times more in research funds is devoted to the diseases most prevalent in the developed nations, notably cancer and heart ailments, than is devoted to schistosomiasis, river blindness, diarrhea, and other afflictions that affect literally hundreds of millions of the people in the poor countries.

26. Insofar as possible, therefore, an important criterion in deciding priorities for research on technology is to determine who will be its chief beneficiaries. Is research likely to benefit first and foremost the already advantaged, as has tended to happen with recent advances in new grain seeds and pesticides? Is research "neutral" in its effect— i.e., potentially usable by both large and small farmers — as with research on nitrogen-fixing grains and plant photosynthesis? Or is it primarily directed toward the poor majority, as would be the case with research on schistosomiasis? Most research in recent years has been

in the first category. Clearly the need is to give greater priority to the latter two, including social science research on how to extend the benefits of technological development to the poor.

27. *Facilitating a more effective and equitable international division of labor in a world of technological advance and shifting comparative advantages.* This goal is closely related to the preceding one, but it focuses on the measures that need to be taken by the advanced countries and the more industrialized developing countries. New production capacities in some developing countries can not only help overcome the worst aspects of poverty in other developing countries but can also contribute to lower inflation, higher-wage jobs, and increasing employment in the developed countries. However, imports from developing countries may undermine certain industries in the developed countries that tend to be labor-intensive, such as textiles, apparel, shoes, electronics, and steel. More effective employment and technology policies are required in most industrial countries, and perhaps in some of the more industrialized developing countries, to secure public acceptance of increased imports from less industrialized countries. Within the OECD countries, more attention should be paid to greater coordination of industrial technology policies. North-North and East-West trade and competition have far-reaching implications on relationships with, and cooperation among, developing countries themselves.

28. *More efficient management of global problems, particularly those relating to natural resources.* In an increasingly interdependent world, individual countries cannot cope effectively with inflation, economic growth, population growth, and poverty unless measures are pursued which deal more effectively with global pressures on food, water, land, energy sources, raw materials, and the environment. On these and other global problems, scientific and technological cooperation between North and South is appropriate and necessary.

29. Such cooperative management of global problems is possible, however, only if all affected countries—both developed and developing—participate in the definition of the problem and the formulation and implementation of the solution. For this reason, it is in the interest of both the developed and the developing countries that the latter have the technological capacity to participate in global efforts.

30. In the case of food, for example, effective global management of foodgrains requires not only the establishment of a food reserve system but also effective use of underutilized resources in Asia, Africa, and Latin America. By 1990, the annual world demand for grain is projected to rise to 1.9 billion tons, 700 million tons above the 1970 level. If current production trends continue, many developing and developed countries will face increasing grain shortages. Any attempt by Canada and the United States to produce enough grain to cover the world shortage, however, will send production and en-

vironmental costs spiraling. Yet India—one of several possible examples—could more than double its grain production at current price levels if it could overcome its own institutional and financial barriers to using the production technology now available.

31. Effective management of food and other global resources could also significantly ameliorate inflation rates, employment levels, and GNP growth rates in both the developed and the developing countries in the 1980s and 1990s.

32. *Achievement of self-reliant, sustainable economic growth in the developing countries within the context of a new international economic order, including a doubling of per capita income and food production by the year 2000.* Without accelerated economic progress within most of the developing countries and a more equitable distribution of the fruits of economic progress, the issues of self-reliance and poverty cannot be addressed simultaneously. Nor will the developing countries be able to gain fully from changes in their comparative advantage relative to the advanced nations, or to carry their full share of responsibility for global management. Thus, the achievement of self-reliance by the developing countries underpins all the goals discussed earlier. The objective of doubling per capita income by the end of the century is consonant with the goal of the International Strategy for the U.N. Second Development Decade (DD II), which called for increasing per capita income by 3.5 per cent annually. The goal of doubling food production is a compromise between the 4 per cent annual increase target of the World Food Council (and of the DD II Strategy) and the 3 per cent target of the World Bank. The targets suggested here represent annual GNP and food production growth rates that are approximately twice those achieved by the low-income countries over the preceding two decades. The experience of some countries does suggest, however, that the targets *can* be met through appropriate national development strategies supported by international cooperation in financing and technology.

33. Achieving self-reliance, equity, and growth will require a major strengthening of indigenous technological capability for research and development in both the social and the natural sciences. The same is true for pre-investment work, engineering, design, management, and associated project-level skills. Achieving these goals will also require special efforts to correct existing biases in national technological systems against less capital-intensive, or traditional, technologies, and the creation of mechanisms to ensure the diffusion of technology to smaller farms and enterprises.

34. Technologies are needed that can help meet more than one of the four goals discussed above simultaneously. For example, large sums are now spent on research relating to the development of plants that will absorb more fertilizers and require pesticides and other inputs as a means of growing more food. But the use of such inputs

raises environmental problems and may also strain the financial resources of small farmers. In comparison, only trifling sums are now spent on research aimed at raising food production by increasing the productivity of plants known to be resistant to the diseases and pests of their environment, or on research striving for higher productivity through nitrogen fixation, increased pest resistance, photosynthesis, or better water utilization.

35. Sustained progress on any one of the four goals depends in part on progress with the others. Thus, overcoming the worst aspects of absolute poverty will be dependent on the level of international cooperation that can be mobilized for advancing self-reliant growth and vice versa. Furthermore, given the many divisions within both the North and the South as well as the continuing tendency of the North to defend the status quo and of the South to be suspicious of the North, there is a need for unifying objectives—such as meeting most basic needs by the year 2000; or assuring stable, expanding, and equitable trade in raw materials; or providing for a more efficient distribution of global industrial capacity. Linking these objectives to the long-term economic self-interests of both the North and the South will, in the opinion of the Symposium participants, create numerous opportunities for mutually beneficial technological cooperation.

IV. Mobilizing Technology for National Needs

36. The Symposium agreed that, to achieve the goals outlined above, people-oriented development strategies and technologies are required. The capital-intensive technologies generally available from industrialized countries are oriented toward minimum use of workers, who constitute the scarcest economic resource in the high-income countries. People-oriented technologies in the developing countries would minimize claims on their scarce capital and maximize job creation so that these countries could take advantage of their most abundant resource: people.

37. Thus, the controversy between the advocates of a policy designed to master the advanced technology needed for industrialization and growth and the advocates of a technology to meet the basic needs of poor people is largely an artificial argument. Both kinds of technology are needed. The real issues are those of balance in the allocation of resources and the extent to which a common technology policy can serve both ends. In certain categories of industry, such as heavy engineering, electronics, heavy chemicals, and some types of infrastructure, there is no substitute for the "latest and best" capital intensive large-scale technology. Yet the owners of a one or two-hectare farm, a family machine shop, or a small retail store need appropriate productive technology no less than the owners (public or

private) of a petrochemical factory, automobile assembly plant, or centralized electric power system. As amply demonstrated in East Asia, one hectare farms (if they are effectively supported by credit and other facilities) can utilize the newest plant varieties and pesticides flowing from the most advanced agricultural resource centers in the world. Developing countries need the largest and the smallest technology, the most complex and the simplest, the most expensive and the cheapest, and the latest and the best as well as the tried and true. The extent to which any of these is used will depend upon the characteristics of the potential user, the particular situation in which the technology is to be used, and the country's stage of development.

38. It must be remembered, however, that the developing world is overwhelmingly a world of smallness. Four fifths of the farms are of 5 hectares (12 acres) or less. Nearly half are just a single hectare. Most business and industrial establishments are family firms or enterprises that employ only a handful of people. Incomes in this world of smallness are low. We now know from the history of a few countries, as well as from experience with innumerable community programs carried on all over the world, that tools and machines can be designed for small enterprises that can make them much more productive than they were when they used traditional technologies. These tools and machines are low-cost and job-creating rather than labor-displacing. Such new technology for micro-enterprises is not a replacement for large-scale, capital-intensive technology. It is complementary. Moreover, such technology is neither second-rate nor second-hand but the "latest and best" for its purpose; it is frequently based on the most sophisticated scientific research. By combining support for vast numbers of micro-enterprises with investment in large-scale industry, a few developing countries (including some in densely populated East Asia) are now approaching full employment while experiencing rapid growth.

39. Few will dissent from the idea that the desirable way to overcome poverty is to create enough jobs to enable the poor to meet their needs through their own efforts. According to the International Labor Office, the number of jobs that need to be created by the year 2000 to achieve full employment in the developing countries is nearly double the number of productive jobs that exist today. To achieve this goal, which was internationally endorsed at the World Employment Conference in 1976, will require enormous effort as well as an open mind about what constitutes "appropriateness" in technology. However formidable the problem may appear, it is not insoluble.

40. The bias against smallness that is still widespread—and that is usually justified on grounds of the inefficiency of small size and the backwardness of small-scale technology—is not supported by either economic analysis or experience. We now know that in labor-abundant economies there is an enormous and mostly untapped potential for increasing production and creating jobs in capital-saving

micro-enterprises *without compromising efficiency*. In countries that have developed high-productivity agriculture on farms that average just a single hectare in size, there are 175 to 225 productively employed farmers per 100 cultivated hectares — and the incomes of these farmers are rising. In the United States, there are only three farmers per 100 cultivated hectares. In Western Europe, the number is several times higher than in the United States but still many times lower than in science-based, small-farm systems. Most important, it is now known that output per hectare and per unit of capital are higher on small farms. Hence, investing in small farms can maximize output, maximize employment, and minimize the capital cost of agricultural advance.

41. The characteristics of many categories of small businesses and industrial enterprises parallel those of small farms. Recent research on such enterprises suggests that the key to increasing industrial production outside the big cities is an effective linking of agriculture, industry, and marketing. If farm income is rising, the potential for labor-intensive rural enterprises is very great. Lower-income groups tend to purchase more commodities produced by capital-saving technology than do high-income groups. Lastly, output per unit of capital is often higher in small, labor-intensive industrial enterprises than in many larger, capital-intensive industries.

42. It is worth noting that appropriate technology also is gradually becoming an issue in the rich countries, where nearly all "modern" technology originates. The energy crisis demands energy-conserving, capital-saving technologies based on renewable energy sources. The environmental crisis demands a less rapacious use of resources, and technologies both in industry and agriculture that are non-violent toward living things. Social tensions arising from highly centralized technologies call for human-scale technologies and decentralized production. New forms of ownership could reverse the current centralization of economic power. Also needed are new opportunities for creative work and self-reliance. What needs to be considered, therefore, is not one kind of technology for the North and another for the South, or one technology for the rich and another for the poor. The task that confronts North and South, and every individual country, is to develop and perfect technologies that enable men and women to earn a decent and satisfying living in ways that are both equitable and sustainable.

43. In order to provide technologies for small markets and small producers and also to maximize capital-saving, job-creating investment, two courses of action are needed. First, large-scale production processes should be scaled down whenever possible. That this is possible has already been satisfactorily demonstrated in several industries, including bricks and cement, paper, textiles, packaging, sugar, and agricultural equipment. Second, traditional technologies should be upgraded and made more productive.

44. If the poor majority in the developing countries is to be given a chance to work itself out of poverty and to make a significant contribution to national output and national self-reliance, all groups in each society should be involved in mobilizing the technology they need for their own particular situation. Those who select technology should be many, not few. All groups also need to be involved in creating capital—for capital formation is needed in small production units as well as large ones, both in the myriad rural communities and in the handful of metropolitan centers.

45. Technological self-reliance (defined as the freedom to make and implement decisions) is a national goal that can and must be achieved at the national level. It is also a goal that can be approached to a considerable extent at the level of the individual production unit (including cooperatives, and other group organizations).

46. History suggests that agrarian reform, substantial decentralization of development to local organizations (both public and private) and other types of social change will accelerate the achievement of the development goals set forth above. And since unbridled market forces do not often induce the development of people-oriented technologies on a large scale, government intervention on behalf of the poor will be needed to alter the framework in which market forces operate.

47. Countries should examine the different technologies that are available or can be created for both small-scale and large-scale activities. They should examine the capital-intensiveness of different technologies to determine the judicious mix of technologies needed to achieve economic growth with social justice within a given time frame.

48. It is important that national technological capacity not be equated with research capability. The nature of technological capacity varies according to the level of development and the technological sophistication of indigenous enterprises. For instance, in many cases, the function of indigenous technological capacity is the identification of national, sectoral, and sub-sectoral goals, followed by the selection and installation of the foreign technology most appropriate to a particular goal. Sometimes, the function may extend to the country's ability to undertake economic and project-related planning and analysis independently, but more frequently it means the minimum ability to evaluate the planning and analysis performed by outside consultants or development agencies. Occasionally, it may entail mastery of the technology to the point of being able to replicate it with minimum external assistance and the ability to carry out local adaptations. In some instances, it may involve carrying out research independently.

49. Building technological capacity is necessarily a complex, time-consuming process that has to take place at all levels of a society and must be supported by basic changes in the educational system.

The notion that technology is rooted in high level R&D institutions is a narrow view of the innovative process and is historically inaccurate. In countries where development is decentralized and community programs have been undertaken, technological innovation has come from individuals, local governments, farmer cooperatives, and other local organizations. Technological innovation comes from the users of technology as well as from scientists and engineers; it comes from the bottom up, as well as from the top down.

50. Scientific and technological institutions are needed at several levels. Such institutions should include not only sophisticated laboratories staffed with persons of the highest possible professional training, but also field R&D centers that work directly with producers — especially small farmers and small and rural non-farm entrepreneurs—to upgrade their traditional skills and technologies, and to develop new techniques and new tools. All such centers should be autonomous, with adequate financial support to sustain long-term activity. They should work closely with business and other professional communities. They should also be free to seek whatever help they need to do their work, both internally and externally. This is especially important for field R&D centers, since they will probably lack the capacity to do sophisticated research. Universities in the developing countries can improve their educational capacity and contribute to development by increasing their research on the practical problems of their own countries. R&D should be directly linked to production, marketing, and financing systems; otherwise, much new or improved technology may lie about unused.

51. Information systems are needed at all levels to support the work of both the developers and the users of technology. Much more information on sources of knowledge (who is doing what and where) is needed both within and among countries. Also needed is a greater amount of personal interchange among developers of technology, especially those working with capital-saving, small-scale tools and equipment. Moreover, innovation does not occur simply as the result of a need but rather as a response to a demand expressed in terms of willingness to pay for a particular product or service. Policies to foster innovation must therefore be complemented by efforts to stimulate consumption.

52. Training programs at all levels are another essential element of a country's technological capacity. These programs must provide training for the users of technology, for extension agents who work directly with users, for field practitioners, and for those with college and higher degrees. It is difficult to develop ways for people at these various levels to work together, but coordination is essential if the specialized knowledge of a few is to benefit the many.

53. It is a common procedure in management to begin with a needs survey, locate the knowledge needed to solve the problem, carry out whatever design work or adaptation is needed, do the field-testing, and develop the prototype. At this point, a technology is ready for

dissemination and use. This procedure is widely used for large-scale investments. It should be used for small-scale activities as well. However, because of the difficulty and high cost of working individually with large numbers of small producers, common service organizations are needed to achieve economies of scale for certain specific functions. These functions include R&D, marketing, finance, training, and specialized quality control.

Recommendations

54. Both national and international institutions will need to reorient their programs and policies considerably to strengthen scientific and technological capacity to meet national development needs more effectively along the lines discussed above. Recommendations advanced with this objective in mind were:

(1) Existing financial and production institutions, internal and external, public and private, should gear their policies toward greater support of employment-generating investments of activities designed to build up technological capacity.

(2) Bilateral and international assistance agencies should use a larger proportion of their resources to support R&D activities within the developing countries by channeling such assistance to institutions capable of generating and disseminating technology without restriction. The experience of the International Development Research Centre of Canada should be employed broadly by other countries. Some Symposium participants were in favor of establishing a World Technology Bank under genuine international control, with a certain proportion of current assistance designated for distribution through such an institution. This institution should have its own specialized staff and operational policy to handle the complex problems and issues that characterize the technology market.

(3) International assistance agencies should invest a greater proportion of their resources in identifying and testing innovative technological approaches within the developing countries. Such agencies should be more cautious about relying on "proven" technology, since such technology has been "proven" in rich, not poor, countries. This point applies especially to social considerations, primarily employment.

(4) Given that non-governmental organizations (foundations, universities, non-profit agencies, public volunteer organizations) have a proven capability in innovative, risk-taking, and people-oriented activities, more support (both domestic and external) should be channeled to them.

(5) More frequent and improved cooperation among science and technology organizations (similar to those supported by the

Consultative Group on International Agricultural Research) is needed to facilitate the transfer of technology and of supporting scientific knowledge both between developed and developing and, in particular, among developing countries. Useful suggestions in this regard were made at the 1978 United Nations Conference on Technical Cooperation Among Developing Countries.

(6) A dramatic increase in R&D expenditures is required in the developing countries by the year 2000, and a greater proportion of those expenditures should be devoted to meeting the needs of small-scale agricultural and industrial producers and the poor majority.

V. Technology Flows for a New International Order

55. Commercial technology flows — as distinct from the public-domain flows emphasized in the preceding section—were the subject of spirited discussion at the Symposium. Continued differences over the role of the transnational enterprises (TNEs) showed themselves during the Symposium. This was not surprising since, as noted earlier, the driving force behind the General Assembly decision to convene the United Nations Conference on Science and Technology for Development (UNCSTD) was the widespread conviction in the developing countries that the world technological system is not working efficiently or equitably for them.

56. The striking outcome of the Symposium's consideration of commercial technology flows, however, was the strong consensus that emerged on two central points. First, all agreed that the current situation is unsatisfactory and detrimental to the longer-term interests of the developing countries, the industrialized countries, and the TNEs. Second, there was noteworthy agreement on the principal types of action which could help defuse the suspicion in many developing countries that the industrial countries consciously wish to keep them dependent in order to exploit their economic weaknesses.

57. Proponents of the New International Economic Order seek the creation of a new and more equitable structure of economic relationships between the North and the South. Central issues in this restructuring relate to: trade, investment, and ownership patterns; control over decision-making processes and bodies which affect the international economy; control over natural resources and the industrial processing of outputs; and capital flows and the management of international financial resources. Underlying all these issues are considerations of the location of production activities and their effectiveness and relationship to developmental goals, the control of evolving forms of international economic interaction, and the distribution of the benefits derived from such global economic restructuring.

58. International flows of technology have a specific role to play in this restructuring. Technology flows do not take place in isolation but are linked to overall systems of production and company- or country-specific capabilities. The success of technology flows depends on the extent to which they are assimilated by and adapted to local socio-economic conditions, and on whether they complement or displace indigenous technological capabilities. There are important operational differences among different types of flows and among characteristics of technology-importing countries. The impact of technology flows depends on an appropriate mix of other production inputs, including, for example, managerial and marketing capabilities, skilled labor, and capital resources.

59. Technology comes from many sources. One useful but crude categorization of technology is whether it is in the public or in the commercial sector. The controversy over the terms of transfer is primarily associated with the latter, for which TNEs have been the principal means of transmittal. This crude division is inadequate from some perspectives, however; it is argued, for example, that within the commercial category, distinction is needed between proprietary technology and various forms of managerial and other expertise which are not protected by patents or other ownership rights. A developing country may be required to purchase the latter because of its state of underdevelopment or because the TNE makes its sale of proprietary technology dependent on this purchase. In the latter case, the purchaser may feel that he is being charged for expertise that he could purchase locally or is being deprived of an opportunity to develop his own expertise.

60. The flow of commercial technology from the developed to the developing countries is largely related to the capital-intensive manufacturing and extractive industries. The financial and legal terms of commercial transfers are the priority issues in this area. Transnational enterprises seek the most profitable arrangements from their own point of view. The purchaser, on the other hand, seeks to pay less but is often hampered by unequal bargaining power. Another major set of transfer issues concerns the extent to which governments of industrialized countries should reduce incentives for, or impose restraints on, technology flows which allow developing countries to compete with their own industries or which, as in the case of nuclear technology, threaten their security interests. Except for nuclear technology, this issue is only now coming to the fore—as continued recession and high unemployment in industrial countries create additional pressures on governments to restrict technology flows which threaten already weak industries.

61. Other channels for technology flow include the hundreds of thousands of students studying in industrial countries, the tens of thousands of teachers and public sector technicians from developed countries working in the developing countries, the on-site training of Third World personnel in more advanced countries (the principal

means for the now largely forgotten technology flow from the United States to Japan and Western Europe at the time of the Marshall Plan), the purchase of thousands of technical publications and periodicals, and consulting and engineering services, turn-key plants, joint ventures, and management contracts.

62. An adequate understanding of the impact of international technology flows and of their commercialization requires, then, a threefold assessment. The assessment depends on the nature of the technology transactions involved, the uses to which the technology is put, and the specific recipient countries and enterprises concerned. The more technological capability a purchaser has, the greater his ability to negotiate with technology suppliers. The lack of such capability on the purchaser's side may include information gaps (about potential sources of technology, their likely terms in transacting the technological characteristics of the procured knowledge, etc.) and technological weaknesses (lack of expertise, skills, experience, R&D capabilities, etc.), or both. Information gaps and technological weaknesses seriously affect the terms under which productive knowledge is transferred and put to use.

63. The process of transferring technology presents two kinds of issues for both suppliers and purchasers: the costs involved in either selling or acquiring technology and the numerous impacts on the interests or objectives of the parties concerned. The costs can be grouped into three categories: (a) pre-acquisition costs, such as those incurred by the *purchaser* in scanning the international market in preparation for the purchase of know-how or in setting up indigenous technological and negotiating capabilities; or those incurred by the *seller* in generating the transacted know-how; (b) direct costs involved in purchasing the technology itself; and (c) indirect costs and payments for various other inputs and resources tied or linked to technology transactions.

The various types of impact include: (a) the economic effects of the technology in question on, for example, trade patterns, access to markets, the local infrastructure, scarce resources, the natural environment, and industrial restructuring; (b) the structural impact of the technology on the displacement or promotion of local technological capabilities and production structures; (c) the social impact of technology on, for example, consumer preferences, social mobility, class structures, etc.; (d) the political impact of the technology on the composition of elites, foreign penetration and dependence, direct interference through diplomatic and other pressures exercised by foreign governments, etc.

64. Host countries are becoming aware that there is often a clear distinction in international business between ownership and control. While ownership can be secured through nationalization or through agreements which phase out the participation of foreign equity, control is a much more elusive matter. One of the most crucial factors contributing to a country's ability to control its means of production is

the availability of local skilled personnel. Policies designed merely to control foreign business penetration without providing for human and institutional skill formation are proving to have limited effects. Policies on the importation of technology therefore need to be matched by equally explicit policies on local skill, personnel, and institution building.

Future Technological Trends and Shifting Comparative Advantages

65. Advances in technology are shifting the comparative advantages of countries and inducing the relocation of industries. These relocations have been stimulated by governmental policies in the developing countries. As a result, the developed countries may begin to adopt policies to retard industrial relocation which threatens their interests.

66. Among the advanced countries there is increasing standardization of major product lines to make performance more equal. At the same time, however, there is also a growing amount of product specialization — the addition of different options to standardized equipment, as in car models available with either four or six cylinders. Both standardization and the proliferation of specialized options are opening up opportunities for technically capable producers in the developing countries to bid for supply contracts.

67. As some developing countries move to utilize these opportunities and as wages rise, there will be new comparative advantages for other less developed countries with lower wage levels. The newly industrialized countries should be willing to open up their markets to the manufactures of these countries; increased foreign exchange earnings by these less developed countries would serve the export interests of the newly industrialized countries, since many of their products are particularly appropriate in terms of technology and price. In addition, the newly industrialized countries have experience in meeting the problems of lagging sectors (for example, rural/village areas in Brazil and cottage industries in India) that is applicable to the servicing of the internal markets of the least-developed countries. But there are few incentives, few resources, and few channels for passing on such information.

68. In choosing their route to industrialization, countries with natural resources decide whether to direct them to world or to local markets. Export to world markets requires no processing, although processing increases both the value added and foreign exchange earnings. Such processing would have to meet foreign quality standards and would require advanced technologies. Use for the domestic market would also require processing, but not necessarily to such high standards, and the value added would probably be less. The decision about the amount of processing depends partly on the ability of the economy to absorb higher technologies and partly on the market orientation of the country's productive sector.

69. The character of a country's productive sector depends on how its policies are shaping consumer patterns — whether the country is seeking to follow the pattern prevalent in the already developed countries (under the pressure of the demonstration effect) or is seeking to develop on the basis of indigenous values and patterns. Technologies should be available to permit the latter, if desired, without forcing low standards of living.

Areas of Action in the International Flow and Commercialization of Technology

70. The Symposium's participants were able to reach agreement that the broad remedial actions required to deal with the problems outlined above should include:

(a) Enhancing, through a wide range of measures, the negotiating capability of developing countries in their acquisition of foreign technology so as to increase the prospects for effective, stable agreements in the basic interest of all parties;

(b) Strengthening local capabilities to explore technological alternatives and to participate in their implementation;

(c) Reexamining the legal and contractual mechanisms of commercial technology transfer, including the Paris Convention on patents, and establishing international codes of conduct setting guidelines for technology transfer arrangements and for the activities of TNEs;

(d) Improving adjustment mechanisms in the industrial countries, as well as the newly industrializing ones, so as to reduce restrictive pressures on technology flows to the developing countries;

(e) Adopting special measures to facilitate the international flow of technology for the benefit of the least-developed countries.

71. These remedial actions could help defuse the suspicion in many developing countries that the industrial countries consciously wish to keep them in a status of dependency in order to exploit their weaknesses for unfair financial and other gain.

72. Serious debate continues, however, about issues such as mandatory versus voluntary codes of conduct and the extent to which industrial countries should subsidize technology flows competitive with their own industries. Debate over these aspects of commercial technology flows has unnecessarily delayed action in areas of mutual interest and created a climate of controversy and suspicion adverse to the overall interests of the developed and developing countries and TNEs alike.

73. The policies of industrial-country governments toward technology flows affecting their own weak industries is an issue of particular concern. Global economic efficiency — and therefore lower inflation and increased employment for all countries — argues against creating artificial barriers to technology flows.

74. *Enhancing the negotiating capability of the developing countries in their acquisition of foreign technology.* During the last decade, a number of developing countries have acted to improve their bargaining capabilities vis-a-vis foreign suppliers. These actions need to be supported and intensified so as to promote more effective, equitable, and therefore more stable structures in the world technology market. Measures to help strengthen negotiating *power* by increasing *knowledge* on how to negotiate and strengthening the *will* to do so are all needed. These include improved access to information, management skills, regional cooperation, collective procurement of technology, and clear and consistent policies on foreign enterprise. Correlatively, negotiators for the developed countries need to acquire a better understanding of the cultural conditions and development policies of the developing nations.

75. *Strengthening local technological capabilities.* Any policy on foreign technology imports is incomplete unless it expressly incorporates specific measures designed to improve indigenous technological capabilities. Such measures should include policies to popularize science and technology so that the whole population can participate in and benefit from their use, and the specific development of such things as consulting and engineering skills, company-specific technological capabilities, R&D activities in enterprises, and specialized research institutes.

76. *Reexamining the legal and contractual mechanisms of commercial technology transfer.* For the first time in history, the entire world community is deeply involved in examining and modifying the legal and contractual mechanisms by means of which technology and other intangible assets are appropriated and traded. The areas under investigation include the deficiencies of the Paris Convention on industrial property matters, the desirability of effective codes of conduct regarding technology commercialization and the activities of the TNEs, the significance of restrictive business practices in light of the worldwide operations of the TNEs, and the consequences of the increasing share of tied-in and related-party trade goods and services which are linked to the flow of technology and direct foreign investment. The mutal understanding that is being obtained by all parties to the extended negotiations on these subjects has importance in itself, quite apart from the value of the end results achieved.

77. *Improving adjustment mechanisms in the developed countries.* The flow of technology to the developing countries and the adjustment mechanisms and unemployment policies of the developed countries are closely related. Technology is not static but is continuously evolving. Major technological breakthroughs in certain areas (such as micro-processors and synthetic fibers) which are important to developed countries may also seriously and adversely affect commodities or traditional manufactures of the developing nations. The impact of such developments on competitive economic

interests within the North has important repercussions on the North-South flow of technology and the overall North-South economic relationship, particularly with respect to developing-country access to industrialized markets. All of these interconnected and complex issues should be given a higher priority in national policy concern and in international forums.

78. *Adopting special measures to facilitate the international flow of technology for the benefit of the least-developed countries.* A significant number of resource-poor, least-developed countries find themselves outside of the mainstream of technological evolution. These countries manifest specific bargaining weaknesses when they enter the world technology market. Moreover, many existing channels and purveyors of international technology do not cover some areas crucial to their developmental concerns. Concentrated regional and international action needs to be undertaken to provide support in meeting the needs of these countries. R&D in the private sector, while important, cannot be completely effective. International public R&D, including technological cooperation by the industrialized countries, is of primary importance.

Recommendations

79. Implementing the broad remedial actions discussed above will require renewed efforts at the national, regional, and international levels:

(1) Information should be improved and made more available to potential users. Data banks at the national, regional, and international levels need to be expanded, and some should be specialized. Individuals capable of identifying information needs as well as disseminating information must be trained.

(2) In the effort to improve the application of technology, guidelines for transfers will be useful, as will the clear enunciation of national goals and the expectations of suppliers of technology. Governmental screening processes can be useful in facilitating technology transfer and helping users identify and select appropriate technologies.

(3) New educational institutions should be established at all levels in the developing countries, and existing ones should be improved. Transnational enterprises should be encouraged to prepare persons in the developing countries for technical and managerial tasks appropriate to established goals and marketing roles.

(4) Several forums should be established through which a continuing dialogue can take place at the technical and subministerial levels to keep information flowing on needs, available technologies, and emerging patterns of acquisition and use.

(5) More effective institutional means and incentives need to be created for the transfer of commercial technologies to the least-developed countries, particularly from the industrialized developing countries.

VI. Mobilizing Technology for the Management of Global Problems

80. There are a number of global problems on which scientific and technological cooperation between North and South is possible, appropriate, and necessary. Some of these global problems — weather, environment, natural disasters, management of river and ocean basins and deserts — originate in nature. Others, such as poor health, overpopulation, urbanization, drug addiction, racism, unemployment, rural poverty, and lack of mass transportation, are grave social problems. Still other global problems—in areas such as food, energy, and raw materials, for example — involve interdependencies related to the operation of the world economy and affect inflation, employment, and growth rates in both the developed and the developing countries.

81. Because these problems affect all of humanity, they cannot be solved by either the North or the South in isolation. A significant portion of the scientific and technical knowledge needed to solve them is not proprietary information, but knowledge available from public institutions, such as government research laboratories in the health, agriculture, and energy fields, for example, or government weather bureaus. The non-proprietary nature of this knowledge alleviates one of the main causes of North-South conflict.

82. The interests of the North as well as the South are consistent with, and in fact demand the development of a self-reliant technological capacity in the developing countries to enable them to participate fully in the definition and solution of global problems such as those mentioned above. This convergence of interests provides a sound political basis for long-term cooperation between North and South in a joint attack on shared problems. Such cooperation — based on long-term mutual self-interest rather than the paternalistic premises of traditional development assistance — can facilitate a depth of commitment and a scale of effort commensurate with the scope and importance of the problems. There are many fields in which the achievement of the developing countries has attained worldwide standards. These include the accomplishments of individual countries in such fields as low-cost housing, rubber technology, water management, urban traffic control, solar heating, biomass energy, and low-cost health care.

Major Areas for North-South Technological Cooperation:
Food and Energy

83. Some areas of mutual interest to the North and the South — especially food and energy — originate in a scarcity of resources. Unless the situation improves rapidly, the developing countries will fall more and more short of grain self-sufficiency. This increasing shortage will have to be supplied by North America with all the resulting environmental and other difficulties. The inevitably higher costs of this added production will have adverse effects on both the developing and the developed countries. Furthermore, it is unwise for food-deficit countries to become dependent on a single source that is vulnerable to climatic and political variables.

84. The developing countries clearly have the physical resources to meet their increasing demand for food at current world price levels. Technological cooperation that helps to make production technology available to the farmers of the poor countries is thus strongly in the interest of both the North and the South. Such cooperation, if it were in part directed to improving productivity on small farms and in dry-land zones, would contribute to improved rural incomes. It would also help to stem environmental degradation; the most serious ecological problems of the densely populated countries arise from the misuse of marginal lands by poorer farmers.

85. In energy, as in food, demand is outrunning supply. The developing countries, with their underutilized non-renewable resources and their great comparative advantage in renewable energy resources, could play a greater role in providing new sources of supply at reasonable cost levels. Global energy management, however, is complicated by the control of much of the relevant technology in a relatively few private hands, or, in the cases of nuclear technology and oil, in the control of a few governments. In principle, both the developed and the developing countries have a common interest in maximizing the number of alternative sources of fossil fuels, maximizing the number of alternative energy resources, conserving energy, and managing nuclear technology. Greater effort is required to make that common interest a reality.

86. Consumption patterns in the industrialized countries and among the newly affluent in the developing countries are also aggravating the problem of global resource management. Increased consumption of meat, involving a manyfold increase in the use of food grains, is one example. Another is profligate use of energy in the developed countries. The situation is compounded by the spread of industrialized-country consumption aspirations to the developing countries. These patterns, based on energy-intensive and resource-consuming production systems, should be the subject of active and open debate in the 1980s at both the national and the international level. This overdue debate should stimulate a search for more resource- and energy-conserving technologies and should lead to ap-

propriate action by national governments to encourage less
consumption-oriented and wasteful life-styles.

87. Another resource area in need of global management is that of
non-food agricultural commodities. In this field, the main problems
have been competition from synthetic substitutes, lack of adequate
scientific, technological, and promotional inputs, excessive price
fluctuations, and lack of confidence in the long-term future. Synthetics, which are produced mostly in the developed countries, enjoy the
advantages of stable prices, integration of manufacturing and marketing, and massive scientific and technological inputs. This unequal
competition—and a resultant lack of confidence in the future by the
producers of natural commodities that are important to both developing and developed countries—has progressively eroded the technical
and economic viability of many natural commodities. Notable exceptions are rubber, wool, and (to a lesser extent) cotton.

88. Both rubber and wool provide excellent examples of how the
market for a natural commodity can be defended against competition
through production and end-use research, development, and promotion at the national and the international level. Developing-country
governments, international agencies, and interested parties in the
developed world must work to identify other natural products which
could benefit from the same concerted approach. Substantial incentives for this search are increasing chemical and energy prices, which
have already begun to change the competitive environment in favor of
agricultural commodities.

Other Global Problems Suited for International Cooperation

89. Another area of shared North-South interest—and a potential
area for cooperation among the developing countries — is the development of innovations that will permit the transformation of irreplaceable global assets—such as game parks, endangered species and
their habitats, cultural monuments, and geological formations—into
economically productive assets without destroying their unique
character. One of the important irreplaceable ecological assets is the
mature tropical forest, a rapidly diminishing resource in urgent need
of North-South cooperation.

90. The preceding sections merely suggest some examples of a
common North-South interest in technological cooperation in working toward shared long-term goals; many other avenues of technological cooperation should be explored.

Mechanisms for Global Problem Management

91. In the case of food, the recognition of an imminent and shared
danger culminated in the World Food Conference in 1974 and the
creation of the present cluster of international organizations concerned with the international food problem. Together with the Food

and Agriculture Organization (FAO), these organizations constitute a reasonably well-integrated apparatus for global problem management. They include the Consultative Group on International Agricultural Research, which identifies needs for new research programs and funds an expanding network of internationally managed agricultural research institutes; the International Food Policy Research Institute, which carries out economic policy research on world food problems; the International Fund for Agricultural Development, a fund intended specifically for investments in agriculture in the developing countries; and the World Food Council, a political forum for the discussion of food policy issues.

92. The experience of the international community in developing this cluster of institutions to manage the global food problem holds important lessons for future attempts to design institutional frameworks for the management of other global problems. Major efforts are needed to assess the likely impact of any new technology that may emerge from cooperative action in the light of the economic and other constraints facing potential users. Social, institutional, and policy innovations are needed to complement technological innovation. Care is needed to ensure that international machinery is linked to, and strengthens, national capability. It is also important that institutions and individuals from the developing world be actively involved in the design of international efforts. There is likewise a need for continuous, independent technical and economic advice to monitor and evaluate existing programs, identify gaps, maintain contact with the international scientific and technological community (including basic science), identify new problem areas, and propose technological efforts for their solutions.

93. Successful international cooperation in global management will require the strengthening of local capabilities in the developing countries. There must be full and equal involvement of Third World scientists, technologists, and other experts and institutions in the process of identifying global problems and in the design of mechanisms for working on their solution. Only if they participate fully from the start will the developing countries support the solutions that emerge from that process. Moreover, it is through such participation that the developing countries will strengthen their own problem-solving capabilities and thus accelerate the development of their self-reliance. At the same time, however, there must be no artificial barriers to the use of technological resources which are available from the *developed* countries when these are most appropriate to the tasks at hand.

94. The developed countries should commit substantial resources to the development of local capabilities. They should also encourage and support the participation of their own scientists in programs of global scientific cooperation, such as the Tropical Diseases Research Program of the World Health Organization and the Global Atmospheric Research Program of the World Meteorological Organization.

One promising approach would be for the developed countries to fund a set of institutions patterned on the International Development Research Centre of Canada and similar institutions which make grants for technological research and innovation intended to strengthen local capability. A proposal which is currently under consideration in some developed countries recommends that institutions might be established as adjuncts to existing multilateral and bilateral assistance efforts.

95. The establishment of autonomous funding institutions (including non-governmental ones) in the developing countries is an essential complement to this proposal. These institutions would receive funding from developed- and developing-country governments and from diverse external sources, including bilateral and multilateral aid agencies, private sources, and scientific bodies. Such institutions would provide support for high-quality technological research and innovation on the problems of the developing countries. They could provide a link between the development of local capability and programs of international cooperation on global problems. A significant amount of autonomy from both bureaucratic barriers and short-term political considerations is essential for the effectiveness of technological institutions, both in the developing and in the developed world. On the other hand, autonomy alone will not ensure that the activities of these institutions are targeted directly to the needs of the users.

Recommendations

96. The complex and dynamic character of economic relations between the North and the South and the difficulty of defining opportunities for technological cooperation based on shared long-term interests suggests a need to support an independent analytical capability to examine new problems and technological changes.

   (1) An ad hoc independent commission of non-governmental experts, consisting of both thinkers and doers, needs to be established. Members of the commission should include scientists, technologists, economists, financial executives, social thinkers, political leaders, project managers, and representatives of other relevant disciplines, representing all parts of the world. The commission should analyze present and future trends, identify alternative courses of action, define and recommend priority areas for major new programs of North-South collaboration based on mutual self-interest, and recommend institutional mechanisms to carry out the work.

   (2) The commission should have as part of its mandate the promotion of its analyses and considerations among political leaders and policymakers. This is especially important because leaders and opinion makers in both the developed and the developing countries often are not well-versed in the issues dis-

cussed in this report. The commission should have an able staff and should also identify and work closely with existing organizations capable of implementing its recommendations. It should consider the advisability and structure of a permanent mechanism to carry on its functions.

(3) As an example of the type of analysis to be undertaken, the commission might wish to survey and analyze natural raw materials and their synthetic substitutes in order to draw up a list of relevant commodities that merit the concerted attention of both the producing and the consuming countries. The group could also assess the scientific, technological, and economic status of selected commodities and outline the total research, development, and promotional effort called for from the international community.

(4) The recommendations of the commission should lead to the initiation of major programs of long-term North-South technological cooperation based on shared long-term interests. This collaboration should take advantage of scientific and technological resources wherever they may be located—specifically including the developed countries — but should be designed to strengthen the capability of the developing countries and to give as much responsibility as feasible to developing-country participants.

Jamaica Symposium Participants

Co-Chairmen:

Mahbub ul Haq
Director, Policy Planning and Program Review Department, World Bank, Washington, D.C.

Ivan Head
President, International Development Research Centre, Ottawa, Canada

Co-Rapporteurs:

James P. Grant
President, Overseas Development Council, Washington, D.C.

Constantine V. Vaitsos
Fellow, Institute of Development Studies, University of Sussex, Brighton, U.K.

R. P. Baffour
President, R. P. Baffour Associates, Accra, Ghana

Sonja Bata
Chairman, Symposium Working Group on International Technology Flows
Director, Bata Shoe Co., Toronto, Canada

Jack N. Behrman
Professor, Graduate School of Business Administration, University of North Carolina, Chapel Hill, U.S.A.

Hyung-Sup Choi
President, Korea Science and Engineering Foundation, Seoul, South Korea

J. D. Drilon, Jr.
Chairman, Symposium Working Group on Mobilizing Technology for National Needs

Director-General, Philippine Council for Agriculture and Resources Research, Pasay City, Philippines

Cees Eerkens
Director of Agricultural Research, Unilever Research Institute, Zevennar, Netherlands

Jacques Giri
Director of Economic Studies, Société d'Economie et Mathématiques Appliquées (SEMA), Paris

Carl-Göran Héden
Professor, UNEP/UNESCO/ICRO Microbiological Resources Center, Karolinska Institutet, Stockholm

Amir Jamal
Chairman, Symposium Working Group o Global Problem Management
Minister of Communications and Transpor Tanzania; Member of Brandt Commission o International Development Issues

Lovraj Kumar
Director, Bureau of Industrial Costs an Prices, Ministry of Industry, Government India

George McRobie
Director, Intermediate Technology Deve opment Group (ITDG), London

José Mindlin
President, Metal Leve S.A., São Paulo, Braz

Kinhide Mushakoji
Vice Rector for Programs (Human and Soci Development), United Nations Universit Tokyo

Jamil Nishtar
Chairman, Agricultural Development Bar of Pakistan, Islamabad, Pakistan

Jorge Sabato
Member of the Board of Directors, Funda cion Bariloche, Argentina; Visiting Profe sor, University of Montreal, Canada

Francisco Sagasti
International Development Research Centr Latin American Regional Office, Bogot Colombia

Luis de Sebastián
Vice Rector, Catholic University, San Sa vador, El Salvador

B. C. Sekhar
Chairman and Controller of Researc Malaysian Rubber Research and Develo ment Board, Kuala Lumpur, Malaysia

Lowell Steele
Manager, Research and Development Pla ning, General Electric Co., Schenectad New York

Juarez Távora Veado
Director, State Technological Center, Be Horizonte, Brazil

Aaron Weiner
Chairman, Tahal Consulting Engineers, Aviv

Staff

Shelley Dobyns
International Institute for Environment and Development, Washington, D.C.

Sandra Jo Hamlin
World Bank, Washington, D.C.

Jairam Ramesh
Symposium Coordinator
Consultant, International Institute for Environment and Development, Washington, D.C.

Edgar Owens
Development Officer, Appropriate Technology International, Washington, D.C.

David Runnalls
Vice President, International Institute for Environment and Development, London

Charles Weiss, Jr.
Science and Technology Advisor, World Bank, Washington, D.C.

Observers

Anil Agarwal
Assistant Editor, *Earthscan;* International Institute for Environment and Development, London

M. Anandakrishnan
Chief, New Technologies Section, Office of Science and Technology, United Nations, New York

Kyung-Mok Cho
Scientific Attache, Embassy of South Korea, Washington, D.C.

R. R. Clarke
Senior Advisor to the Vice President, External Relations, World Bank, Washington, D.C.

Guy Gresford
Deputy Secretary-General, United Nations Conference on Science and Technology for Development, United Nations, New York

Khadija Haq
Director, Third World Foundation, Washington, D.C.

Ward Morehouse
President, Council on International and Public Affairs, New York; and Visiting Professor, University of Lund, Sweden

Other Contributors

Rex Bosson
Formerly Mining Engineer, Industrial Projects Department, World Bank, Washington, D.C., and Assistant General Manager, Chase NBA-New Zealand Group, Ltd., Aukland, New Zealand

G. K. Helleiner
Professor, Department of Political Economy, University of Toronto, Canada

David A. Henry
Assistant Director, Renewable Energy Task Force, International Development Research Centre, Ottawa, Canada

Bension Varon
Senior Economist, East Africa Department, World Bank, Washington, D.C.

José Israel Vargas
Secretary for Industrial Technology, Ministry of Industry and Commerce, Government of Brazil

II. The Nature and Consequences of International Technology Flows

Development as we know it today is hardly possible without technology. Moreover, the technological level necessary for the attainment of any delineated developmental process is more easily reached when there are relevant precursory developments in science. Technology is in most cases a product of some sort of science.

The question, insofar as technology is concerned, that the least-developed countries are asking — or ought to be asking — is how to contend with technology that is a product of industrialization efforts in countries other than theirs. The least-developed countries need to industrialize, and to do so they need technology. The snag is that industrialization as we now know it is the result of a complex spiralling process firmly rooted in the highly industrialized countries. Within the industrialized world this process has inevitably developed its own logic. The fact that industrialization in capitalistic countries is spearheaded by "market" forces whereas in socialist countries it is contained within the framework of a planned economy does not make any difference to most of the least-developed countries which have to import technology. The phenomenon of interaction between science (and/or technology) and the demand for material satisfaction emphasizes this predicament.

There are, of course, variations between countries in the types of systems that characterize their respective economies. But, quite indisputably, in both the advanced capitalist and socialist countries there is a discernible mass of technology which is both the product and the propeller of the whole process of industrialization. To state the obvious, industrialization is the engine of growth and development of most advanced economies today. This is not surprising, given that, historically, technological development was geared toward the production of military hardware and software, the pursuit of communications techniques, and reliance on cheap energy sources — all this, of course, in support of satisfying the demand for material consumption and protecting such consumption. Thus, both means and ends are fairly well understood, if not deliberately defined, by most of the

Chapter 1

The Consequences of Technological Dependence in the Least-Developed Countries

Amir Jamal

advanced countries that have pushed for industrialization through technological advances.

It may be relevant here to observe that the industrialization of the developed countries has been an organic process which has not only developed its own logic but also taken its own time. The replacement of feudal, agrarian society with industrialized society has been an "internalized" process. Industrial technological know-how has been developed within the confines of the same society, thus providing it with the logistics permitting the development and dissemination of technology within its confines. This was done through the operations of financial institutions and capital markets which, over a period of time, formed a strong alliance with the technological base. As more and more countries gained independence and came to be known as developing countries, this total alliance between finance and technology was well-placed to extend its activities, in the form of transnationals and consultants, along the path already laid down.

Is Technological Dependence Inevitable?

Without going into the political background — spanning centuries — which characterized the securing and sustained transporting of raw materials and cheap fuel, without which no technological development was possible in the industrialized countries, let us now look at the receiving end, that is to say, the developing countries, particularly the least-developed ones.

Before gaining political independence, these countries, whether landlocked or not, had already been penetrated with infrastructures and services which depended on the technology of the industrialized world. Almost certainly, there were bound to be in place internal combustion machines, power generating plants, telecommunica-

*Revised version of a paper delivered at a conference on Development Policy in Wiesbaden, West Germany, September 1977, organized by the Social Democratic Party.

tions, airports using radar, and the like. And, depending on the country, there was probably a railway system or a seaport operation, or both, that depended on a range of products from the industrialized world.

When independence came, these technological installations became the immediate concern of the new nation state. How could a government afford to endanger the transportation system, let alone jeopardize vehicular travel by ministers of state, or the telephone system, or the water supply whose pumps were operated by electricity supplied by the power company? Naturally, there were foreign emissaries and visitors from abroad to join the country's independence celebrations, and so the airports were rather important, as were all the attendant services ensuring safe landing and takeoff of airplanes. Membership in the United Nations followed; no state could afford not to be a member! A nation had to be represented at General Assembly sessions and to be in contact with its beneficent agencies, with the International Monetary Fund and the World Bank. In any case, what choice was there? A nation had to sell its cotton, its coffee, its spices to the industrialized world, and all these activities called for logistical support, i.e., transportation, telecommunications, and so on.

To ensure the perpetuation of this inherited dependence on technology that had evolved in the industrialized world, no indigenous cadres existed to man these "vital" centers within the newly independent country. Foreigners therefore had to be induced to stay on or come to help run them while the local educational system was put on a "crash program" basis to churn out administrators, and, later on, technicians to take care of these essentially urban technologies, which inevitably multiplied in the meantime.

The initial period of independence was thus taken up with the deliberate stimulation of the inherited educational system to train people able to manage the technological operations already given priority. This period also saw the advent of travelling salesmen, feasibility experts, advisers, tourists and others, all of them directly or indirectly contributing to greater demand for those very services — telecommunications and transport, urban water supply and sanitation, and electricity — and their attendant social and financial infrastructure.

The newly trained and educated cadres of the country became the most powerful supporters of the whole developmental process. They themselves, by virtue of their positions in the workforce, multiplied the demand for services dependent upon foreign technology. And in due course, their resourcefulness, their ingenuity, their energies became directed towards learning and mastering the efficient use of the machines and equipment that met their needs. Now, to top it all, there are those who envision electronics industries in the developing countries that will meet an already existing "demand," even though the vast majority of the local people still have no means by which to reach the nearest health center in time to save a precious life!

Behind the whole range of technology were the transnational enterprises, which had already made projections regarding market expansion based on firmly laid foundations. The transnational enterprises made their own deliberate contribution in training and research and development which, in almost all cases, simply meant ensuring that the local elite became the purveyors of their hardware and software and the protectors of their patents. And if this, in turn, meant ever-increasing dependence on spare parts and modifications, and on the generation of new technology which made the existing technology obsolete, so much the better.

In an environment dominated by deeply entrenched urban consumption groups, it is extremely difficult to undertake reform of the social, political, or educational systems to meet the needs of a rural society. The advocates of modernization and progress receive powerful support from those who argue in favor of maximizing the returns from any given investment by adding just a little more to that investment. The appetite for investment returns increases, and policymaking itself becomes conditioned by it. The countryside is far too remote and, in the eyes of the urban elite, its populace too apathetic. The assistance and loan packages offered from abroad contain rather indigestible stuff for the rural population, and so the urban development process is left to itself to continue accelerating at the expense of rural concerns.

It is often taken for granted, for example, that main roads have to be engineered, paved, and maintained so that secondary roads can be used to take farm crops out of rural areas and bring products in. But the entire mobilization of road construction is urban-centered and often modeled on the road system in an industrialized country. All the major economic activities generated—the engineers and the managers employed, their supply organizations, the urban water and sanitation services they depend on, the telephones and electricity they use, the port capacity they strain, the consumption of urban products by the families involved, the financial institutions which engage themselves in the process—all these and more in turn demand a share of urban services, as do visiting salesmen, consultants, etc. All these demands interacting upon one another further entrench the urban sector and increase the marginalization of the rural population by taking hold of the limited financial and skilled human resources available to the wretched country.

Any suggestion that these operations should be based in a rural environment would be dismissed by the financial analysts and the engineers as either irresponsible or absurd. They would say they must depend on many essential services, including maintenance facilities already available in the towns. In any case, there is a built-in reflex within a national developmental process, whereby no skilled technician trained in heavily-engineered road construction, for example, would want to go and live in the villages without his family and without his minimum standard of living assured. (A singular exception to this is the building of the Tan-Zam Railway, which established scores of non-urban local units.)

If investment in highways, which are considered a national priority, can contribute so clearly to the polarization of society, what, then, is the total impact of so many interacting investment decisions which depend on urban centers for their implementation?

Thus a climate has been firmly established in which the debate is not between improvisation and adaptation to meet local needs, on the one hand, and imported technology on the other, but between contending foreign technologies. All who are in positions of responsibility for decisionmaking speak the same language. They advocate more telephone connections, more sophisticated airports and harbors, more urban water supply and sanitation facilities, more electricity for more capital-intensive activites as well as for increasing urban consumption. The military defense chiefs, too, quickly begin to look for more modern hardware, the products of a whole range of technological development rooted outside the country's boundaries, yet paid for and maintained by the country's rural producers. The feasibility experts, the U.N. advisors, the consultants, the packaged offers of "assistance" — all pile up more and more of this and that technology, new and not so new, on a group of admiring "modern" men and women, now eager to process their primary products locally by using capital-intensive foreign technology for which the country has neither the social, cultural, nor economic base.

In its totality, therefore, this development process calls for significant capital investment, mostly borrowed from the outside. The pattern of foreign trade inherited from colonial days becomes even more accentuated because these things have to be paid for sometime, somehow. Dependence on foreign users of primary products, raw or processed, increases sharply, and the vicious cycle continues, both nationally and internationally.

Toward a New International Order

The foregoing has demonstrated to some extent that the overpowering environment which envelops the developing countries, particularly the least-developed ones, is a direct function of accelerating technology rooted in the "pre-emptive strike" of colonial penetration.

Without detailing here the compounding of this process by the industrialized countries as their capital and technological resources are made available to strengthen the forces of reaction and oppression, one can readily imagine the distortions that these policies and actions impose on the already committed developing countries. "Bow and arrow" technology is no answer to electronically guided missiles, and so a further twist is delivered to the national economy. The pricing of imported technology, with all its manifestations and implications, and the lack of equity in international exchange, both in terms of prices and access to markets, are further problems to be reckoned with.

It is no wonder that Tanzania's economic prospects for the next ten years, according to the World Bank, make such sombre reading—even on the agreeable assumption of a 6 per cent annual growth in agricultural production. On this basis, the Bank's assessment is that Tanzania's rural income will rise by some 30 per cent in the coming decade—from the present annual per capita income level of U.S. $120.

The message is loud and clear. Developing countries, particularly the least-developed, are caught in a poverty trap. Time itself has a different significance in the two worlds of wealth and poverty, and these worlds are diverging.

Fortunately, there has been in recent years a deepening awareness in the world that the widening economic gap between poor and affluent nations cannot be allowed to continue along such a predictably disastrous course. It is now generally agreed that the peculiar schizophrenia historically induced in the developing countries, particularly the least-developed ones, by their continuing struggle to achieve internal economic and political stability in the urban and rural environments—which call for a variety of weaponry and technical know-how — must no longer be allowed to reach a point where tensions cannot be contained within the geographical boundaries of the states concerned. There is also an increasing awareness that the question of manufacturing arms — the armaments race itself — is not just a philosophical one. In this age of space satellites encircling the globe, there is increasing awareness that the industrialized societies themselves are not immune to the tensions of unbridled technological development. The so-called "cold war," and its now popularized antithesis "detente," are nothing less than byproducts of these existing tensions.

Chaos is not here as yet, mercifully. But neither is time our ally. Immediate action is required on the part of the world community in the form of some clear policy decisions. The following are some areas of concern that need a worldwide response:

(1) While affirming that the developing countries must accept responsibility for planning their own development, we must also recognize that history has drastically limited their options in this regard.

(2) Significant resource transfers from the richer to the poorer nations are needed, not as an act of charity but as an integral part of a worldwide effort to build up the capacity of the poorer nations to contend with the economic imbalances of their urban and rural areas. One would like to believe that democratic societies have a special obligation to ensure that economic assistance is not predicated on ideology, that ideology is not used as an excuse for marginal action on their part. Only when the democratic process is concretely applied to the fulfillment of the rising expectations of developing societies will the meaning of "democracy" become comprehensible to those disadvantaged peoples who have had little experience in self-determination.

(3) Fortunately, certain international institutions have evolved

that can be harnessed to meet the challenge facing the world community. The International Monetary Fund and the International Development Association (IDA) must be restructured so as to become the main instruments for channeling resources where they are most needed. These two institutions should not be controlled by one powerful country or group of countries. Their mandate, derived from the total world community,must be to receive resources and redistribute them in accordance with the adjustment problems of developing countries in an intelligent and realistic manner, by fully taking into account the peculiar factors which affect the performance of these developing societies. The IDA should become an institution in its own right, the international mechanism for pursuing development policies with maximum decentralization of powers and functions.

(4) The United Nations Conference on Trade and Development (UNCTAD) should be given the means and the authority to establish a framework for equitable exchange of goods and services, and this framework should replace the General Agreement on Tariffs and Trade (GATT).

(5) Specific action should be taken to establish and develop local science and technology centers in various regions in the developing countries, with emphasis on need- and resource-oriented work. Training — through economic production based on locally evolving technology — should be a priority commitment both for the developing countries and for the international development agencies. All relevant U.N. agencies will need to respond to this priority requirement. Research on energy, for example, must not lead to new burdens for the developing countries, which are barely able to contend with technology based on the use of fossil fuels. Information about world resources collected by means of space satellites must be made available to the countries concerned as a matter of right. Science and technology, now more than ever, need a human face.

(6) Finally, developing countries must accept the disciplines involved in the utilization of world resources and build such disciplines into their national codes of political, social, and economic management.

The present international framework within which societies interact cancels out the effects of any ad hoc endeavor, however well-meaning. If development policy is not to be frustrated but is to be pursued meaningfully, a new international order is urgently needed. It will not come about by the waving of some magic wand. Nor will 150-odd countries sit together on one auspicious day and promulgate such an order. Like all human achievements, it will come through leadership. One man in a village can inspire hundreds to follow him toward purposeful action. The world itself is now a village. A few nations and societies determined to bring about a new order have it in their power to give leadership, which the rest of the world will, of necessity, follow. Such leadership cannot come from selfish, inward-looking regimes; only social democracies, committed to bequeathing their children a just and stable order, will be able to provide it.

In one sense, all countries — including underdeveloped countries—today have "appropriate technologies." The technologies currently available in all countries are, in general, the technologies most appropriate to the economic interests of the ruling social groups. To think that the situation is otherwise would amount to denying rationality to the dominant groups in their quest for the greatest economic benefits.

El Salvador, a case in point, is a small country with extreme development problems. Yet the techniques currently employed in the private sector of the economy are modern, profitable, and seemingly satisfactory to the owners of the means of production. The technology used in the cultivation and processing of coffee in El Salvador is said to yield returns as high as in any other country. The technologies used in sugar production and in the harvesting and canning of shellfish — the country's main exports — are also modern and profitable.

Further, it can be taken for granted that the technologies used by the multinational firms (Texas Instruments, Philips, Bayer, IBM) or by joint ventures (Unilever and De Sola, Rockefeller and Todos, Sheraton with Camino Real and Hyatt) are technologies that, while not necessarily the best in their home countries, are found to be economically adapted to the proper operation of these enterprises in El Salvador. Their technology is appropriate technology — appropriate for them.

Similarly, it can be safely assumed that local private enterprises function, in general, with the market-acquired technologies which contribute most to maximizing their profits, increasing their share of the market, or achieving whatever else their immediate economic objective may be. Even the buses in San Salvador, while being utter mechanical wrecks, constitute the technical answer best suited to the private interests of the entrepreneurs, who cannot ask more than 8 (U.S.) cents per ride.

There is no quantitative proof for these assertions; their validity is a question of common sense and direct observation. If we consider the logic of the capitalist firm, we cannot but accept that all such firms operating in El Salvador adopt the type of technology which best

Appropriate Technology in Developing Countries: Some Political and Economic Considerations

Luis de Sebastián

leads them to the achievement of their economic goals (which normally amount to maximizing their profits). On the other hand, one might hope that the public sector in El Salvador would use a technology suitable (appropriate, in this sense) to economic objectives that could be easily and quantitatively measured.

Moreover, the production and distribution of some public goods is carried out in El Salvador with almost the same efficiency as in developed countries. The modern electric power system, the international telephone service, the main roads between large cities, the port activities at Acajutla, and the international airport are some examples that come to mind. The technology used in the production and supply of these public goods is the only one currently available for the efficient attainment of local objectives. Thus, the production and supply of these public goods, which are more likely to benefit (via external economies, for example) the interests of the elite, are also brought about with modern, efficient technology.

This surely is the case in El Salvador, and probably in all developing countries with a bipolar, oligarchic-dependent social structure. If the technology adopted both by private firms (national or international) and some public enterprises were not appropriate to the interests of the owners of the means of production, that technology would not be in place. The private cost-benefit analysis of the capitalists and the economic power that they so effectively exercise, particularly in a developing society, ensure the application of these technologies.

Defining "Appropriate Technology"

In this paper, the concept of "appropriate technology" differs from the conventional sense commonly understood and applied by participants in international gatherings. There are different terms of refer-

*Revised version of a paper presented to the II International Symposium on Appropriate Technology, sponsored by the Central American University "José Siméon Cañas," held in San Salvador in February 1979.

ence for a definition of "appropriateness." If we make these terms of reference into variables to be maximized, we can define appropriate technology as that type more apt to maximize such variables as the employment of human labor, the national (or some sector's) product from a given stock and given relative prices of factors of production, the overall growth rate of the economy, the economic surplus to be invested, the economic autarky of the country, its war potential, and the welfare of specific social groups.

In discussions of the problems of developing countries, the appropriateness of technology is usually understood with reference to the overall availability of productive resources (almost never to their distribution), to the relative prices of marketable factors of production, and, in the final analysis, to the basic and most urgent needs of the majority of the population. The discussion, in other words, focuses on the poverty of the country and of certain social groups. The approach adopted here, however, is to focus on the rich and powerful within and outside the developing countries.

The question of appropriate technology, like all other issues concerning development, has to be defined with reference to the different economic groups, in order to determine as clearly as possible not only the needs of some but also the obstacles that others put in the way of meeting those needs.[1] From this point of view, it becomes obvious that the technology to be found in the developing countries is, in general, appropriate for the rich and powerful but highly inappropriate for the poor who constitute the majority. To deal with technology simply as it relates to a country, a continent, or a hemisphere, has little operative value.[2]

If we accept the view that the technology now installed in the developing countries is appropriate to the national or international groups which rule their economies, we cannot hold great hopes for technological change, either through an autonomous development process or through the transfer of technology. We must ask ourselves where the initiative for technological change is going to come from, if those who control the economy do not feel a need for it.[3]

The Universal Presence of Inappropriate Technology

No developing country has the set of technologies appropriate to solving the basic problems of the majority of its population: malnutrition; lack of adequate health care, housing, and education; insufficient opportunities for stable employment; low income. Their technologies are not predominantly of the type required for efficient production of basic goods, private and public. This is, obviously, a posteriori assertion. The technology actually available in the developing countries is not appropriate to solving their problems, because if it were their problems would have been at least partly solved and would not have become more acute, as seems to be the fact in many countries.

In El Salvador, the available technologies have not been able to eliminate dramatic problems of malnutrition, unemployment, illiteracy, endemic diseases, excessive population growth, alcoholism, crime, and so on. Obviously, this situation exists because the technology in use is not applied effectively to the solution of social problems. In the final analysis, the problem resides in the fact that the economic organization of an underdeveloped country has purposely been made appropriate to the interests of the ruling groups and highly inappropriate to the destitute majority.

The underdevelopment of any country is not a functional phenomenon but a structural one. The structure of the economy of an underdeveloped country is formally different from that of a developed country. Because technology is an element of the economic structure and its ultimate significance derives from the structure to which it belongs, it follows that the technology of an underdeveloped country is different from the technology of a developed country; the technologies belong to different structural realities, even though their physical composition is the same.[4]

Whether the structural formulation is accepted or not, it is clear that technology is not an independent, exogenous variable in any given social system.[5] Technologies are developed, disseminated and, above all, applied within a given social context in such a way that the technological stock is not independent of the values, objectives, and organization of that society. Even in countries that are merely importers of technology, this connection is not the result of some historical accident, nor is it imposed by some unspecified necessity. It is closely interdependent with the type of economy and society that has been chosen or is being promoted. Technological choices are, almost necessarily, the result (given the state of technological knowledge) of previous choices relative to the values, objectives, means, and instruments of the economic system. The technology of any country, therefore, will be appropriate for some of its citizens and inappropriate for others, according to the economic and social structure in which it is implemented.[6]

False Problems in Determining Appropriate Technology

The following diagram shows the linkages between four types of choices, each of them conditioning the ensuing choice.

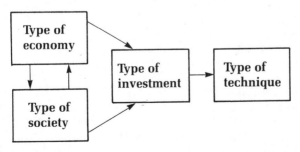

Most discussions of appropriate technology focus, rather narrowly, on the last of these categories, as if an autonomous choice were really possible. Fortunately, however, there is a growing body of knowledge which analyzes the technological problem as only a limited aspect of the whole social system.[7]

The real and the false aspects of the problem are illustrated in El Salvador, where a new international airport is being constructed with the latest technology. Many have raised angry voices against the use of capital-intensive technology in a country with so much unemployed labor. But the technology used in the construction of the Cuscatlan Airport is not the major problem. It is, at most, only a marginal one. The real issue is that $150 million has been expended on a new airport instead of building more hospitals and schools for the rural populace. The problem lies, then, in the choice of the investment project and not in the type of technology used in the construction of a modern airport, an activity which does not allow for much freedom of technological choice anyway.

Ostensibly, a modern airport was chosen over equipment and services urgently needed in the countryside because the exporting segment of the economy required an airport to increase non-traditional exports and the dependent segment of society needed to promote tourism. Moreover, convenient financing for the project was offered to the Salvadorian government by Japan, apparently in view of the logistical advantages that the new airport will provide to Japanese trade along the Pacific coast. It is inconceivable that a foreign country would have granted financing on the same terms for a rural hospital. Thus, the discussion of capital-intensive construction techniques in this case fails to recognize the true nature of the problem. The choice of technology only becomes a problem when the choice is not appropriate to overcome structural causes of underdevelopment in a country.

By the same token, it seems absurd for a developing country to embrace a life-style reflecting the consumption patterns of an affluent country and, at the same time, to reject or even to criticize the technology necessary for those consumption patterns. If the dominant groups of El Salvador decide to live like the inhabitants of Coral Gables or Santa Monica, and the government approves and supports this choice, there is not much margin for further technological choice. The technology implicit in the automobile, the motorboat, the private airplane, will impose itself in spite of every consideration of its appropriateness to the country. This technology is, quite obviously, inappropriate to a country where basic needs are massive and extreme; but the problem once again resides in the choice of consumption patterns, not in the choice of technology.

Furthermore, the choice of technology as such — the selection of production techniques for goods and services in a country — has no definite impact on development. Consequently, a more appropriate choice (appropriate in the traditional sense) is not enough in itself to change substantially (or even partially) the situation of underdevelopment. The importance of the *right* choice of technology has sometimes been exaggerated. There are many examples which should make us more cautious.

The famous "green revolution," for instance, can only solve the nutritional problems of a developing country, if, in the words of Norman Borlaug, "the Government defines and carries out, from the highest level, a suitable economic policy."[8] Moreover, it has become evident in several countries that without an adequate redistribution of land ownership the benefits of this important technological innovation will be unevenly distributed, and the "green revolution" will not achieve its primary objective.[9]

Two examples from El Salvador show the limited effect that technological innovations can have when they take place without structural changes. With U.S. technology and advice, El Salvador installed ten years ago a system of educational television that was to alleviate the pressure of a great number of young people upon educational resources. The results so far have been disappointing. According to an evaluation team from Stanford University, educational television has not made a significant impact on the educational system of El Salvador. The system continues to be inadequate.

The other example is provided by the Salvadorian Foundation for Development and Minimal Housing (FUNDASAL). The technology used by the Foundation is appropriate not only in the traditional sense of being adapted to the availability and relative prices of productive resources, but also in the structural sense of building housing for the more needy and developing a different type of society. FUNDASAL's designs of housing units and its methods of construction provide a great deal of employment to the beneficiaries of its projects. Nevertheless, FUNDASAL has not managed (in spite of the fact that it builds more housing units for the poor than the central government) to make a substantial impact on the housing situation. In spite of all its innovative efforts in design and financing, the Foundation's work does not benefit the very poor. There are people in El Salvador who have such a low and unstable income that they cannot take upon themselves any debt, not even the minimal one necessary for the acquisition of a housing unit in a "sites and services" project.

Without profound structural changes, the prospects for choosing technology capable of overcoming the underdevelopment of any country are very limited. It is much more fundamental to decide first what kinds of goods and services are going to be produced and consumed, who is going to produce them, and how their production and distribution are going to be organized. Only then can it be determined which of the many existing and adaptable technologies are appropriate to the goals of the reformed social system in its struggle toward development. This seems to be the main issue, and the question of appropriate technology should not divert us from confronting squarely and sincerely the social problem of underdevelopment.

With respect to the choice of technology, a well-known economist from a developing country has aptly commented that "as a general rule, there should not be in an underdeveloped economy different choices from those which would be made in a well industrialized country; the most efficient technique must be chosen: the one that maximizes the economic surplus at the level of factor remuneration which is actually practiced."[10]

This is the general opinion of those who look upon economic underdevelopment as a historical process with a structural result which has neither isolated individual causes nor panaceas. The choice of technologies must be, in their opinion, an important, although partial, factor in carrying out a global strategy to transform the economic structure of underdeveloped countries. Without this transformation process, the question of choice is almost irrelevant.

New Wine in Old Wineskins

"Appropriate technology" is the latest, or one of the latest, strategies devised to soothe the social conscience of the affluent countries, which do not cease to protest against the enormous human suffering that economic underdevelopment perpetuates — suffering that cohabits in this world with exaggerated and, so to speak, insulting luxury.

What has occurred for decades can be likened to new wine being poured into old wineskins: new technological stretegies being poured into the same old, dependent, autocratic social structures of most underdeveloped countries. Unless deep-rooted changes in the social structures of the developing countries take place and are accompanied by fundamental changes in the attitudes of the developed ones, all partial strategies — basic needs, mass education, fertility control, "sites and services," "the green revolution," and others—are doomed to have only limited success. Let us face the facts. All these strategies have been tried before, in one form or another, in the past twenty-five years. In fact, we have hardly any new solutions for the 1980s. Not even the wine is new. What in most cases is missing is the determination to act. Both local and international powers and decision centers (such as the Pentagon, ITT, and the like) are unwilling to change radically a social structure that is cumulatively beneficial to a handful of people but that inexorably damages the vital chances of the majority and is at all times compliant with the economic interests of the developed countries. It is, however, extremely difficult to generate this *determination to change* in a world that is still strained by the fear of communism and still owes its prosperity to the present international division of labor.

Notes

[1]It was a constant preoccupation of the classical political economists, from Adam Smith to Karl Marx, to ask themselves what would be the effects on the different "ranks of people" of a change in the variables which define equilibrium at a given point in time. See, for instance, on the technological question: David Ricardo, *Principles of Political Economy and Taxation*, third edition, chapter 31, "On Machinery"; John Stuart Mill, *Principles of Political Economy*, Book IV, chapter 3, "Influence of the Progress of Industry and Population, On Rents, Profits and Wages"; Karl Marx, *Das Kapital*, B.I., k.13 "Machinerie und grosse Industrie." For the need to return to the great visions of the classical writers in matters of economic development see Irma Adelman, "On the State of Development Economics," *Journal of Development Economics* 1, 1974, pp. 3-5.

[2]"Poverty has to be defined in terms of people rather than nations." Jagdish Bhagwati, ed., *Economics and World Order* (New York: The Free Press, 1972), p. 14. On the important change in perception, see the recent study by David Morawetz, *Twenty-Five Years of Economic Development* (Washington: The World Bank, 1977), p. 9 and passim.

[3]The entrepreneurs in underdeveloped countries usually complain about the prices they have to pay for importing technology. See Harry G. Johnson, "The Efficiency and Welfare Implications of the International Corporation" in *The International Corporation*, Charles P. Kindleberger, ed., (Cambridge: The M.I.T. Press, 1970), page 39. The question of its appropriateness to the country as such does not normally enter into their calculations.

[4]This is not Marxist thinking. The idea of structure and reality used here is taken from the Spanish writer Xavier Zubiri. On this subject, see Ignacio Ellacuria, "La idea de estructura en la filosofía de Zubiri," *Realitas*, I, 1974, pp. 71-139. In the English summary of this article we read: "The whole of reality should be seen from the essence, and essence in the last analysis is a structural principle."

[5]Against Schumpeter's notion of technological change (as invention) being a phenomenon exogenous to economic development, the idea of change (as innovation) being a function of demand and dependent on the actual process of economic development has been highlighted by many modern writers. See, for instance, Jacob Schmookler, "Economic Sources of Inventive Activity," in *The Economics of Technological Change*, Nathan Rosenberg, ed., (Harmondsworth: Penguin Books, 1971), pp. 117-137; and Nathan Rosenberg, *Perspectives on Technology* (Cambridge: University Press, 1976), pp. 260-79.

[6]As an expert in this matter put it, "The economic decision processes that determine the technology and the level of employment in a given economy depend on the pattern of ownership of the means of production and the relation between the different economic classes." Amaryta Sen, *Employment, Technology and Development* (Oxford University Press, 1975), p. 60.

[7]Frances Stewart, *Technology and Underdevelopment* (London: Macmillan, 1977).

[8]Norman E. Borlaug, "La revolución verde y despues," *Facetas* 5, 1972, p. 28.

[9]India and Mexico are no doubt the countries best studied in this connection. See D.P. Chaudhri, "New Technologies and Income Distribution in Agriculture," in *Agrarian Reform and Agrarian Reformism*, David Lehmann, ed. (London: Faber and Faber, 1974), pp. 157-89.

[10]Samir Amin, *Le Développement Inégal: Essai sur les formations sociales du capitalisme périphérique* (Paris: Les Editions de Minuit, 1973), p. 201.

G lobal interdependence is a fact of late 20th century life. We are all riders on Spaceship Earth—but alas, a small proportion of humanity travels first-class and the rest are down in steerage. Melancholy evidence accumulates that the "benefits" of international cooperation for development flow unevenly both within and between countries. This is hardly surprising when the rules of the game have been set by the more powerful actors in the international economic and political system.

Although all the riders on the global spaceship share an ultimate concern for improving the human condition, it is manifestly *not* in the short-term interest of the powerful actors in the international system to surrender willingly their superior capacity for generating and using technology to produce goods and provide services. The technology they do generate, furthermore, is designed to serve their needs and is largely irrelevant to the needs of poor countries. Behind the facade of international cooperation in science and technology for development lies a harsher reality: the preoccupation of some of these more powerful governmental and corporate actors with using their superiority in science and technology to force the poor countries into a dependent relationship and thus maintain dominance and control. ("Policy leverage" is the polite phrase in superpower documents).

North-South negotiations over the past decade underscore this harsh reality. Where vital interests are at stake, negotiations yield little for the poor but crumbs off the table *except* when the weak organize themselves to bargain effectively with their more powerful adversaries. And vital interests are at stake in some key areas of technology generation and application. But not in all areas: one obvious task in North-South discussions on technology and development is to identify those sectors where less vital interests are involved and more meaningful international cooperation may be possible.

The Unholy Alliance: Power, Privilege, and Technology

Underlying the irrelevance of most technological change to the unmet social needs of a majority of the Third World population is the unholy

Third World Disengagement and Collaboration: A Neglected Transitional Option

Ward Morehouse

alliance between the rich countries, which collectively generate their own technology, and the 10 to 20 per cent of the population of poor countries who have adopted rich-country consumption patterns. The needs of these largely urbanized middle- and upper-income groups in the Third World are thus well served by rich-country technology.

Such groups feel little compulsion to break the links tying them to technological development in the advanced countries through investment, trade, and other economic and political ties, which are the carriers of technology from North to South. Since these middle and upper-income groups include most of those with political and economic power and the privileges which go with that power, and since those in rich countries with whom they interact — political leaders and senior officials of banks, multinational corporations, and international agencies—also occupy positions of power and privilege in the industrialized countries, we are confronted with an alliance of those within rich and poor countries who determine the direction and character of technological change in order to maintain their own status and power.

The systemic character of technological development, with productive activity based on one kind of technology frequently requiring complementary activities based on similar technologies, means that this unholy alliance becomes all the more pervasive in its impact on technological change in poor countries. Alternative technologies designed to meet the needs of those now largely excluded from the benefits of technological change would also raise serious questions as to the efficiency of the existing system of productive activity. The pervasive influence of this unholy alliance spills over into the economic infrastructure and social services, which are required to operate a productive system based on advanced country technology, and thus absorbs most of the resources available to build up and maintain such infrastructure and services.

In similar manner, the influence of this unholy alliance pervades the political and economic systems of both the developing and the developed countries. As Frances Stewart puts it:

To the extent that governments consist of individuals who benefit from, and represent those who benefit from, the political economy in being, they may not wish or be able to challenge it. An alternative technology at a macro level involves an alternative political economy — a different distribution of the benefits of the economic system. Governments which have developed in one system may not be powerful enough to choose an alternative system. . .

The effective pursuit of an alternative appropriate technology would threaten interests in the advanced countries . . . who are currently benefiting from the use of advanced-country technology in developing countries. The continued use of advanced-country technology is at the heart of the continued dependence of the poor countries. It maintains the advanced countries' lead in technology and therefore permits, indeed necessitates, the continued sale of technology, goods and managerial services to poor countries, on terms favorable to the rich countries.[1]

The Global War on Poverty: A Late 20th Century Myth

Notwithstanding this unholy alliance, most Third World political leaders are pro-poor at the rhetorical level. They really want to eradicate poverty from their lands — without, to be sure, paying the political and economic price of doing so. But the sad fact is that their maneuverability is limited.

The commitment of Northern elites to fighting poverty in the Third World is even more doubtful. Their compulsions are less intense, and the domestic political costs are likely to outweigh by far the marginal economic and social benefits to their own constituents. Given these circumstances, bold talk about mounting a global war on poverty lacks credibility. Carlos Diaz-Alejandro of the Yale Economic Growth Center puts it this way:

> Why not argue for a world-wide war on poverty and oppression? To those familiar with the rise and fall of the Alliance for Progress, the answer is obvious: no Northern government has both the credibility and the resources to launch and lead such a program seriously and globally, not now and not in the 1980's. Proposed global bargains between Northern and Southern elites of the types more aid in exchange for redistribution and democracy are, at best, utopian; at worst, a new version of an old confidence game. The sincerity with which some Northern individuals deplore poverty and oppression in the South is to be respected: but it strains the imagination to believe that major Northern governments, particularly those of large countries, could place such concerns at the center of their policies toward the South in any sustainable fashion in the near future. Indeed, much more needs to be done by some governments on their home front to eliminate poverty and injustice.[2]

A Hobson's Choice for the Third World

Most Third World countries are confronted with a Hobson's choice in the coming decade. Too heavy an emphasis on meeting basic needs, narrowly defined as satisfying minimum requirements for survival, is likely to result in relegating the developing countries to second-class economic and political status if it involves opting primarily for small-scale village technologies. If this emphasis also involves acceptance of large-scale food aid and other international assistance to the rural poor, the dependence of these countries on a politically capricious international dole will be increased.

Too heavy an emphasis on a strategy which seeks to strengthen national economic and political autonomy through aggressive acquisition of high technology may, paradoxically, lead not to greater technological autonomy but to greater dependence at a qualitatively higher level. India's recent difficulties in supplying one of her nuclear power stations (itself an aberration in India's generally autonomous atomic energy program) with imported fuel from the United States is a case in point. The United States has proposed unilaterally to impose conditions unacceptable to India, thus seeking to use India's dependence on external fuel sources to exercise "policy leverage" over India's atomic energy program. An imitative industrial strategy, furthermore, is not likely to meet the minimum needs of most of the people. Few countries — even those which claim to control technology imports—have been able to avoid the socially distorting effects of a pattern of economic growth based on foreign technology (or even on indigenously developed derivative technology) and geared primarily toward meeting the needs of the urbanized middle classes.

India again comes to mind as an example, although there are many others. From 1966 to 1976, private sector industrial employment hovered between 6.5 and 6.8 million, while industrial production grew substantially through increased capital investment and improved technology largely imported from the industrialized countries.[3] India's modern industrial sector thus succeeded in soaking up scarce capital while doing nothing for one of the most critical social problems facing the country — unemployment, underemployment, and employment at very marginal rates of productivity. From 1961 to 1971, the number of landless and almost landless agricultural laborers affected by these conditions increased by 90 per cent. What lies ahead is far worse: by 1984 the male labor force alone is expected to total 196 million, compared to 152 million in 1974.[4]

Lack of productive employment is only one part of the equity crisis in the Third World, which will reach epic proportions by the mid-1980s. In many Third World countries, sharply increasing income inequality is another. For instance, from 1960 to 1970, while Brazil was aggressively importing Western technology to maximize export earnings, the share of the national income going to the top 5 per cent of the population went from 27 per cent to 35 per cent, according to official Brazilian statistics.[5] (Private estimates claim that the top 5 per cent received as much as 46 per cent of the national income by 1970.)[6]

Acute material deprivation is yet another aspect of this crisis. In India, estimates place up to 54 per cent of the rural population (and 40 per cent of the total population) below the poverty line, defined in one instance as income sufficient to acquire enough calories of food just to stay alive.[7] This situation can be found in other Third World countries as well.

A Likely Scenario for the 1980s

Because of the interlocking alliance of power, privilege, and technology, the pursuit of a trickle-down development strategy based on an expanding modern industrial sector remains strongly tempting to Third World political leaders and is actively encouraged by some Northern elements. The temptation is compounded by the bleak character of the alternatives, but those in the Third World opting for this strategy would do well to ponder the implications for their fragile modern industrial economies of emerging trends in Western technology.

Let us assume we are now in the mid-1980s. The most industrialized Southern market economy countries, which are generally regarded as the more advanced within the Third World in terms of industrial and allied technological capacity, such as Brazil, Mexico, and India, are still characterized, as they are today, by sharp inequality of income and massive rural unemployment but with a substantial modern industrialized sector. Meanwhile, however, the leading industrialized countries, responding to continuing pressure to increase the productivity of labor because of rising labor costs, will have automated much more of their production technology, created more and more synthetic substitutes for Third World raw materials, and moved toward an increasingly self-contained industrial system. These trends, which will weaken manufacturing operations in those developing countries, may be accelerated by rising labor costs within such developing countries and their growing assertiveness on international economic and political issues.

These developing countries will have become increasingly integrated technologically with the industrialized countries, especially through multinational corporations, which seek to rationalize production on a global scale to minimize costs and maximize profits. But these developing countries will lack the capacity to innovate because they have never had to try and because that capacity is a carefully guarded monopoly of the multinationals and their home country governments. The Mexicos and Brazils and Indias of the 1980s, if they persist in their present policies, will be like the proverbial emperor in his new suit of clothes—all dressed up but with no place to go. They will have a production capacity that will become obsolete virtually overnight, they will have only limited internal markets because of income inequality and mass poverty, and they will not have the ability to adapt quickly to cataclysmic changes which are externally determined without reference to their own needs. In short, they will be left high and dry.[8]

Disengagement as an Alternative Strategy

Consider a possible alternative scenario, involving those developing countries which in the 1960s and 1970s recognized the critical importance of strengthening their autonomous capacity for choosing technology to meet their own needs. They placed heavy emphasis on creating local technology systems to improve productivity in rural areas for the purpose of meeting minimum needs. In their industrialization efforts they concentrated on processing their own raw materials and avoided or deemphasized the role of providing relatively low-cost labor for the labor-intensive phases of the production of consumer and intermediate goods.

These same countries concentrated on buying technology abroad in the most disembodied form possible, even though it usually cost more initially, while simultaneously investing most heavily in their own research and development in precisely those areas where they were buying foreign technology so as to be able to improve upon what they acquired elsewhere. When technology was acquired from abroad, the highest priority was given to technologies which would better enable the country to meet the minimum needs of the majority of its people. At the same time, these countries sought to strengthen their trade with other developing countries, participating in Third World multinational enterprises which pooled capital and technological skills available from within the Third World in order not to be more vulnerable than necessary to changes in the economies of the major industrialized countries.

These countries, although remaining very much a part of the world market system, will clearly be in a markedly different situation a decade hence than the Mexicos and Brazils and Indias, assuming the latter continue to follow a pattern of technologically dependent economic growth. As long as the capacity for technological innovation remains concentrated in the industrialized countries, the developing countries will be vulnerable to technological choices made elsewhere. This would be tragic, because the choices of the industrialized countries are unlikely to be made in order to protect the interests of developing countries. The net result will be increased dependence.

A strategy to maximize the autonomous capacity for technological change in the Third World will obviously vary from one country to the next. But at least four major characteristics can be identified:

(1) A conscious and deliberate effort to break away from past dependence on external sources of technology, perhaps through a ban on technology imports (subject to exceptions noted below). Gradual disengagement appears difficult to achieve because policies leading to greater autonomy are undermined by economic and political interests within the country which benefit from maintaining existing links.

(2) Selective acquisition from external sources of high priority technologies in the most disembodied form possible, with emphasis on capital goods technologies for meeting the minimum

material needs of the poor majority and on technologies to increase the value added component of exports based on local raw materials. The extent of disembodiment will depend on the level of technological competence within the country; the higher that level, the more disembodiment possible.

(3) Diversification of trading partners to avoid excessive dependence on a small group of countries, especially large industrialized countries, the superior economic strength of which always makes small countries (rich or poor) vulnerable. Diversification means efforts to strengthen trading links with other Third World countries, but given the extreme imbalance in the existing international economic system, this will be no panacea. This strategy also implies increasing the value-added component of primary commodity exports (as suggested in the preceding paragraph) and deemphasizing foreign trade in an attempt to meet local needs as much as possible through local productive effort. This step is probably more feasible for larger developing countries.

(4) Most important of all, vigorous support for local innovations to solve local problems. This may require opting for less "efficient" technologies in the short run in recognition of the longer-term benefits to be gained from learning to solve one's own problems without continued dependence on outside sources and the confidence this generates to tackle larger, more complicated problems in the future. Support for local innovations also means a commitment by the country's political leadership to use them.

These components of a policy to strengthen technological autonomy are not given in any order of priority, but the last element is of basic importance. A strategy for increasing technological autonomy is in any event but a subset of more comprehensive economic and social policies which depend above all else on the commitment of political will over an extended period of time. The significance of technology policy within this broader context lies in its potential as a means of "kicking the habit" of continued dependence on outside solutions to local problems and breaking out of the vicious circle of dominance/lack of autonomy.

Technological Self-Reliance and Social Equity

Disengagement and greater emphasis on internal development of the autonomous capacity for technological change are therefore important for poorer countries, individually and collectively. The beachheads of technological competence built up within the Third World in the past two decades, even in high technology areas such as space, electronics, and computers, make Third World collaboration a more meaningful possibility in the decades ahead if mechanisms for genuine sharing can be devised.

Selective delinking for varying periods of time (leading to a more autonomous relinking as local capacities are strengthened) should not be dismissed by setting up the straw man of technological autarky, clearly a foolish strategy in the contemporary world. Although we have no assurance that greater autonomy will necessarily lead to greater equity within poorer countries, few developing countries have gone very far in meeting the minimum material needs of most, if not all, of their people on a self-sustaining basis without a substantially increased capacity for autonomous technological decisionmaking.[9]

The task of mobilizing technology for development will be done a disservice by glossing over the harsh realities surrounding North-South technology flows and by neglecting such options as disengagement and Third World collaboration. These are not substitutes for North-South cooperation but means of making that cooperation more honest and meaningful in meeting the most urgent needs of the poorer countries.

We may, in fact, be confronted with a paradox. The movement toward a more just world order may be more certain in the long run if the poorer countries disengage themselves to varying degrees in the short run from an international system in which they are now weak and dependent actors. The critical question is whether, by such disengagement, they can move more quickly and surely toward strengthening their autonomous capacity for solving their own problems, thus laying the foundation for a more balanced and equitable international order.

Notes

[1]Frances Stewart, *Technology and Underdevelopment* (London: Macmillan, 1977), p. 277.

[2]"Delinking North and South: Unshackled or Unhinged?", *Rich and Poor Nations in the World Economy*, by C. F. Díaz-Alejandro, et al. (New York: McGraw-Hill, 1977).

[3]Employment figures are taken from the Government of India, Ministry of Finance, *Economic Survey: 1976*, Delhi: Division of Publications, 1978. While there was some growth in the public sector during this period (9.4 million in 1966 to 12.5 million in 1975), much of it was in clerical and service activities and not production.

[4]K. N. Raj, "The Economic Situation," *Economic and Political Weekly*, July 3, 1976, p. 995.

[5]James H. Weaver, Kenneth P. Jameson, and Richard N. Blue, "A Critical Analysis of Approaches to Growth and Equity" (Paper prepared for the International Studies Association Annual Meeting, March 1977, St. Louis).

[6]Ibid.

[7]Pranab K. Bardhan, "The Pattern of Income Distribution in India: A Review," *Sankhya: The Indian Journal of Statistics*, Vol. 36, Series C, Parts 2 and 4 (1974), pp. 103-138; and V. M. Dandekar and N. Rath, *Poverty in India* (Poona: Indian School of Political Economy, 1971).

[8]Some critics of the strategy of increasing integration of the modern sector of Third World economies into the global production system dominated by industrialized country multinational corporations carry the argument further by pointing to an accelerating "deindustrialization" of the Third World, which is already occurring at an alarming rate and bids fair to get worse. Extraction of mineral resources, and the increasing reorientation of Third World agriculture toward production of cash crops and non-food products, are in many cases driving the poor from the land. Environmental degradation, which is destroying the productive capacity of the land, is making the problem still worse. See, e.g., Claude Alvares, "Development against People," *Development Forum*, July 1978.

[9]Díaz-Alejandro has properly cautioned against overloading external relationships of poorer countries with too many expectations for more equitable economic and social growth in his "Delinking North and South," *op. cit.*

III. Commercial Technology Flows and Transnational Enterprises

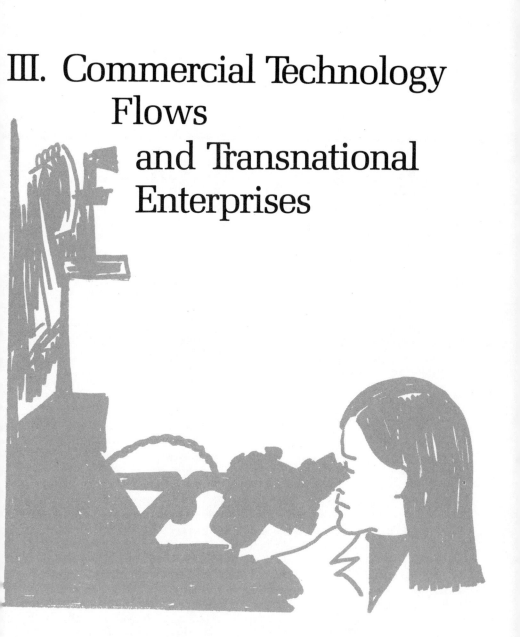

Although no one minimizes the importance of foreign exchange earnings, capital inflows, or domestic savings, recently there has been a relative shift in emphasis in the less-developed countries toward the role of technology in development efforts. In many less-developed countries, the difficulties of raising capital either at home or abroad now appear less formidable than the problems associated with technological progress. The consequence of these new perceptions is a new set of issues for international debate and resolution — issues that, unlike those of commodity policy, market access, monetary reform, or aid, were scarcely heard of only a decade or so ago.

Technology "gaps" exist everywhere. In few sectors of the world economy is it reasonable to assert or assume that the same technology governs production possibilities everywhere (that is, that all producers operate on the same production function). It is this very fact of *differences* in the level of technology, between countries or between segments of the same country, that has bred the whole discussion about the "transfer of technology." (That is not to say, however, that observed differences in production techniques — measured by indicators such as the capital-labor ratio — necessarily reflect differences in access to technology; they may simply reflect different relative factor and input prices.)

Even within the developed countries, technology is far from uniform. Since the frontiers of knowledge are constantly being pushed back in all sectors by ongoing research and development in both the public and the private sectors, everyone everywhere must run quickly to stay abreast of the most recent technological breakthroughs. The process of technology diffusion is thus by no means simply a matter of transferring "shelf" knowledge from rich to poor countries. Indeed, in this as in most other aspects of their economic participation in the world economy, the importance of the developing countries is small. The process of diffusion or transfer of technology to poor countries is of relatively little consequence to most owners of technology in the developed countries. Because of this, the institutions and legal ar-

Chapter 4

International Technology Issues: Southern Needs and Northern Responses

G. K. Helleiner

rangements that affect or govern technological matters in the developed countries have been constructed by and large with the interests of only the developed countries in mind. In the market economies of the West, moreover, more attention probably has been paid historically to private property rights than to the interests of society. In the developing countries, however, *social* objectives are today universally espoused as the goals of economic development.

Those most concerned with the interests of the less-developed countries therefore have been led to assess (1) the size and nature of the effort to transfer technologies that are particularly well-suited to the problems of the less-developed countries; and (2) whether and where the technological "system" of the developed countries, with its great influence on the international economy, is harmful or beneficial to the less-developed countries.

Although it is difficult to make *general* assessments of these issues, it is worth noting at the start that the expressed general view of the less-developed countries on these issues is that (1) existing efforts to transfer technology to them are severely flawed and far too small, and (2) that the present technological "system" of the industrialized countries is biased and fraught with imperfections that reduce the gains that might otherwise accrue to the less-developed countries. These perceptions underlie all policy positions.

Market incentives have not, by themselves, generated much effort by the commercially motivated firms that develop and sell technology to devote special attention to the needs of the less-developed countries. Rather, such firms have tended simply to offer for sale the technologies already "on their shelf." Both the production and consumption technologies[1] of these firms therefore frequently have been judged "inappropriate" in the sense that they are not adapted, or are insufficiently adapted, to the particular physical, economic, and social environments of the less-developed countries. Such efforts as

*Excerpted and revised from *The New International Order: The North-South Debate,* ed. Jagdish N. Bhagwati (Cambridge: The MIT Press, 1977), pp. 295-316, by permission of the publisher. Copyright 1977.

have been made to transfer suitable technologies to the less-developed countries frequently have been undertaken by agencies not geared to the profit motive, notably charitable foundations and governments.

The principal point to be made concerning the present system of technology development and diffusion is that most of the technology made available to the less-developed countries is not so much "transferred" as "sold." The market for technology is a highly imperfect one in which information is limited, and monopoly, while sometimes mitigated by inter-technology substitution possibilities, is common. Existing international legal conventions grant wide-ranging rights to the owners of intellectual property but impose few developmental obligations upon them. As net purchasers of imported technology, the less-developed countries understandably seek to increase competition, eliminate restrictive business practices, and reform the international conventions that govern technology trade and development. Their goal is the creation of new institutions and new means of producing and supplying technology — involving specialized firms that are prepared to deal at arm's length, governments, and international agencies.

To a considerable extent, the debate about international trade in technology has been conducted as part of the general debate about multinational firms and the possibility of antitrust action on an international scale. On both the left and the right, some observers see technology questions as indivisible from overall issues of international business enterprise, and they lament the "excessive theorizing" that has led to their separation. This interrelationship between technology and multinational firms stems from the fact that much of the recent transfer of technology to the less-developed countries has been effected through direct investment by multinational firms.[2] Yet there is now increasing experimentation with the "unpackaging" not only of what direct investment traditionally has supplied (capital, technology, management, marketing) but also — notably in the Andean Pact — of the technological packages themselves. One reflection of this has been the change in the nature of the disputes involving U.S. firms abroad. In the period 1960-1971, over 71 per cent of those disputes had to do with nationalization or expropriation. Between 1971 and 1973, however, only 22 per cent of the disputes involved either of those questions. The bulk of the disputes had to do with contractual and managerial disagreements.[3] As "unpackaging" has proceeded, it has become evident that the principal contribution of private multinational firms to host countries, and the main source of their market power, is their technology. Technology, in the words of one study, is the multinational firm's "trump card."[4] It may also constitute an important element in the national advantage of the countries in which its owners are based.[5]

There nevertheless is a lot to be said for the maintenance of direct investment as a means of transferring technology to developing countries. Wholly owned subsidiaries of multinational firms undoubtedly do have smoother, more automatic, and sometimes even (socially)

cheaper access to technology — in the form of ongoing advice, information, and personnel — than licensees or one-time, "arm's length"
purchasers of "shelf" technology.[6] The policy bias toward this form of
private technology transfer to the less-developed countries — a bias
engendered by most present investment guarantee programs of the
developed countries — probably stems more from inertia than from a
careful assessment of the alternative institutional forms which this
trade now takes. Nor is there any developmental rationale for the
restrictions frequently placed on projects that qualify for such guaran-
tees (such as restrictions in the U.S. program that forbid support of
firms in which governments have a majority interest).

In any case, there is no mistaking the recent trends and therefore no
escaping the technological issues now on the international agenda.
As consumers of imported technology, the less-developed countries
are engaged in a vigorous international "consumerism" effort, the
object of which is to raise the quality and lower the price of what they
buy. This means that their individual shopping efforts entail more
careful screening of products and harder bargaining over prices. At
the international level, the less-developed countries seek to stimulate
competition among the sellers of technology and cooperation among
the buyers while increasing the flow of information generally.

No one in the developing countries expects owners of technological
property to give up their income. Since these firms have invested in
the production of technology, they are acknowledged to deserve a fair
return on their investment. Private firms are engaged in the pursuit of
profit, and it is unrealistic to expect them to act otherwise.[7] Although
private profit is frequently consistent with social objectives (for
example, in training and in some local subcontracting) this will not
always be the case.

Many governments of less-developed countries therefore employ
official screening mechanisms to assess contracts involving the importation of technology, but this screening has been a rather imperfect
process so far. Although the economic and legal aspects of new
technology contracts have been relatively easy to assess, the analysis
of possible alternatives typically remains beyond the limited
capacities of the screening agencies. Efforts to control technology
imports (rather than only direct investment) nevertheless can be expected to continue in those countries which already have such
policies and to spread quickly to other countries as their expertise and
administrative capacity improve.

All things considered, these and other domestic policies of the
governments of the less-developed countries are likely to have a
greater impact on the use and development of appropriate
technologies than international conventions or the policies of the
developed countries. Because the terms of international technology
trade will be very much influenced by the policies of the importing
countries, the technological issues now placed on the international
agenda by the developing countries will require thoughtful responses
from the developed countries.

Commercial Technology: Non-Aid Issues

The three principal non-aid issues in international technology trade are the revision of the Paris Convention governing patents, trademarks, and other industrial property, the introduction of a code of conduct to regulate the international transfer of technology, and the limited information available to purchasers of new technology.

The Paris Convention: Patents, Trademarks, and Other Industrial Property

Many of the issues surrounding the international debate concerning patents, trademarks, and other industrial property have to do with national policy rather than international agreement. Over 90 per cent of the patents granted by developing countries are foreign owned; an equally high percentage of these patents is never employed in the developing countries that have granted them. These two facts suggest that the patent system's role is more to preclude the employment of technologies in developing countries than to encourage their development and use.[8] Moreover, in the absence of advice on alternative options, many developing countries have adopted a Model Law on Inventions, created for them by the World Intellectual Property Organization (WIPO).[9] Analysis of this model law suggests, however, that it is probably injurious to the developing countries.[10] Industrial property legislation and conventions in developing countries therefore are matters for early reform.

Such reforms do not necessarily (nor should they) involve the total repudiation of conventional industrial property rights. On the contrary, the recognition of such rights—at least in selected areas—may be crucial to the development of technologies tailored to developing-country needs. Such recognition is likely to be of greatest importance to newer and smaller foreign firms rather than to established transnational enterprises, which have their own systems of knowledge protection. It is from the newer and smaller firms (other things being equal) that the less-developed countries can hope to extract better terms.

The details of reform are matters on which the less-advanced developing countries could use informed technical assistance. Among the principles that reform certainly ought to incorporate are: developmental criteria for patentability, limitation of patent privileges to local products (rather than as at present, to imports as well), identification of key sectors where patents will not be granted, simplified administrative procedures for granting and enforcing industrial property rights, and shortened duration of patent privileges.[11] Appropriate changes in the Paris Convention would ease the introduction of such domestic reforms and might also achieve systemic change significant enough to induce greater numbers of less-developed countries to join the Paris Union. At present, the Union has only forty-five members among the less-developed countries. In the absence of reform, their numbers may well decline. Many more, of course, recognize international patent conventions.

The basic objectives of a revision of the Paris Convention seem to have been agreed upon already. The discussions that have been under way for some time in the U.N. Conference on Trade and Development (UNCTAD) and WIPO have led to agreement on the preamble to a revised convention; it contains recognition of the need to balance the objectives of development against the rights of industrial property owners, to promote the use of inventions in each less-developed country in which rights are granted, to facilitate the transfer of technology from industrialized to less-developed countries on fair and reasonable terms, and to improve the institutional infrastructure in developing countries to permit them to assess industrial property questions effectively. At the same time, there is agreement that more technical assistance in this area should be provided for developing countries. There is therefore room for some optimism with respect to the prospects for a serious revision of the Paris Convention in the course of the next few years.

A Code of Conduct for the Transfer of Technology

There has been extensive discussion at the international level of the possibility or desirability of a code of conduct to govern the transfer of technology to developing countries. The overlap of technology issues with the multinational corporation issue already has been noted. Codes of conduct for multinationals and international antitrust efforts — *without* specific reference to the transfer of technology — are being discussed at the international level. But (with UNCTAD pressure) the technology code has made more progress than the broader objectives. Rival drafts have been prepared by the "Group of 77" developing countries and by the developed countries. Since these drafts contain substantial areas of agreement, the question now does not seem to be whether there will be a code but what its specific content and modes of operation will be. The main points still at issue between the developed and the developing countries are the following:

> (1) which precise "restrictive business practices" are to be prohibited by the code (the most recent draft from the Group of 77 lists forty items under this heading);
> (2) whether the code should be legally binding and backed by national laws or merely offered in the form of voluntary "guidelines";
> (3) whether the code should incorporate the principle of special preferences for the less-developed countries;
> (4) whether such legal problems as arise in technology contracts should be subject to international arbitration or to resolution by the courts of the importing or exporting country;
> (5) whether the code should include guarantees that suppliers must offer to purchasers (say, that the technology supplied is "complete");

(6) whether the code should include general prohibitions and restrictions as to the terms of technology contracts (limits on royalty payments to parent firms, time limits on licensing agreements, and so forth).

Questions can be raised, of course, about the purpose of such a code. After all, with or without a code, individual governments possess the power to control technology imports and to prohibit related restrictive practices *if they choose to exercise it*—and many less-developed countries already do so. Less-developed countries also can set up joint rules for negotiations and contracts with foreign technology suppliers without a universal code and without the compliance of the developed countries, and some (notably, the members of the Andean Pact) have done so. In recent years there also has been considerable exchange of experience and information with respect to technology import policies among the less-developed countries, with "latecomers" sometimes modeling their practices on those of the "veterans." Why, then, the intense pressure from the developing countries for an internationally accepted code of conduct? And why the vigorous resistance to the idea on the part of international business firms?

There undoubtedly *is* a case for jointly imposed rules that would raise the developing countries' share of the rent accruing to technology owners (that is, reduce its price) and assist the weakest of the developing countries. What is the case, though, for involving the developed countries in the enforcement of such a code? The developing countries' desire for developed-country involvement can be ascribed to three factors: (1) the desire for formalized legitimacy of policies that will be pursued in any case; (2) the desire for assistance in data collection and in enforcing provisions of technology contracts (which would be more likely if there were agreement at the international level as to the "appropriateness" of their contents); and (3) the desire to develop international controls over transnational enterprises—in particular, to extend to the international arena the antitrust laws of the United States and other developed countries.

Apart from arguments attributable to special interest, opposition to a code rests upon two basic but mutually inconsistent premises: (1) that it will be unenforceable, and (2) that it will reduce the volume, or increase the cost, of technology transfers.[12]

The debate over enforcement involves both disagreement as to whether a code could, even in principle, be legally binding and the practical problem of adequate enforcement. The questions raised are difficult, but hardly unfamiliar. Few of those who argue against the code have urged the end of the General Agreement on Tariffs and Trade (GATT) or the Paris Union. Whether the code would be enforceable would depend on the same set of imponderables that affect all other efforts at international regulation. It should be noted, however, that the United States now favors a firm international agreement, backed by national legislation, governing certain other activities of multinational firms (relating to bribery and political influence).

It can be assumed that if the code is unenforceable, it is unlikely to affect significantly the current scale or terms of technology sales to developing countries. On the other hand, business economists and spokesmen for the developed countries argue that a code that does have some "teeth" may not be in the interests of the developing countries that are pressing for it.[13] They contend that too many limitations on the rights and profits of technology owners will lead them either to forego sales in the Third World entirely or to demand higher prices (perhaps indirectly). It may also be that, if a code comes into existence, firms that have, in effect, supplied technology on an ongoing basis to subsidiary or related firms abroad will identify such transactions as deserving of reimbursement, although they never did so before.

These, of course, are arguments against more stringent policies rather than against a code as such. Similar arguments have consistently (and incorrectly) been raised with respect to attempts to extract higher resource rents from foreign mineral exporting firms and attempts to bargain more effectively with foreign sources of direct investment in other sectors. There is no doubt that some investment and some technology are lost through harder bargaining. But there is also no doubt that larger proportions of rent accrue to host countries and that increased development results are realized from the investment and technology flows that continue. At issue is the true shape of the supply schedule for the technology that is of greatest interest to the developing countries. There are strong grounds for the view that the schedule is highly inelastic in the present range of prices, which far exceed the marginal cost of supply.[14] Whether on balance the better controls would increase the welfare of the host countries remains to be seen, but that judgment in any case seems best left for them to make. A learning process is likely to be required if host countries are to employ their regulatory and tax powers most effectively. A certain amount of time must elapse before final judgments can be offered. But there is no *a priori* reason to take the gloomy forecasts of businessmen and spokesmen for developed countries too seriously, since they are obviously interested parties.[15]

Whatever the eventual outcome, it is more likely to be favorable to the less-developed countries if they coordinate their policies and adopt common positions than if they remain divided. Hence the importance of a common and generalized code. In the view of the international business community, it is the attempt to implement a *general* code that is so potentially damaging. A case-by-case approach in which the screening agency considers each case entirely on its own merits is less likely, they argue, to produce rigidities, delays, and inefficiencies. They contend that a willing buyer and a willing seller generally should be allowed to strike a bargain without regard to preestablished norms and without the necessity of dealing with another level of bureaucracy. But case-by-case, as opposed to general, approaches carry implications for the relative bargaining strengths of technology suppliers and importing countries (whether governments or firms). In particular, case-by-case approaches are likely to favor the more powerful parties to these bargains. Bargaining strength depends primarily upon knowledge, experience, and political power, and these qualities are often limited among the negotiators of developing countries compared to those of multinational firms. Thus, the weakest of the developing countries clearly stand to gain the most from a generalized approach and a common code. Even businessmen in relatively strong importing countries have noted that they derive increased bargaining power vis-a-vis foreign firms from minimum legal requirements in contracts.

Reservations concerning the code on the part of some of the less-developed countries — generally countries that are relatively experienced and knowledgeable in the technology sphere — stem from the risks some of them see in establishing international norms that are less attractive to them than the policies they would otherwise pursue (or that they are already implementing).[16] A code acceptable to the developed countries, they suspect, may well contain undesirable and unnecessary limitations on the policies of the technology-importing countries. They also fear that the *minimum* conditions that a code imposes on the suppliers of technology will rapidly be taken to be the *maximum* conditions. It is also unlikely that countries like India, Mexico, Argentina, Brazil, or the members of the Andean Pact, for example, would give up their own recently introduced technology screening procedures to comply with a code designed primarily for the weaker importing countries.

At the same time, anxiety is also expressed about the potential impact of a code on the weaker developing countries, whose freedom of maneuver in attempting to offset their relative unattractiveness to foreign business might be inhibited by too rigid a code. These countries, however, do retain the possibility of influencing the many other dimensions (such as taxes, disclosure, local procurement, and training) of their relations with foreign firms — relations that, in any case, are more likely to involve capital as well as technology.

Even with a code, conditions for investment and technology sales by multinational corporations can be expected to vary from country to country. Tax treatment of fees and royalties, foreign exchange controls, and the strictness with which the code's rules are applied would all leave room for considerable competition among developing countries in technology and capital markets.

It seems safe to conclude that any code that could at present gain the agreement of both rich and poor countries would be rife with escape clauses and would almost certainly not be legally binding. If these conclusions are correct, one might wonder whether establishment of a code might not simply generate a new international agency with imprecise functions and limited power. Whether such a bureaucracy would have sufficient value to justify its existence would inevitably remain a matter for judgment. Clearly, however, a new agency *could* increase the pressure for a future institution—paralleling the General Agreement on Tariffs and Trade (GATT) in the field of trade—focusing on the multinationals and internationalized antitrust action, and serving to gather objective data on international business. Alternatively, *existing* institutions, such as the U.N. Centre for Transnational Corporations, WIPO, UNCTAD, or GATT, could monitor the code's application.

It may, however, be more realistic to regard discussion of the code as essentially *educative* in purpose. The more advanced host countries have technology contract assessment procedures firmly in place and are already learning by doing. International discussion of a code, whether or not it actually generates one, will inform the less advanced of the less-developed countries of the issues and create legitimacy for the other countries that have developed or are developing policies in this sphere.[17] The "process" is more important than the end product.[18] From this standpoint, there is no urgency about reaching agreement. The object is simply to keep the discussion going.

Information Services

The greatest source of imperfection in technology markets is the limited information available to buyers. In part, the problem is inherent in the nature of knowledge markets; if one had sufficient information to be able to assess the value of the knowledge one was purchasing, the purchase frequently would be unnecessary. To a larger extent, however, the limited information available to buyers in the less-developed countries is a remediable problem. Their present sources of information — coming from technology and equipment sales, advice or recommendations of aid agencies, or consultants — are all consciously or unwittingly biased toward the technologies of the developed countries they know best.

It is never easy for decisionmakers in the developing countries to obtain a general impression of the entire range of technological possibilities relevant to a new undertaking, or to learn about new processes, techniques, or products related to existing projects. It is especially difficult, because of the North-South orientation of traditional communication flows, to learn of technologies developed or employed in other less-developed countries (unless the technologies are owned and transmitted by multinational corporations). A systematic canvassing of technological possibilities can usually be contemplated only for major projects and even then, the sheer volume of printed material may be so great that the cost of such an effort may be prohibitive. Therefore a strong case can be made for the creation of international, or perhaps regional, institutions that can avail themselves of economies of scale to meet the informational needs of many less-developed countries that could not otherwise afford such services.

Consulting, information, or referral services, and exchanges of experience, are all much discussed means of increasing consumer power in technology markets. Legal, technical, and economic information concerning the terms of contracts, the abilities of firms and consultants, and so on, might be centrally screened, organized, stored, and made available to individual less-developed countries on request. Difficulties might, of course, arise from the unwillingness or legal inability of individual governments to disclose the full terms of their àgreements to outsiders. Moreover, formal institutional arrangements, such as libraries, might prove too rigid or too distant to be useful. Advisory services, through which individuals experienced in particular sectors could be supplied on request, might therefore prove more effective; instead of drawing upon an "information bank," governments could employ expertise. Such service agencies might also be able to draw up model technology contracts on a sector-by-sector basis for use by a wide range of government or private clients in the less-developed world.

Technology data banks, in which information about available technologies and their sources would be stored, also have been suggested. This is difficult to envisage, given the diversity and quantity of technological activities. It might be best to store information as to where to go for relevant information while relying on trade associations, consultants, and traditional channels for specifics, although joint "shopping services" and referral services might be established in particular priority sectors and/or among cooperating countries. Some of the sectors in which such services deserve priority are pharmaceuticals, food processing, and agricultural inputs.

The U.N. Industrial Development Organization (UNIDO) and the Food and Agriculture Organization (FAO) already have services of this sort in their respective fields of interest, and UNCTAD and the International Labor Office (ILO) have proposed the establishment of new institutions for developing appropriate technology, exchanging information, and improving the terms of technology trade. To the extent that these various measures and institutions would tend to perfect international technology markets and to assist the developing countries, they must be counted as beneficial. If such new institutions were financed primarily by the developed countries — in addition to their present levels of development assistance — they would, of course, be especially attractive to the developing countries.

Non-Commercialized Technology and the Role of Aid

Technology transfer problems differ greatly from sector to sector, even though most of the international discussion in this area relates to industrial technology of a sophisticated nature. One must not lose sight of the issues surrounding the transfer of technology in agriculture, health sciences, and services, as well as in more basic industrial technology. In these sectors knowledge is relatively free from private claims on intellectual property, and the institutions for technological development and diffusion are therefore less often commercially motivated. In these sectors, furthermore, the importance of reforming the Paris Convention and developing a code of conduct is relatively slight. These sectors thus may offer some indication of the problems that would remain if major reforms in technology trade were achieved.

Agricultural research and extension efforts have brought about dramatic changes in the technology employed in the developed countries. Progress in medicine and health has been no less dramatic. Much of the organization and financing of these efforts has been undertaken by national governments, and much of the knowledge developed has been, and can in the future, be transferred to less-developed countries through non-commercial channels — provided that firm decisions to do so are taken.

In these transfers, particular responsibility rests with governmental authorities and international agencies, since crucial importing decisions usually are uninfluenced by commercial considerations. Although the developed countries cannot expect to have much influence over decisions made by the governments of the less-developed countries, their own domestic development assistance and related programs — and those of the international institutions to which they belong — should incorporate policies that encourage "correct" decisions, or at least do not encourage "incorrect" ones. However, the tendency to encourage incorrect decisions is not infrequent, and it is often combined with pious declarations concerning the need for more appropriate technology, more attention to poverty, and wiser decision-making. Both procurement restrictions (which limit the use of local goods and services) and "project fixation" have tended to bias the character of the technology transferred under the aegis of official development assistance toward import-using and large-scale techniques. Given the paucity of efficient labor-intensive techniques in the aid-supplying countries, the restrictive conditions in these flows probably have also produced a bias against labor-intensive technologies. As technological capacity increases within the Third World, it will become increasingly important to retain and expand the provisions in aid contracts that permit procurement locally and in other less-developed countries. Abandoned in 1971, the international discussions on the possibility of untying and otherwise easing the conditions surrounding official development assistance might now be resumed under the banner of improving the price and appropriateness of imported technology.

Technology transfers also occur under the heading of "technical assistance." Although much of this assistance has been invaluable, particularly in the least-developed countries, it has often carried technological biases into local demand structures and decisionmaking. Not surprisingly, familiarity with the production techniques and consumption standards of the developed countries has influenced the technical assistants' advice, with the result that inappropriate consumption and production technologies have been transferred to less-developed countries. Thus technical assistance, even in the best of circumstances, may improperly influence the demand side of technology policy and choices.

Apart from these impediments to the free flow of technology, aid also affects the relative price of different techniques. Those offered on concessional terms, other things being equal, are more likely to be purchased. Export credit and investment guarantee programs in the developed countries also distort incentives in the less-developed countries in such a way as to reduce the adoption of labor-intensive, small-scale, local, input-intensive techniques. In some instances, the relevant laws of developed countries are explicitly protectionist in intent and designed to deflect activity in foreign countries away from the use of technologies that would improve their comparative advantage in particular sectors. For example, the U.S. Investment Insurance program (OPIC) will not insure technology contracts or investments in textile operations engaged in exporting to the United States.

Although there may be fewer imperfections in knowledge markets in sectors that seem to be free from commercial secrecy, there may still be imperfections in the markets for inputs required to employ a particular technology. The channels through which information about new medical or agricultural technology flows are not totally frictionless and neutral. Producers of inputs associated with certain techniques will be active in efforts to "sell" those techniques—both by fair means and through the illegitimate purchase of influence—to potential users in the Third World and to technology transmitters in aid agencies and international bodies. Many of the resulting transactions in equipment and inputs are far from being "pure" market transactions in which consumers express their preferences in textbook fashion. Rather, they are frequently the result of administrative decisions taken by governments or by research institutions. Such agencies do not face market tests and therefore are susceptible — especially in the weak administrative systems typical in developing countries—to "marketing" efforts of the more dubious sort. Tractors and mechanical equipment for government schemes and research stations at least must face some sort of market test when they are offered to farmers for adoption (albeit sometimes with subsidies). But in the case of medical equipment and pharmaceuticals, buying decisions of the relevant authorities are unlikely to be influenced by efficiency criteria. Thus the need for improved information services in the fields in which technology is not wholly commercialized is every bit as great as in others.

Notes

[1]Consumption technology relates to the characteristics of products. See Kelvin J. Lancaster, "Change and Innovation in the Technology of Consumption," *American Economic Review* 56(1966): pp. 14-23. For further elaboration of the need for distinguishing between production and consumption technologies, see G.K. Helleiner, "The Role of Multinational Corporations in the Less Developed Countries' Trade in Technology," *World Development* 3(1975): pp. 161-189.

[2]See Helleiner, "The Role of Multinational Corporations."

[3]See "Nationalization, Expropriation, and Other Takings of United States and Certain Foreign Property since 1960," U.S. Department of State, 1971; and "Disputes Involving US Foreign Direct Investment, 1st July, 1971 through 31st July, 1974," U.S. Department of State, 1974.

[4]See John M. Stopford and Louis T. Wells, Jr., *Managing the Multinational Enterprise* (New York: Basic Books, 1972), p. 177.

[5]See Carlos Alfredo Rodrigues, "Trade in Technological Knowledge and the National Advantage," *Journal of Political Economy* 83(1975): pp. 121-135.

[6]See Jack N. Behrman and Harvey Wallender, "Technology Transfers to Wholly-Owned Affiliates: An Illustration of the Obstacles to Controls," a paper presented to the International Studies Association, Toronto (1976).

[7]Harry Johnson has recently summarized the behavior of private business in this sphere:

> Its capacity to make profits derives essentially from its possession of productive knowledge, which includes management methods and marketing skills, as well as production technology. It has no commercial interest in diffusing its knowledge to potential native competitors. Nor has it any interest in investing more than it has to in acquiring knowledge of local conditions and investigating ways of adapting its own productive knowledge to local factor/price ratios and market conditions. Its purpose is not to transform the economy by exploiting its potentialities (especially its human potentialities) for development, but to exploit the existing situation to its own profit by utilization of the knowledge it already possesses, at minimum cost to itself of adaptation and adjustment. . . . Hence, it will invest in technological research on the adaptation of its technology and in the development of local labour skills only to the extent that such investment holds a clear prospect of profit.

See Harry Johnson, Technology and Economic Independence (London: Macmillan, 1975), pp. 79-80.

[8]See Edith Penrose, "International Patenting and the Less Developed Countries," Economic Journal 83(1973): pp. 768-786.

[9]Formerly called the United International Bureau for the Protection of Intellectual Property, WIPO is a non-governmental body based in Geneva that concerns itself with laws on patents, trademarks and the trade in proprietary technology.

[10]See Constantine V. Vaitsos, "The Revision of the International Patent System: Legal Considerations for a Third World Position," World Development 4(1976): pp. 85-102.

[11]Ibid.

[12]To the extent that avoidance of enforcement involves real costs that can be passed on to the developing countries, these premises may not be wholly inconsistent.

[13]See Council of the Americas and Fund for Multinational Management Education, Codes of Conduct for the Transfer of Technology: A Critique (New York: n.d.); and Jose de Cubas, Technology Transfer and the Developing Nations (New York: Council of the Americas, 1974).

[14]See Constantine V. Vaitsos, "Bargaining and the Distribution of Returns in the Purchase of Technology by Developing Countries," Bulletin of the Institute of Development Studies, Sussex, England (1970).

[15]There is already some evidence of substantial gains to technology importing countries following the introduction of technology vetting procedures. It has been estimated that Mexico saved $80 million in payments for foreign technology for the duration of contracts that were revised in direct consequence of the application of its new technology law in 1973. See Miguel Wionczek, "Notes on Technology Transfer through Multinational Enterprises in Latin America," Development and Change 7(1976): pp. 152-153. The Japanese experience is, of course, a better known historical example of success with such policies.

[16]See Constantine V. Vaitsos, "Foreign Investment and Productive Knowledge," in Guy F. Erb and Valeriana Kallab (eds.), Beyond Dependency: The Developing World Speaks Out (Washington: Overseas Development Council, 1975), pp. 87-88.

[17]Jagdish Bhagwati has commented that there is no reason to assume that those in the forefront in this sphere are doing sensible things. (No doubt views on this differ.) If they are not, however, their experience should be as instructive to latecomers as if they were.

[18]See Howard V. Perlmutter and Taghi Saghafi-nejad, "Process or Product?: A Social Architectural Perspective of Codes of Conduct for Technology Transfer and Development," a paper presented to the International Studies Association, Toronto (1976).

Transnational enterprises (TNEs) today constitute an intrinsic element in the world economy. They profoundly impact upon, and often dominate, the evolution of scientific and technological achievements in the countries in which they operate. In foreign direct investment activities; in non-equity technological, managerial, and marketing contractual relations; in the procurement of machinery, components, plants, and services—in all of these areas a country's technological evolution must reckon directly with the crucial role played by the TNEs.

Developing countries receiving TNE technology need to adopt policies that will enhance the development of their own technological capabilities as they are affected by TNEs. Following are some general ideas to consider:

(1) Production knowledge is, of course, crucial to a country's economic performance; it is also a key instrument, often the distinguishing one, of the TNEs in pursuing their objectives. Recognizing that the development of expertise and capabilities by TNEs is not altogether for the benefit of society but rather for the benefit of specific corporate interests, nations need to consider how these benefits are distributed.

(2) Knowledge is power that provides economic as well as social and political leverage. It is in the interest of the TNEs to safeguard their technological monopolies to maintain their knowledge captive within the corporate system in order to make a global impact. TNEs do not seek to transfer their technology, since this would preempt their power. Yet they need to use their technology internationally to enhance their interests. Thus, TNEs concentrate their research and development activities in their home country while using the generated know-how across national boundaries. These conflicting practices create opportunities in the developing countries for government policymaking and negotiations with the TNEs.

(3) Regardless of its source, technology is not neutral. Its properties reflect the needs and resource endowments of those who create it, and

Government Policies for Bargaining with Transnational Enterprises in the Acquisition of Technology

Constantine V. Vaitsos

it is dependent upon the characteristics of consumption. The policy issues of concern to a host government involve not only selecting from different production technologies or from varying sources of supply, but also making decisions about the products and services needed within the context of development.

(4) The deployment of technological capabilities in international business is an integral part of a broader package of corporate strategy and business conduct. The capacity of the TNEs to synthesize a variety of theoretically distinguishable but in practice undifferentiated inputs (managerial skills, capital, marketing practices and assets, opportunities for resource and market access internationally, etc.) is a major advantage and key contribution to the world economy. But it is also the cause of monopoly and a concomitant displacement of locally originated activities in host countries. Because the TNE contribution is "complete," recipient countries must forego the developmental process of "learning by doing." It is in this area that serious policy instruments need to be introduced by host countries.

Policy Criteria and Guidelines

With these four broad conceptual areas of policy concern in mind, we can proceed to enunciate some policy criteria and guidelines that host governments need to apply in their dealings with TNEs in the sphere of technology:

(a) Contrary to traditional economic principles, the TNEs should not be granted automatic entrance to a host country. Various host countries — both industrialized and less-developed — have come to recognize that the nature of TNEs and the characteristics of the markets within which they operate require the establishment of explicit bargaining structures involving specific criteria and policy instru-

---

*Revised and edited version of a draft note prepared for the United Nations Centre for Transnational Enterprises, January 1979.

ments on the basis of which a host country can evaluate, negotiate, approve, regulate, and monitor TNE operations.

(b) Host government policies, whether in the sphere of technology or in any other of the key issues involving TNEs, require a certain degree of comprehensiveness to be effective. Isolated or partial policies can prove to be counterproductive, given the multiple degrees of adjustment available to these firms because of their transnationality and their "packaged" form of operations. At the same time, though, host government policies also need some degree of selectivity. The choice of key sectors, main enterprises, and crucial policy issues is highly relevant. The high degree of concentration in TNE operations means that their ability to contribute, or to do more damage, to the host economy (depending on its stage of development and degree of foreign penetration) tends to be quite pronounced. Focussing comprehensive policy approaches on key sectors, enterprises, and issues has a large pay-off and avoids unnecessary bureaucratization of the host economy.

(c) Policies on imported technology or on other key issues in the conduct of TNEs include (i) direct approaches and instruments, usually referred to as "treatment of foreign enterprises," (ii) sectoral policies which affect not only the TNEs but also other enterprises in a specific sector, and (iii) certain key macro-economic policies with implications for the entire economy. These three levels of policy concern should be viewed in an interdependent and integral manner.

(d) Two infrastructural requirements are needed to manage the policies mentioned above. First, an intelligence system must be developed to collect, process, and qualify information relevant to the operations of the TNEs. Certain minimum requirements for information disclosure by TNEs must therefore be established. Second, a host country needs expert personnel who understand both the functioning of international business and the technology utilized by the TNEs in order to interpret their actions and negotiate intelligently with them.

(e) The defensive regulatory policies that a host government needs to establish in dealing with TNEs must be accompanied by positive policies which link the import of foreign know-how to the process of local technological development—i.e., explicit policies for assisting local capabilities in consulting, engineering, R&D, and local enterprise promotion. Such policies need to be designed so that foreign know-how comes to support and complement the process of local technological development rather than serve as a substitute for it.

Basic Bargaining Principles for Technology Payments

There are five basic principles which developing countries should heed when bargaining over payments for technology with the TNEs:

(a) Since TNEs provide a package of resources, only one of which is technology, the individual channels of income remission (e.g., royalties, inter-affiliate debt servicing, dividends, transfer pricing on inter-affiliate sales, etc.) are only nominal accounting categories. They do not reflect the effective monetary cost to the host economy in acquiring technology, capital, goods, and services. (In fact, TNEs do not usually enter into single sales of individual inputs.) What is relevant is the total sum remitted through all channels for the whole package. Individual bargaining in one category of inputs may prove counterproductive if not coordinated with other categories. The net income position of the foreign supplier may remain unaffected while the host economy ends up worse off, with the benefits going to a third fiscal jurisdiction.

(b) The above-noted fungibility in income remission is generally conditioned by two broad sets of considerations. First, the sectoral characteristics within which a TNE operates are likely to suggest the channels which create the major opportunites for income remission. In the automobile and pharmaceutical sectors, for example, transfer pricing in imported intermediates is likely to be crucial. In the petro-chemical industry, the pricing of machinery and plants will be a key channel for income payments and a source of fiscal loss for the host economy because of high depreciation charges. In large-scale, continuous-process industries, capital costs (in addition to machinery prices) will be pivotal. Second, the diverse government policies applicable to TNEs will tend to affect the latter's preference for channels of income remission (e.g., requirements for joint ventures reduce the attractiveness of profit declaration, and income is remitted indirectly through other channels). High tariffs on imported intermediates, on the other hand, significantly reduce the overpricing of such goods imported from foreign affiliates by TNEs.

(c) The distribution of benefits between a host country and the TNEs is not based on any a priori arrangement. Rather, it is affected by a number of sometimes implicit, sometimes explicit, negotiable policies which countries set or agree to set for the operations of their productive sectors. Thus, the amount of income is interdependent with its distribution. For example, host country tariff and non-tariff protection on import substitution, or subsidies on export promotion, affect both the size and distribution of income related to the activities of TNEs. Such broader policies need to be considered in conjunction with other issues at the negotiating table.

(d) The structure and costs of the technology market depend not only on the nature of the suppliers (i.e., TNEs) but also on the characteristics of demand (i.e., the host countries). The more capable and advanced a technology purchaser, the greater his ability to negotiate with TNEs. The lack of capabilities on the purchaser's side may be of two types: information gaps (about potential sources of technology supply, their prices, their technological properties, etc.) and technological weaknesses (lack of expertise, skills, experience, R&D, etc.). Information gaps and technological weaknesses usually are interrelated. The former require explicit policies by the host country in setting up explicit information mechanisms to search and monitor the possibilities offered by the international market system in key sectors.

(e) Given the size of its market and resource endowments, one of the main sources of negotiating power of a host country is its ability to unbundle the technology package (or the overall investment or project package, in the case of the TNEs). The correct identification and evaluation of different production inputs, and their cost in comparison with other sources of supply (both local and foreign), constitute an essential part of bargaining strategy. The skills involved in such unpackaging involve a combination of economic-accounting, legal, and purely technological capabilities. The development of such skills by the negotiating team of the host country constitutes a sine qua non of effective negotiating.

Control Issues

Among the many considerations which affect control over the management of enterprises and the functioning of markets, two merit particular consideration. Since technology is intrinsically non-appropriable by a single user (due to the possibility of imitation by others), the suppliers of know-how tend to impose contractual obligations on users. In other words, the sellers condition the economic applications of their know-how. These contractual obligations are traditionally referred to as restrictive business practices. In the last five to ten years, individual host countries, regional groups, and international organizations have declared such clauses contrary to established principles of anti-monopoly legislation.

Although laws and agreements against restrictive business practices can have a significant effect in transactions between unrelated firms, their application to the conduct of affiliated enterprises is quite limited or nil. Actual control is exercised through other mechanisms, while the exclusion of restrictive clauses from technology contracts could have little impact on the activities of such enterprises.

To tackle the issue of restrictive business practices, individual governments or groups of them need to enter into direct bargaining with foreign suppliers. Criteria other than those of a clearly legal nature constitute the most effective mechanisms for limiting such restrictions.

Host countries are becoming increasingly aware that there is often a clear distinction between ownership and control in international business. While ownership can be secured through nationalization or fade-out formulas for foreign equity participation, control is a much more elusive matter. One of the crucial factors contributing to a country's capacity to control its means of production is the availability of skilled personnel with knowledge of and access to managerial and technological capabilities. Policies designed to defend against foreign business penetration without providing for human and institutional skill formation are proving to be of quite limited impact in a number of sectors. These policies need to be matched by equally explicit policies and commitments of resources to the training of local skilled personnel and the development of local institutions to deal with technological issues.

Bargaining Power in Relation to the Acquisition of Technology

A host country confronts certain given constraints in its acquisition of technology, such as the availability of natural resources, the size of its population as a determinant of the size of its market, international competition in the sale of given technologies, the rate of change and diffusion of technological improvements, and so on. There are also certain overall policy implications which affect the level and distribution of a country's income, the degree of its local market protection, its access to foreign financing, etc., all of which can seriously affect the terms under which it is able to acquire foreign technology.

In addition, certain policies of host governments have a direct bearing on their bargaining power vis-a-vis the TNEs. The following are some crucial ones:

(1) Since TNEs deal with a number of government institutions in a given country, a country needs to harmonize criteria among its key governmental agencies prior to negotiating with foreign enterprises. Experience has shown that conflicting interests and uncoordinated actions by different government agencies severely limit a country's bargaining power.

(2) In dealing with TNEs, industrialized countries have often used the government's procurement power as a means of influencing the negotiations. Many developing countries have yet to develop an explicit strategy which utilizes their public sector as a concentrated and forceful tool in bilateral negotiations.

(3) Regional cooperation among countries in their technology dealings with TNEs can sometimes weaken their bargaining power and at other times significantly increase it. The dilution of host country power tends to occur when regional cooperation is confined simply to liberalizing regional trade barriers. In those cases, the position of the TNEs is strengthened; they are able to play one country against the other while still maintaining the authority to decide where they will locate their productive activities within their corporate system. If, on the other hand, regional cooperation includes a combination of regional industrial policies, common fronts with respect to foreign investors, common procurement of technology, the exchanging of information, and so on, a host country's position can be significantly improved.

(4) Certain internationally induced policies have tended to strengthen the position of the TNEs in their dealings with host countries. Such policies include (a) legal monopolies in technology — for example, the present system; (b) legal management of the foreign investment environment — for example, international courts and international settlements of disputes; and (c) legal protection of market-

ing assets, such as commercial trademarks. National, regional, and international actions need to be introduced in these areas to shift the institutionally imposed balance of power in favor of the host countries.

The Impact of Foreign Technology

A large volume of importéd technology does not necessarily imply a disadvantage to the importing country. For proper evaluation of the effects of foreign technology, two additional structural elements need consideration. First, it must be ascertained whether the imported knowledge has encouraged, or been substituted for, local technological efforts. Second, the use of foreign technology and its net effects must be examined.

Unbundling Imported Technology Packages to Promote Local Technological Development

One of the most important measures a host country can take in its technology dealings with TNEs is to set policy directed at unbundling investment and technology packages. This disaggregation can have direct and important effects on the cost of a foreign investment package, as well as on the assimilation, adaptation, and generation of technology in a host country.

There are two types of unpackaging:

(a) *Differentiation between, and separate evaluation of, the various inputs present in the investment-cum-technology package.* These inputs include equity investments, non-equity inter-affiliate financing, intermediate inputs, imported capital goods, technical assistance and technology sales, patent and trademark licensing, etc. In contrast, the commonly practiced capitalization of intangibles in foreign direct investment operations is often designed to inhibit unpackaging.

(b) *The unbundling of the technology package.* This includes differentiating between core technology elements, as in process know-how and basic engineering, and peripheral ones, such as computing, design engineering, technical assistance in plant construction and lay-out, civil, electrical, and other engineering, choice of equipment, and preinvestment technical services.

The purpose of directly intervening through such means is threefold:

(1) Unpackaging helps the host country strengthen its negotiating capacity in selecting suitable technology and other foreign inputs under convenient financial terms. (2) Unbundling can generate a clear and direct demand for the use and promotion of local capabilities in consulting and engineering, intermediate and capital goods suppliers, R&D institutions, etc. (3) It is also intended as an instrument for identifying and negotiating with the TNE about the

training of local personnel who can master the technological and business activities in which they are involved. Actions at the national, regional, and international level can assist host countries in developing: competent national agencies to back up local industry in negotiations with technology suppliers; information systems to provide detailed data on international and local technological processes; local engineering consultancy and service firms; local personnel trained to carry out research, development, and product or process design, engineering, etc.; and local research institutes to complement the scientific and technological activities of technology users.

The Appropriateness of Imported Technology

There is an abundant literature of diverse viewpoints on the issue of "appropriateness." In a narrow context, "appropriateness" may mean greater use of local labor and materials. In the broadest sense, though, appropriateness is linked to normative socio-political structures (an "appropriate" society will use "appropriate" products made with "appropriate" techniques). Between these two extreme cases there exist a number of definitions of "appropriateness."

Empirical evidence suggests that although TNEs may introduce minor adaptations of techniques and products as well as some scaling down of their operations in host countries, they generally relocate their operations from developed to less-developed areas without changing the technology. Furthermore, there is no convincing evidence that foreign firms are better or worse at adapting technologies to local conditions than local firms. "Foreigners" as such do not seem to be a major factor in determining techniques. Yet "foreigners" tend to strongly affect the geographical distribution of procurement practices for intermediates and other inputs.

With respect to choice of technologies, host government policies are not likely to significantly affect the actual practices of the TNEs. Far more important are decisions on choice of products and consumption patterns. These latter choices are not strictly technological ones but involve important socio-political and cultural preferences and commitments. The influence of the TNEs needs to be seen in the way they affect such socio-political and cultural directions, rather than in the use of technology. It is to the former area that host government policies need to address themselves.

Furthermore, TNEs should be judged — and used — for the functions they have been created for, and not for all the multiple objectives that a society may have. These firms operate to create profits from their worldwide activities and not to maximize employment or use more "appropriate" technologies which fit the resource endowments of host countries. If there are limits to the bargaining power available to a host government (as there always are), the power available should be applied in the areas where maximum impact can be obtained, particularly where TNEs have a certain set of productive advantages.

Local R&D Activities

Considerable attention has been drawn to the fact that a coherent technology policy cannot function without a serious commitment of resources to local "learning by doing" and local technological and skill generation. In this area, a host country needs to rely basically on its own institutions and enterprise. For both strategic corporate reasons as well as important externalities and economies of scale, the TNEs are not likely to shift the location or share their basic capacities in knowledge creation with the less-developed countries. The recent experience of India in confronting the major TNEs on these issues demonstrates the extent to which transnational enterprises are unwilling to change their established practices.

Conclusions

There are very few developing countries with sufficient market size and resources to advance development through exclusively inward-oriented policies and in relative or complete isolation from the rest of the world. Although China was able to achieve this, and many consider it feasible for India, most of the other Third World countries will find it necessary to take into account their relation (dependence) to the industrialized world.

The joint objectives of power formation and enhancement of knowledge to achieve a more equitable international economic structure necessitate a certain set of conditions in the Third World. These conditions include the political will and commitment to achieve such objectives, a certain degree of unity of action (including exchange of information) leading to new, non-spatial forms of economic integration, the development of expertise to advance knowledge and promote self-reliance, and the elaboration of variant characteristics and possibilities at each stage of economic development.

Even if these conditions are fulfilled, however, a restructuring of the power relationships between the developing countries and the transnational enterprises (or their home countries) will not necessarily and by itself lead to a restructuring of power relations within the nations of the Third World. The gains obtained will benefit only a small part of the population in the developing countries unless internal changes take place. Nevertheless, the two issues are not unrelated. External dependence affects internal inequality. Hence, policies which redress such external relations are necessary, even if not sufficient, for social and economic development.

Descriptive and analytical statements made about the role, behavior, and impact of transnational enterprises (TNEs) frequently display a lack of historical perspective, almost invariably are overly simplified, and often are distorted or incomplete. They provide a theoretical view of the process of generating and applying technology that is remote from practice, and they often are stated in pejorative terms that do not foster constructive discourse.

This paper was prepared in draft form in Ocho Rios under the direct stimulation of the discussions that were occurring at the Jamaica Symposium. The paper attempts to address some of the misconceptions and oversimplifications that were reflected in some of the comments being made. The paper also attempts to explain some of the views of businessmen regarding technology transfer and economic development in terms of their experience in the commercial world and the values that underlie a commitment to the private enterprise system.

The Need for Historical Perspective

TNE's have existed for centuries — the world would be a far more primitive place without them. Technology transfer has been an intrinsic part of their activities from the beginning. All too frequently in discussions of technology transfer, the most important of all forms of technology transfer — trade in goods — is left out of consideration. Trade makes one aware of what others have done and leads one to view his own resources and opportunities with new insight. Businessmen see this byproduct of commercial exchange as an important contribution whose value is often overlooked. Virtually all forms of technology transfer in use today — joint ventures, minority investment, licensing, joint manufacture, partial processing by foreign "associates," etc. — have been around for decades. Consequently, the subject is not some sudden new phenomenon that must be studied and understood.

Chapter 6

Transnational Enterprises and Technology Flows: A Business Viewpoint

Lowell W. Steele

The role and impact of TNEs on technology transfer should be viewed in that historical perspective, but they rarely are. TNEs undoubtedly display the full range of behavior associated with all business activity—indeed, with all human behavior, from paternalistic to predatory. Almost any assertion made about them can in all likelihood be verified in specific instances, but no comprehensive studies exist to describe with statistical accuracy the range of behavior and its impact. Ethical businessmen, at any rate, believe that the conduct of transnational enterprises is, in the great majority of cases, beneficial to host countries. As this paper will note later, businessmen are committed to the values that accrue to both parties by aggressive pursuit of advantage in the process of exchange. Consequently, from their perspective, "exploitation" should not be used as a pejorative term to describe differing interpretations of value received. Sorting out the sustainable charges from those that arise from different interpretations of behavior, particularly when the behavior grows out of different cultural backgrounds, is a difficult task. To a considerable extent, the resolution of different interpretations will require greatly increased understanding by all concerned. Ethical businessmen deplore predatory practices, and they take pride in their contributions to human progress.

Study of the impact of TNEs over a considerable period of time is badly needed. Anecdotal evidence indicates that the impacts are diverse, widely spread over time, and not always readily visible. In addition to their tangible products, the TNEs provide markets for and stimulus to local suppliers, they finance and frequently construct parts of the industrial infrastructure, they train workers, they influence educational curricula, they enlarge career aspirations, and they stimulate supporting services, such as finance and distribution. They also stimulate increased savings by providing more secure and attractive investment opportunities for local banks. All of this is an evolutionary process, and neither the host country nor the TNE can foresee in advance the actual course of events that will follow from embarking on commercial activities and technology transfers.

Many discussions of this process of technology generation and transfer — despite protestations to the contrary — tend to distort the way in which it is understood and managed in actual practice. Businesses do not create technology simply to sell it or transfer it. They create it to provide the basis for a business opportunity. Technology is licensed rather than embodied in a product only when analysis indicates the latter is not feasible — i.e., licensing is not the preferred mode of capitalizing on technology. R&D is not planned in isolation; it is an integral part of a business plan. R&D resources are not allocated in isolation, they are allocated as part of a business plan. Consequently, discussions of technology transfer or R&D that lack a specific context are regarded by businessmen as simplistic abstractions.

From a business standpoint, technology is regarded as an asset that has been created as a result of investing in a highly risky process. Commercial application of that technology involves an even larger risk. The value of the technology is determined not by the cost of generating it but by the utility it achieves in the marketplace. That value is exceedingly difficult to determine, because it is a derivative of the commercial success achieved by the products made possible by the technology. Thus, technology's value is a function of the commercial opportunity it makes possible, modified by the alternative technologies available to the prospective purchaser. There rarely is anything even resembling a "market" in technology, and "value" must be determined by negotiation. The entire system of goals, measurements, and rewards in business is predicated on determining exchange values, and then determining whether or not mutual benefit can be derived from the exchange. Cost does not determine value, but it *does* influence whether production will continue. Since R&D is seen as an investment that must be made on a continuing basis to insure the future of the business, businessmen believe that obtaining a return on a successful investment is necessary to obtain funds to make additional investments in R&D.

Much R&D comes to nought. Much technology never finds a viable application. Indeed, investment in R&D can be one of the easiest ways to waste money. Studies indicate clearly that the greatest cause of failure in commercializing new technology is inadequate coupling with the market. Consequently, proposals by developing countries that R&D be divorced from business considerations and be treated as an activity in its own right, or that it be initiated in advance of the creation of a local business base that can guide it and capitalize on it, are regarded as ill-advised.

The development plans of countries by definition have as their goal the introduction of change, i.e., the creation of innovation. Technological innovation is a much broader and more complex process than R&D or technology transfer, and it is more analogous to the development process in developing countries. Consequently, a study of this process to determine the principles that make it effective could well be more productive than a narrower focus on R&D or technology transfer.

An understanding of a businessman's approach to technology transfer must begin with an understanding of his approach to any commercial transaction. The whole concept of business rests on the principle that mutual advantage is possible. TNEs recognize that they must provide value if they are to survive, and they pursue the negotiation of exchange aggressively. But determination of value, especially the value of technology, is complex and elusive; it requires identifying and balancing both tangible and intangible considerations as well as balancing both long-term and short-term factors.

No one would argue that the present system is totally satisfactory, or that no changes are needed. TNE behavior has not always been exemplary, and corrections should be made. Ill-advised agreements have been reached through inadequate information, lack of experience, or failure of foresight on both sides, and those agreements should be modified. TNEs have not always obtained adequate knowledge of the values and aspirations of their customers, and this has sometimes led to unconstructive experience.

But businessmen are perhaps the ultimate pragmatists, and they do seek to understand and respond to their environment realistically. Better sensitivity to local circumstances and local aspirations is being achieved. The determination of mutual benefit must be subject to continuing reexamination and redefinition. The entire experience of the businessman leads him to approach this process aggressively, and it is unrealistic to expect otherwise. When a businessman settles for something other than the most attractive arrangement he can negotiate, he no longer has a standard with which to measure his performance. He regards such behavior as incompatible with the basic tenets of a market system, and he is exceedingly uncomfortable when asked to adopt such behavior. What many people in the developing countries may not appreciate is that bargaining in the developed countries is "hard-nosed" and aggressive. It is only by the aggressive pursuit of self-interest on both sides that a realistic perception of the areas of mutual self-interest can be established.

Thus, when arrangements are proposed that threaten to destroy the prospects for mutual advantage, TNEs can be expected to object, to seek alternative arrangements, or to withdraw their participation. The first goal of business is to make a profit. Without that, other goals become unattainable. The search for profit is a relentless taskmaster that drives the businessman to a continual quest for opportunities and to a creative, flexible pragmatism in negotiating arrangements. His belief in the value of economic progress makes him exceedingly sympathetic to the development goals of less-developed countries. He sees their progress as providing both an improved quality of life for them and additional opportunity for him.

The Process of Technology Transfer

Let us now turn to the process of technology transfer. This subject suffers from the uncertainty and misunderstanding created by imprecise and frequently non-existent definitions of terms. The term technology itself has been broadened to cover a range of disciplines from management to public administration. In this paper we are deliberately choosing a narrower, more nearly classical definition. Technology is taken to mean the body of knowledge, skill, and lore that provides the capability to produce goods and services, to design and develop new ones when appropriate, to apply them to the specialized needs of the customer, and to install and service them. In choosing this narrower definition, we recognize that effective application of technology requires the availability of commensurate capability in management, marketing, finance, and so on.

The term "technology transfer" also has a variety of meanings — from the movement of technological development along the path from basic discovery to commercial application, to the transfer of technology from one social/economic/cultural/political context to a different one. For the purposes of this discussion we take technology transfer to mean the latter. This transfer almost invariably requires a skilled modification of the technology to match a different scale of operation, a different mix of factor inputs, and a different set of customer needs and expectations. This modification requires close and effective collaboration between the supplier of the technology, who can best determine when modification may fatally compromise the basic integrity of the technology, and the intended user, who alone has the necessary understanding of local circumstances and requirements.

It is crucial to recognize that, even under the most propitious circumstances, technology transfer is a complex process. Even when the transfer is within the same organization, it requires what many regard as inordinate time and effort by skilled and dedicated people. The process is uncertain, and failures are frequent. Consequently, it is misleading to talk about the "flow" of technology. One should not regard technology transfer as a process that will occur naturally if one just stays out of the way. On the contrary, technology transfer requires energizing and facilitating interventions at various steps along the way.

In many respects, technology can be regarded as an item of commerce whose transfer (or exchange) has similarities with all processes of exchange. The entire transaction has as its objective the determination of value as perceived by both the supplier and the prospective customer, and the mutual decision that a basis for exchange can be established. Of course, it also reflects relative bargaining power. At the same time, however, the exchange of technology has some special features of its own:

(a) The value of the technology is exceedingly difficult for *both* parties to ascertain. The supplier very rarely understands, in a conscious explicit sense, the full body of knowledge that he draws on in developing the technology; the prospective user cannot know in advance all of the information that he needs to apply the technology, nor can he know how effective the technology will be. Furthermore, technology is a depreciating asset; its value diminishes with time, frequently in an unpredictable manner. Of equal importance, as noted earlier, there rarely is a "market" in technology. This compounds the uncertainty that both buyer and seller must confront.

This uncertainty means that one-time transfers are particularly difficult to negotiate. The likelihood of being wrong, and therefore of receiving inadequate value for consideration given, is high for both parties, and the opportunity for redress is dependent either on exceedingly skilled foresight in writing the contract or on good faith ex post facto adjustments. The problem, for example, may result from contracting to buy a plant on a so-called "turn-key basis," where the supplier hands over a new plant ready to operate, or it may result from outright purchases of technology with no provision for continuing interaction. The key ingredient in achieving transfer under such circumstances is a good faith commitment to "make it happen" and to achieve equity on the part of both parties. In contrast, continuing relationships provide an effective mechanism for building the requisite faith and mutual understanding.

(b) Effective negotiation requires a reasonable match between the knowledge, skill, and experience of the participants. Where the disparities are too great, the party in an inferior position may be immobilized by fear of being trapped in a "one horse — one rabbit" exchange. Furthermore, the communication of substantive information will be arduous and ineffective among parties with substantial differences in technical background. Unfortunately, the technical community has few "translators" for bridging such gaps and no systematic process for training them. The absence of a body of people specifically trained to bridge these gaps is one of the most serious barriers to effective technology transfer and to the attainment of self-reliance on the part of the developing countries.

Key ingredients for success in negotiating and accomplishing the transfer of technology in any context include the following:

(1) Both parties must perceive sufficient potential benefit to warrant the expenditure of effort that the transfer will require.

(2) The transfer itself will involve costs in time, effort, and money to both parties.

(3) Success requires continuing follow-up effort by both parties.

(4) Success is never assured, for there is an irreducible area of uncertainty in all technology transfer.

(5) The values and priorities of the parties are very rarely identical, and their interests in effecting the transfer are rarely commensurate with each other.

(6) Actions and commitments are carried out by people, not by organizations, and a transfer which may be small in the context of the organization typically constitutes a significant event for the particular people who must accomplish the transfer.

(7) In many cases, a significant part of the information that must be communicated is kinesthetic rather than verbal, and direct "hands on" participation may be required.

These and similar micro-factors frequently determine success or failure irrespective of more global institutional or structural considerations or disparities in bargaining power. Just as in the case of a business in the private sector of a developed country, technology in a developing country does not stand alone. Even while it is a means to an end, the body of technological capability that can be brought to bear on a country's problems should also be an ingredient in helping to define what ends will be sought. Furthermore, as noted earlier, the effective application of technology requires the availability of commensurate capability in management, marketing, finance, and other areas.

Specifying Technological Objectives

Specification of the objectives of the development process must precede the identification of technological needs. Effective consideration of technology transfer issues requires subdividing the technical requirements for development into more specific categories. These include: (a) technology to meet a minimally acceptable level of human needs for food, shelter, clothing, health, and energy; (b) technology for agricultural and non-agricultural natural resource products for local consumption; (c) technology for agricultural and other natural resource products for export; (d) technology for the manufacture of products for local consumption; (e) technology for the manufacture of goods for export; (f) technology for the creation of an industrial infrastructure: transportation, communication, power, public services, factories, and repair and maintenance; and (g) technology for creating a self-sustaining technological infrastructure: education, craft training, indigenous technical capabilities, measurement and control instrumentation, or information storage and retrieval.

Specific technologies must be tailored to each local situation. The modes of acquisition will differ for each technology, as will the manner in which they are applied and the types of control exercised over them by the receiving country.

The technology required to meet minimum survival needs is unlikely to be readily available in the highly developed countries, especially in the private sector. This special problem lies outside the purview of the normal technology transfer process that is the subject of this paper. Although private enterprise may play a peripheral role in transferring this technology, the principal thrust will have to come from governments and other public institutions.

The same comment applies to technology to support local production of agricultural and non-agricultural natural resource products. The need to optimize inputs of land, labor, and capital in terms of local conditions will typically require technology different from that used in capital-intensive agriculture and capital-intensive natural resource industries in highly developed economies. Scientific and technical knowledge can help make the necessary modifications in some technology, but private enterprise is unlikely to play a central role. It is in this area, however, that educational institutions can play a critical role by developing special curricula to educate people to address the problems of this particular kind of technology application, i.e., the selection and adaptation of more advanced technology.

Technology for agricultural and other natural resource products intended for export is much more likely to be closely linked to advanced technology in the developed countries. Technology transfer involving the agribusiness industries from the private sector may be important for achieving goals for export. Less-developed countries may well be concerned about the second- and third-order effects of such technology on social structure, transportation, employment patterns, and other aspects of village life. Much needs to be learned about such effects, but the degree of control that the less-developed country would wish to exert over technology transfer in this area may well differ from the areas discussed above. Difficult questions regarding the extent of vertical integration within a country will also have to be resolved in some cases.

Perhaps the most controversial of these technologies is technology for products for local consumption. The question "what is appropriate?" often arouses emotion. Much technology that has been applied for many years in more highly developed economies will turn out to be the most cost-effective for many purposes, but developing countries sometimes feel that a loss of face is involved in using such older technology. They insist on being provided with only the most modern technology available. A much more productive approach would be to take a very pragmatic attitude toward the question, "what will best suit our needs for economic growth, providing jobs, managing trade balances, building infrastructures, etc.?" Frequently, it will be a technology which has been available for some time. What developing countries may not appreciate is that much technology which has been available for years is still the most viable that can be used. Technology is changed only if there is an economic justification for using new technology. Although older technology can frequently be obtained from firms in the private sector, much of it is in the public domain and thus available to any country with the indigenous capability to select and apply it. If such capability is lacking, its creation should have the highest priority. In the meantime, it may be most expeditious to purchase not only the technology but also the know-how for applying it. One would expect this to be an area in which hard bargaining is likely in the long run to result in the most equitable relationships between parties, since the number of products produced only for local consumption tend to diminish over time. As an economy grows, customer expectations regarding cost, performance, and quality tend to rise to international standards.

Technology for manufacturing export goods is the kind most needed in developing countries, and this technology is most likely to be found in the private sector. Technology transfer in this area should be closely linked with the creation of a local industrial infrastructure.

Without this latter development, the advanced technology acquired to capitalize on some domestic advantage — e.g., low labor rates — in world trade will have no synergistic effects on the rest of the economy. A development plan must include the gradual creation of such an infrastructure, and the technology available from the private sector in developed countries is central to this process. The key problem for developing countries is to specify the scope and thrust of the technology to be transferred in such a way that the domestic economy is left with a strengthened and viable technological capability.

The concept of a technological infrastructure is less well articulated, but its absence is a key factor in the "brain drain" of technically trained people from the developing countries. The specialized educational requirements for the new skills needed to support a growing technology are not yet well understood. The dynamics and phasing of the education and training activity with other elements of technological development need more attention, and the private sector can play an important role in this process. In many cases, applicable technology is available or the necessary modifications are straightforward. Overall direction and control of the process of development must come from the developing countries. The process requires the participation and cooperation of governments in both the developed and the developing countries, the private sector, educational institutions, and other public agencies.

Recognition of the varying characteristics of these different classes of technology, of the roles that various parties should play with respect to each class, and of the place of each class in the total development process will help to simplify the discussion of technology transfer and thus focus on relevant issues.

Conclusion: The Need for Self-Reliance

In considering the application of technology to the development process, it is necessary to establish the nature of the mix of objectives and priorities that will be sought. Of at least equal importance is the necessity to understand the ancillary changes that must occur if the development goals are to be realized.

The entire process of technology transfer must rest on a realistic appreciation of what is meant by self-determination or self-reliance. Self-reliance must always be defined in relative terms as meaning the attainment of the indigenous capability to manage one's own destiny in a world community in which both self-determination and interdependence operate in creative tension. The term "self-reliance" unfortunately often is taken to connote autonomy or even autarky. Increased economic development, however, typically goes hand in hand with increased interdependence with other nations or, in the case of industry, other companies.

The key step in this process as far as the developing countries are concerned is to develop the capability to define and adjust the framework of negotiation in such a way as to maximize the leverage of indigenous strengths and advantages. In order for the process of development to proceed, there must be a gradual increase in areas of strength or advantage.

Although the need to do so may not be recognized or made explicit, some additional conditions must also be satisfied — conditions that involve changes in self-perception or values rather than changes in factors directly associated with technology transfer. These include:

(1) A growing sense of equality at the bargaining table, of being able to cope with events.

(2) A growing sense of ability to manage the dynamics of a bargaining process for indigenous advantage.

(3) Adoption of the goal of perennial improvements in costs, productivity, and performance as the condition for survival in international trade.

(4) Recognition of the necessity to adopt measurable goals and to evaluate progress.

(5) Recognition of the need for relentless pragmatism in modifying goals and mechanisms in the light of experience.

(6) Recognition of the need for a local institutional framework that fosters entrepreneurial behavior by providing adequate rewards for success and that matches work assignments with capabilities.

(7) Recognition that progress results primarily from disciplined pursuit of specific near-term goals rather than from vague movement toward distant visionary goals.

(8) Recognition of the inherent incongruity in commercial relations, i.e., that they are a complex and dynamic mixture of cooperation, interdependence, and competition, and that creative tension among these elements fuels the engine of progress.

Perhaps the most striking aspect of this entire discussion is the obvious parallel between the management of technology in a large corporation and management of technology by a developing country. In both cases, the technical community should help to formulate sound goals by making evident what is physically attainable and then should play an important role in helping to achieve those goals.

T he present paper is addressed to two main topics: the policies of the U.S. government that relate to the support and encouragement of transfer of technology to developing countries, and U.S. company initiatives which respond to specific concerns of the developing countries in the process of technology transfer.

The processes and problems of technology transfer are different among the various industrial sectors — manufacturing, service, agribusiness, and extractive. The types of technology transferred, the reasons for transferring the technology, and the channels of transfer are different in each sector. They also vary among companies within the same industrial sector, depending on company policies, preferences, and products. Industrial sectors and companies assess the host country environment differently. Furthermore, the infrastructure for the use of technology is different in each host country. As a result, the technological contributions made to the host country vary. The obstacles to transfers and the impacts of technology transfer differ according to the outcome of negotiations between companies and governments as well as between licensors and licensees. A number of trade-offs are made as a result of these negotiations, and the trade-offs differ according to industrial sector, company policies, and government negotiating abilities. Each of these aspects of technology transfer needs to be examined separately for each of the major industrial sectors in order to develop sound policies.

The strong differences among the various industrial sectors as to their activities, objectives, contributions, and reception abroad lead to the conclusion that U.S. policy cannot be an "overall" or "general" one. No overall policy which seeks to guide or constrain technology transfers will fit the many different situations that exist. Therefore, attention to specific problems and a search for specific results should compel the adoption of a policy that takes into account the different industrial characteristics of U.S. companies and the different levels of technological development among recipients. Although it is contrary to traditional U.S. foreign economic policy to adopt discriminatory

118

International Technology Flows for Development: Suggestions for U.S. Government and Corporate Initiatives

Jack N. Behrman

policies, distinct policies *are required* if specific objectives are to be achieved.

U.S. Government Initiatives

There are at least four ways in which the U.S. government can help in supporting and encouraging the transfer of technology to the developing countries: (1) by reshaping the dialogue with the developing countries; (2) by supporting the development of appropriate infrastructures in the developing countries to receive technology and utilize it; (3) by assisting developing countries to create mechanisms for the selection of technology, including the development of an indigenous scientific and technical base; and (4) by encouraging U.S. R&D activities here and abroad to promote technological development in the Third World.

Dialogues with Developing Countries

Much of the dialogue on technology transfers and the role of foreign companies has taken place at the political level, as though the problem were one that required strategies of conflict resolution rather than strategies of technical cooperation. It would be desirable to shift the level and the nature of the dialogue to that of cooperative efforts at the technical level, for this is the true nature of the problem. It is, of course, impossible under the U.S. system to *force* U.S. companies to engage in technology transfers, or to force them to develop a particular technology. The system itself must induce both of these, since political arguments will do neither.

Dialogue should cover the problems of transferring and absorbing technologies while giving full recognition to distinctions among the

•Excerpted in revised form from Jack N. Behrman, "Industry Characteristics and Policy Suggestions: Manufacturing, Service and Agribusiness," *Public Policy and Technology Transfer*, Vol. 2: *Industry Characteristics* (New York: Fund for Multinational Management Education 1978), pp. 17-68.

industrial sectors mentioned earlier. Only by focussing on these distinctions can appropriate policies be developed. The dialogue should be directed toward the varying contributions from the different sectors and the special role that is played by managerial know-how. In addition, emphasis should be placed on the various technical contributions in manufacturing, the protection and incentives provided by a patent system, and the role of trademarks in raising quality standards in production.

The dialogue should include an extensive analysis of the trade-offs which are likely in the various contractual relationships between licensors and licensees, given the restrictions imposed by governments, with special emphasis on the trade-offs likely under requirements for debundling or joint ventures, or for local investment of returns from licensing, all of which increase the risk exposure of the licensors.

It is also necessary to emphasize in the dialogue the role that the movement of people plays in the transfer of technology, and the desirability of facilitating such movement. Similarly, the movement of a variety of teaching aids and equipment required for solving technical bottlenecks is also necessary, and its role in facilitating technology transfer should be explained thoroughly. For example, it is frequently difficult to get training movies, samples, dyes, or small equipment for teaching or laboratory or testing purposes into a developing country. To do so frequently requires elaborate subterfuges and bribery in order to achieve what should be eagerly sought by the developing countries.

Many of the above problems arise from the fact that the developing countries simply do not have enough information about how American companies operate and what their mutual interests are. Information — its nature and scope, availability, and interpretation — is the most fundamental unresolved problem concerning foreign investment and technology transfer, and it needs thorough airing among governments at the technical level. This is a problem that the U.N. Center on Transnational Corporations has not yet adequately handled, despite the fact that the Center has been in operation for nearly two years. It has not even been able to design an appropriate information system, much less begin to collect data. Yet without adequate information, developing countries will continue to feel that they are operating blindfolded.

Support for National Infrastructure Needs

No developing country can make adequate use of technology unless it has an appropriate scientific and technical infrastructure in the public, private, educational, and corporate sectors. It is of no value to develop a technical training system or R&D institute when companies are not interested in using them. Conversely, it is of no value to interest local companies in technical advances which are not available from the scientific community. Among the initiatives that can be taken in this area are: (a) reorientation of university programs; (b) exchange of professional personnel; (c) stimulation of repair and maintenance services; (d) development of technology centers in the developing countries; and (e) support for small business through appropriate financing institutions.

Many of the universities in the developing countries are staffed by professionals who have been trained in the advanced countries, particularly those of Europe, and have developed a scientific research orientation rather than one concerned with problems of industrial technology and product innovation. Assistance to universities, particularly engineering schools, to develop industrially oriented programs can be achieved through exchange of professors, joint projects, and internships in industry for students, plus company support of supplementary education for its own workers and technicians. Numerous suggestions have been made along these lines, but funds have not been available to make an adequate breakthrough.

One of the best means of inculcating a technical orientation is through exchange of personnel within corporations as well as through private institutes and between universities and industry across national boundaries. Measures must be taken to be certain that this does not become a new "brain drain," but it is feasible if the program is carefully constructed.

At another level, one of the problems in many of the developing countries is the absence of adequate maintenance and repair services and the lack of spare parts for machinery and equipment, which causes much modern equipment to stand idle or actually deteriorate beyond use. Small businesses need to be encouraged to provide such services and to produce spare parts under licenses. To achieve these goals, an emphasis on their importance in industrial development must begin in the educational system itself.

Technology centers for agricultural and health areas were developed under the Point Four Program after World War II. These were known as "servicios." These should be reinstituted as technology and productivity centers, using local personnel with assistance from the United States, possibly in the form of retired technical and executive personnel. These centers would assist in raising productivity in local business as well as in adapting foreign technologies for use by local companies. The centers could also serve to advise companies as to their needs regarding technology and potential sources of it. They would be supported by the local government and would receive payment from the companies they served. The U.S. government could also provide some initial funds for their creation, but they should not be so independently financed that they forget that their purpose is to serve local industry.

A major problem with regard to small business is the lack of financing available for small capital requirements, such as a single machine, truck, or tractor. Much greater attention needs to be paid to small business financing and to related management and control problems. Although development banks have long been in existence in many of the developing countries, they have not been staffed to provide a full range of assistance, including loans, to small businesses.

Mechanisms for the Selection of Technology

One of the most critical problems facing the developing countries is the selection of technology for industrial development. This cannot be done by either the private sector or the government without a prior determination as to the nature and scope of industrial development. This determination is increasingly the responsibility of governments, largely because of the small size and limited resources of many of the countries and the lack of a history of entrepreneurship in industrial development. Such entrepreneurship as exists is more oriented toward trading than toward the development of business institutions. In addition, given the scarcity of resources and the smallness of the market, care must be taken to provide the appropriate infrastructure for whatever industrial sectors are promoted. This is the pattern of development used by Japan, a pattern which is being followed with some success by South Korea.

The selection of industrial sectors to be developed in a host country depends on the factor endowments of the country, the markets to be served, the priority given to basic human needs, the pressures for military development, the ties to regional associations, the openness of the international markets, and other factors. Not enough is yet known about alternative approaches to industrialization and different infrastructure requirements to make optional selections. The creation of an international institute to assist in developing such information and experience has been proposed, however. Such an institute needs to be funded for several years and to have the cooperation of both advanced and developing country governments so as to help generate the information necessary to set national priorities for the development of industrial sectors.

To adopt technologies appropriate to the industrial sectors that they have selected, developing countries also need considerable knowledge about sources of alternate technologies, and the creation of technology data banks has been proposed. The United Nations Industrial Development Organization (UNIDO) and the U.N. Centre on Transnational Corporations have moved into this field, but inadequately. A mechanism for making available sufficient information on alternate technologies and their sources should be supported by the United States and other members of the United Nations.

Most developing country governments recognize that even after they have identified the technologies they need they must negotiate for their transfer, and many officials are not adequately prepared for these negotiations. Longer lasting and better contracts result when all parties to the agreement have access to relevant information and the skills necessary to use it effectively. The United States can promote improved contract negotiations by financing "negotiation simulation" sessions for foreign government officials. Such training sessions are currently offered by the U.N. Centre for Transnational Corporations, the Fund for Multinational Management Education, some university business schools, and private consultants.

A technology triangle, based on (a) government policies that support technical advance; (b) universities oriented towards industrial research and development; and (c) corporations structured to generate, receive, and utilize technical advances has been the base of rapid technical advance in developed countries. This triangle does not exist in most of the developing countries and needs to be created. To stimulate its development, it would be useful to send "technology teams" to developing countries to identify local "change agents" who could,with appropriate assistance, help stimulate the development of a technology triangle.

Support for U.S. Research and Development

For its own national development purposes but also to be able to assist the developing countries, the U.S. government needs to reexamine its policies on the R&D activities of U.S. corporations. Current tax policies do not sufficiently support R&D activities in the United States nor the transfer of resulting innovations. In fact, they often hinder them. In addition, priorities need to be set for the development of technologies among the different industrial sectors, so as to be most helpful in responding to the requests of the developing countries.

U.S. Corporate Initiatives

The companies that have technologies available for transfer, or that can supply the needed know-how, can undertake initiatives in four different areas, in order to play a more effective role in meeting the concerns and needs of the developing countries. First, they can develop much more effective means and channels of communication by participating directly in the North-South dialogue. Second, they can make certain that their technologies are made available on reasonable terms. Third, they can assist in technical training in the developing countries, and finally, they can assist in the development of an indigenous scientific and technological infrastructure in the developing countries.

Communication

Multinational companies have not done a good job of explaining what they are doing and why. Nor have they recognized the concern of developing countries for appropriate information. The companies should recognize that information is the basis of good decisionmaking and that better contractual relations arise when both parties have access to adequate and relevant information and know how to use it.

Many multinational companies have accomplished striking results through varied programs of manpower development and technology transfer. Though individual stories told by the companies themselves might appear to be suspect, there are ways of making clear what transnational corporations are doing by relating the similar experiences of several companies and avoiding any particular interpretation of which tactics or approaches are more or less relevant or useful.

The creation of the U.N. Centre on Transnational Corporations was a reflection of the desire to have more information on objectives, policies, and worldwide operations of the companies. Presently, there is no meeting of the minds between the U.N. members, particularly the Group of 77, and the companies themselves as to what information is needed and how it should be gathered and used. The companies should enter this dialogue fully to make certain that appropriate information is provided and that it is used without pejorative interpretation. The precise concerns and needs of the developing countries should become clear fairly quickly in such a dialogue, and the companies should then be able to explain how they might meet them at the least cost and with the least interference in the desired operations.

In order to enter the North-South dialogue, many companies will have to assign effective officials to this task and provide them with a direct channel to top management so that corporate policies will reflect the results of the dialogues. While many companies do not have officials at headquarters who are charged with this responsibility, some of their affiliates are attempting to set up such a dialogue within individual countries, for example, through the American Chambers of Commerce in Brazil, Mexico, and Venezuela. Since many of the issues, however, are regional or international, and therefore involve the total operations of the companies, it is necessary for these dialogues to be coordinated at headquarters so that corporate representations can be made at top governmental levels and in the United Nations.

Finally, the multiple opportunities for dialogues should be grasped through participation in conferences on particular issues, such as energy, hunger, nutrition, agribusiness, development of tropical plants, attacks on tropical diseases, urban development, and so forth. Rather than seek to keep a "low profile," it will become increasingly necessary for multinational companies to stand on what they are doing and to explain why they believe their activities are desirable in achieving the mutual goals of companies and host countries.

From the standpoint of company communication with the U.S. government, a basic need is to have dialogues which assume that most goals are mutual and that they can be reconciled when they conflict. The adversarial nature of government-business dialogues in the United States for the past hundred years is no longer appropriate. Cooperation, rather than conflict, is required. Still, extreme care will be needed to make certain that cooperation does not become special privilege for the companies.

Availability of Technology

One of the primary concerns of the developing countries is that they do not know what technologies are available or how to assess the value of alternative technologies. Companies therefore need to make certain that developing countries know what the alternative technologies are and what is required to adapt them to local needs. Companies should cooperate with data banks in the collection of such information and create "technical service" subsidiaries to give priority to the identification of technologies available within the company for use in the developing countries.

Apart from what is available through governments themselves, the companies are the sole source of industrial technologies. Yet the myriad types and number of companies is confusing to developing countries, which may be aggressively pressed to accept a particular technology without having the ability to use it effectively. Small companies in host countries have a particular problem in determining alternative sources of technologies and in making considered judgments. Therefore, transnational corporations should make certain that adequate information is available about the technologies they have available for transfer and provide this information to national, regional, or international data banks.

The companies also should be ready to discuss alternative technologies. If they are not willing to do so, technical expertise will have to be developed at governmental institutes — national laboratories, national technology centers, ministries of science and technology, development banks, international lending institutions, U.N. technical assistance units, and others. Since technologies developed for advanced countries may not be precisely adapted to the needs of the developing countries, the companies should stand ready to make appropriate adaptations, either from their own investigations or on the basis of dialogues with developing country officials as to their needs.

Technical Training

Although almost all companies engage in training of technicians or workers in order to make certain that activities overseas (including those of licensees) are successful, it is probable that more could be done both inside and outside of the companies to expand the technical base.

Technical training within companies frequently follows programs developed at headquarters, and much of it is quite specific to the tasks at hand. Training that opens up avenues of promotion for workers is sometimes offered, but is not always part of the training program. Many companies offer support for education outside of the company, but few really encourage its use by persuading workers or technicians to take advantage of the opportunities. Discussion groups composed of management and workers might elicit greater response on the part of the work force so as to elevate their technical skills through both inside and outside programs.

To make certain that programs outside of the company are available and appropriate to developing the technological infrastructure, companies could work with local training institutes, both technical and managerial, and with universities to develop appropriate programs. Some of the university programs could be brought into the plants in the evening, with consequent greater attendance and application to company needs.

Technical training opportunities could also be offered to government lab technicians who need to know more about what is being done in the companies with which they work. This is already being done by some of the pharmaceutical companies in working with government medical labs and hospitals, but it could be expanded, particularly if the technology centers proposed above are put in place.

Assistance to Science and Technology Infrastructure

As indicated earlier in the section on governmental initiatives, there is considerable need for the development of an appropriate scientific and technological infrastructure in the developing countries. Companies should cooperate with the initiatives taken by the U.S. government and also take some on their own to develop that infrastructure.

A technology corps, following the lines of the International Executive Service Corps, has been proposed and could certainly be useful, particularly if it drew on retired personnel rather than on technical personnel at the early and crucial stages of their own development. Some companies have a roster of retired personnel from which they draw for these purposes within their own worldwide operations. These retired personnel could readily be instructed to assist developing countries in promoting a technological orientation among local companies, in developing technology centers, and in providing direct assistance to local companies seeking to adapt foreign technologies.

Among the most critical contributions are assistance to universities and technical institutes in developing professional or technical programs that will prepare new entrants for industrial research and technology programs. Companies could offer their own scientific and technical personnel for teaching on a regular basis, for lectures, seminars, or simply consultation with professors studying industrial research or management in the United States or Europe who plan to return to teach these skills in local universities.

Along with assistance to the universities, companies could supply scholarships to graduate students to develop research skills through summer internships or work-study programs, inculcating the technical needs of the companies into study programs at an earlier stage.

Finally, in order to spread a "technical orientation" among local companies, foreign-owned affiliates could institute industrial seminars on a variety of technical issues—quality control, safety, customer service, production scheduling, inventory control, accounting control. Many of the companies already have meetings among top managers through their various associations. Much less is done at the technical level to make certain that an appreciation of the usefulness of new techniques is spread among workers. Some companies achieve this through their own customer and supplier relations, and this is, of course, a significant contribution. In line with this objective, companies should encourage host governments to adopt international quality standards or, at least, to adopt some national standards looking toward the international standards, so as to begin to gradually improve product quality to the point where products can be exported more readily to advanced-country markets.

Conclusion

All of the above activities require more than an intensification of what is being done. Rather, a new orientation is needed in which the companies accept a responsibility to enter actively into the North-South dialogue to demonstrate the role they are playing and to alter it sufficiently to meet the concerns of the developing countries when they can do so without raising costs unreasonably. Where costs are raised beyond what should be accepted by the companies, cooperative programs need to be developed with host and U.S. government agencies. These initiatives would themselves support a realization that cooperative orientations and efforts are being undertaken to replace the standoffish or adversarial postures which have led to the present tensions.

IV. Mobilizing Science and Technology for

National Needs

erhaps more significant than the present array of fantastic new technologies that have sent man to the moon is the emergence of new perceptions about the role of technology in society. For a long time technology was viewed as a common good having only positive value, and for that reason, it was sought after and often unconditionally accepted and praised. But more recent experiences in the development and deployment of technologies give evidence that technology does not always fulfill its purported objectives. If there is today a growing apprehension about technology's role in the world economy, it is because we have learned that technology is no more and no less than one important means to many different ends.

In discussing the role of technology in the developing countries, we should take note of two conspicuous tendencies. The first is the tendency to advocate "optimization" of the factor endowment (that is to say, achieving industrialization by making the most efficient use of the available resources, technology, capital, and markets of a given country); this approach invariably results in the deployment of less sophisticated, capital-saving, labor-intensive technologies variously termed appropriate, intermediate, or frontier technology. The second tendency is the treatment of development issues at the local community and business firm level as though they at all times represented a microcosm of national needs and objectives. Both of these approaches take more for granted than is necessarily true.

Some of the leading industrial sectors in a developing country are geared primarily toward breaking the inertia of underdevelopment. They introduce technologies which are quite advanced relative to the country's absorptive capacity. But the "feeder" industries that support these leading sectors do not necessarily require such advanced technology. It is therefore desirable to look at development from both the national and the local points of view, so that what is thought to be the ideal — not "mass production," but "production by the masses" involving both leading and feeder industries — can be realized.

In discussing the role of technology in development tasks, this chapter uses the Korean experience as an appropriate illustration.

Chapter 8

Technology for Development: The South Korean Experience

Hyung-Sup Choi

Attention is given to the role of technology at the national level for national development tasks — not to advocate a highly centralized system but rather to emphasize the impact that technological choices can have at the national level. The crucial question is what kind of role national governments should play during the various stages of development with respect to general development choices as well as specific choices among available technologies on the basis of selected economic and social criteria.

Industrial Development in Korea

The success of any industrialization effort hinges on a country's factor endowment. The following statistics give some idea of what conditions were like in Korea around 1959-61, the period preceding the launching of the country's industrialization effort under the First Five-Year Economic Development Plan. First, Korea's GNP growth rate averaged 3.3 per cent per year, and population growth was 2.9 per cent. The per capita income was under $100, and a severe dichotomy existed within Korea's economic structure: 65 per cent of the total work force was in primary industries, while secondary industries (mining and manufacturing) employed only 6.9 per cent. In terms of per capita output, using an index of 1.0, primary industries represented 0.65 and secondary industries 2.60. This meant that a mere 7 per cent of the total work force was engaged in relatively productive sectors. The domestic savings ratio to GNP was only 3 per cent and, perhaps because of that, the Korean economy was from the beginning an open one. This was necessary in order to obtain the foreign investments which accompanied a rise in foreign imports of goods and services, and also, to some extent, a rise in exports to pay for the imports. On the whole, then, Korea offered a perfect example of an underdeveloped, stagnant economy.

*Revised text of a keynote address prepared for the third Inter-Congress of the Pacific Science Association, July 12-18, 1977, Bali, Indonesia.

Initially, Korea opted to develop light, labor-intensive industries by absorbing the labor force from the primary sector. The effective demand in the primary sector for industrial products was, however, all too slight, so it was necessary to look elsewhere in search of capital, markets, and technology. Instead of initiating a pattern of import substitution followed by exports, the two were undertaken almost simultaneously, particularly when the first five-year plan went into effect. The apparent success of this bold approach can be attributed to several factors: (1) the capacity of the labor force to deal with technologies which were relatively sophisticated; (2) close trade relations with the United States and Japan, both of which are big markets; (3) full exploitation of the technical advantage of being latecomers in industrialization; and (4) the capacity to adapt to the international economic environment — a capacity that was actively supported by the government through the creation of a favorable climate for foreign investment.

The most conspicuous constraints on the scheme for rapid industrialization were deficiencies in the social service sectors. The infrastructure for industrial development was very poor, and the government placed greatest emphasis on the building of roads and ports, communications, and other essentials to development, including expanded educational facilities, particularly for training. About 50 per cent of the total foreign capital in Korea, as well as over 70 per cent of the total public loan funds from overseas, were spent on infrastructure.

During the first five-year plan (1962-1966), there was considerable debate — all justifiable — in the course of choosing an appropriate technology. The essential criterion, however, was that the choice of technology had to fit the scale of a project. For instance, the construction of an innovative, integrated iron and steel plant with an annual production capacity of less than 400,000 tons was contemplated. This, however, was less than the optimum size required for the introduction of modern production methods. Since it was virtually impossible to set up an efficient, integrated operation, the establishment of such a plant had to be deferred until the second five-year plan, when a plant could be established with a capacity sufficient to justify, for instance, a tandem rolling mill. The introduction of the L.D. converter was in itself a breakthrough for those who had experience only with open hearth or electric furnaces. But it was necessary to wait another several years before a highly sophisticated, continuous casting mill could be added to the steel-making plant, and before sufficient experience had been acquired in the operation and maintenance of conventional methods.

The Second Five-Year Economic Development Plan (1967-1971) placed emphasis on initiating the "lead sectors" approach and pushed forward with the development of basic chemical industries (such as fertilizers, cement, and petro-chemicals) as well as the iron and steel industry. What was attempted through these sectors was the initiation of a growth momentum that would make itself felt within all Korean industry. These industries are highly capital-intensive and need a huge infrastructure which has to be supported by the government, but they are essential to the foundation upon which the high-linkage industries can be built. In formulating the second five-year plan, a series of bold quantitative tools for constructing development models was introduced. These models were most important in articulating Korea's socio-economic goals, identifying potential industrial growth patterns and major constraints in reaching those goals, and formulating investment programs.

The idea behind the "lead sectors" approach, along with the use of foreign experts, was to allow greater latitude for debate on the plan so that a defensible strategy would necessarily follow. It is noteworthy that the experts often turned out to be too conservative at both the micro- and macro-planning levels. The dynamism of a developing-country economy — if it ever does achieve real momentum — is difficult for the experts to accept. The problem of excessive conservatism can be very troublesome if it occurs in the planning for a key sector, because the forward motion of the whole effort may be brought to a complete halt. Becoming overly optimistic can also be troublesome, however, since it may result in tying up non-productive capital in excess capacity. This too can slow the forward momentum, which, once lost, is extremely difficult to regain.

One pressing question in developing lead-sector industries was whether or not they could operate at full- or at least near-capacity. It was found that the range of choice was extremely small because the cost of capital for these industries, which for the most part originated abroad, was very much higher than for the advanced countries. Recognition of this hard fact of life had much to do with the makeup of any industrial project.

The Third Five-Year Economic Development Plan (1972-1976) followed more or less the same direction as the earlier ones but with greater economies of scale in agriculture and social services, capitalizing on the previous experiences of the advanced countries and the improved capacity of the home country itself. This orientation necessitated the introduction of unprecedented numbers of newer and higher-level technologies into Korean industry. The decision was irreversible insofar as scientific and technological development were concerned. It was an issue of survival or extinction in ever-increasing international competition. Korea's experience in the past decade, particularly with reference to the relationship between commodity exports and royalty payments for foreign technologies, indicates that a close correlation exists between the two: an adequate supply of appropriate technologies is the essential factor in enabling industry to produce the goods and services demanded in international markets.

For this reason, Korea's science and technology development policy today hinges on the proper selection, assimilation, and adaptation of imported technologies. Throughout the first development periods, foreign technologies were often accepted along with the inflow of capital, largely because of the strongly felt need for foreign capital. (Statistics, therefore, tend to underestimate the amount of imported technology). The range of technological choices was often limited, and technology itself was treated as though it were only of secondary importance. But the situation has changed. The specific need for technologies, as distinguished from capital, has been recognized. The achievement of a so-called comparative advantage, which in reality relies heavily on low labor costs and the use of manual workers, is untenable in the long haul and is obviously a direction that should not be taken. For many developing countries, the day for achieving a balance in the employment of manual laborers and highly skilled workers is not and should not be in the distant future.

The three successive five-year economic development plans culminated in success beyond our expectations. GNP growth averaged 10 per cent per annum in real terms. The manufacturing sector alone attained, on the average, a 20 per cent growth rate per annum. Exports, 90 per cent of which consisted of manufactured goods, amounted to (U.S.) $8 billion in 1976 compared to $55 million in 1962, increasing approximately 150-fold in 15 years.

By the time the Fourth Five-Year Plan ends in 1981, it is envisaged (with some optimism) that the Korean GNP will reach $58.7 billion ($1,512 per capita) representing a twofold increase in net terms compared to 1961. The export target for 1981 is set at $14.2 billion in 1975 constant prices, representing an annual growth rate of 16 per cent after correcting for inflation.

Developing an Infrastructure for Technology

Depending on a host of problems, such as the lack of institutional frameworks within which people can function, the lack of legal bases for providing incentives to develop technology, and most of all the lack of qualified people, various approaches can be devised (perhaps differing from country to country) for developing appropriate infrastructures conducive to the development of technology.

It has been said that the development of technology within a developing country is, for all practical purposes, out of the question, and many have treated the subject as though any such concept were simply an intellectual exercise. It is often asserted that any need for sophisticated technologies easily can be met through the transfer of technology from developed countries, as though it could simply be picked off a shelf. This kind of thinking is not without some justification, but it grossly oversimplifies to the point of collectively condemning what in fact may be worthwhile, necessary, and even noble initiatives on the part of the developing countries. A pressing need to possess indigenous sources of technological development in tune with national requirements is widely felt in the developing countries. Many approaches to the problem of development encompass more than technical considerations. For instance, one of many formidable questions that need to be addressed is: What kind of technology should a society seek to develop?

The literature on appropriate technology is replete with elaborate treatises on the attributes of technology, but there is less on the attributes of development tasks themselves, which cannot simply be translated into terms of employment or income distribution, no matter how pivotal their importance. It is not difficult to achieve a consensus among people of different backgrounds that the appropriateness of the technology depends to a great degree on needs and capabilities. We can further conclude that needs must be identified *before* formulation of any plan for technological development—or, on an even broader scale, any aspect of national development. The pivotal problems are how to ascertain needs and how to assess latent capabilities so that they can be translated into development programs. These tasks are most difficult for developing countries, since such capabilities are often inadequate or even lacking. It is especially in this area that international cooperation should play a supplementary and complementary role if any real progress is to be made.

The appropriateness of technology is often measured in terms of the labor/capital requirement ratio, the level of requisite labor, and the necessary material input. These considerations stem from the assumption that technology is to be chosen only *after* goals have been delineated. There is nothing wrong in doing so, but it fails to take note of another vitally important role that technology should play, that is, the process through which goals are defined. The mere assessment of the appropriateness of the technology, using conventional yardsticks, often fails to take into consideration various other important factors, such as a developing country's absorptive capacity, which depends on many institutional, legal, cultural, environmental, and even ecological factors.

Perhaps the biggest problem facing developing countries with respect to appropriate technology is that of establishing harmony between rapidly rising aspirations and the slowness of progress. The cost to the developing countries — both in political and economic terms — of exercising a degree of patience rather than allowing rapid growth to skew development in the lead sectors will vary from one context to the next. In all contexts, however, the attempt to balance immediate needs against long-term goals requires political will and sound leadership that goes beyond technical considerations.

Korea's creation of an institutional framework was comprehensive, including, among other institutions: (1) the Ministry of Science and Technology (MOST) established in 1967 as the central planning, coordinating, and promotional body in the government; (2) the Korea Institute of Science and Technology (KIST), established in 1966 as an autonomous, multidisciplinary, industrial research institute chartered as a contract research organization; (3) the Korea Advanced Institute of Science (KAIS), founded in 1971 as an autonomous institution supported chiefly by the Ministry of Science and Technology, with the mission of training high-caliber professionals in selected applied sciences and engineering; and (4) a great number of vocational training institutes and technical high schools to meet the rapidly rising demand for skilled workers and technicians.

The new Ministry of Science and Technology spearheaded the enactment of several laws of great importance for the development of

science and technology, including: (1) the Science and Technology
Advancement Law of 1967, which defines the basic commitment of
the government to support science and technology and to provide
policy leadership; (2) the 1972 Law for the Promotion of Technology
Development, which, among other things, provides financial incentives to private industries for technology development; (3) the Engineering Services Promotion Law of 1973, which promotes local engineering firms by assuring markets on the one hand and performance
standards on the other; (4) the National Technical Qualification Law of
1973, which, through a system of examinations and certifications,
promotes the abilities and professional status of those in technical
fields; (5) the Assistance Law for Designated Research Organizations
of 1973, which provides legal, financial, and fiscal incentives for
research institutes in specialized fields on which the government and
private industry place particular emphasis (e.g., shipbuilding, electronics, communications, mechanical and materials engineering, and
energy and related areas); and (6) the Law for the Korea Science and
Engineering Foundation of 1976, which provides a legal basis for the
Foundation to act as the prime agent for strengthening research
(mainly university-based research) in basic and applied sciences as
well as in engineering, and to facilitate more rapid application of
science and engineering to national needs.

The Ministry is in charge of formulating, and to some extent implementing, plans for the development of science and technology as
an integral part of the nation's five-year economic development plans.

The Korea Institute of Science and Technology (KIST) was brought
into being to bolster the industrial sector, particularly in areas emphasized by the national economic development plan, by eliminating
bottlenecks that hinder further growth. Through special legislation,
the Institute was made a contract research organization — to make
researchers problem-oriented and to help make underwriters of R&D
aware of the importance of its results.

Before it undertook research of any kind, KIST carried out a comprehensive study to ascertain the actual needs of Korean industry. A
study was made of 600 industrial plants and related organizations
covering 25 industrial sectors. This study took eight months to complete and involved 80 specialists, 23 of whom were brought from
overseas. The survey helped to identify the main areas of concentration for the Institute during its initial period of operation. They
included: (1) materials and metallurgical engineering; (2) food
technology; (3) chemistry and chemical engineering; (4) electronics;
(5) mechanical engineering; and (6) industrial economics and management. This selection of areas of concentration then guided important decisions concerning the Institute's staffing, equipment, and
facilities. Studies similar to this initial comprehensive survey are
carried out periodically to ascertain industry's ever-changing requirements and to maintain the Institute's capability to solve them.

Among the operations set up within the Institute were: (1) a project
development department to promote the concept of scientific research among industrial firms and to help industry formulate ques-

tions to ask the Institute, (2) a cost accounting system to compare input with performance, and (3) the establishment of a large endowment fund to enable the Institute to undertake long-term research for which no particular client could easily be found. To avoid the rigidity inherent in departmentalization, a multidisciplinary approach was emphasized throughout the Institute.

As industry grew, its technological requirements increased in level and diversity. Some of the Institute's laboratories, such as those in shipbuilding and petrochemicals, were no longer able to render the necessary technical support to their industries. An independent research organization specific to each industry and problem area thus became necessary. Creating completely new organizations would have been a formidable task, so some of KIST's existing laboratories were spun off the mother institute. Thus, they inherited not only the knowledge that had already been accumulated, but also a workable and working management system and philosophy, which all too often are missing or amorphous in a new organization.

The vast importance of industrial research has only recently been recognized. It not only provides support for economic development, but, even more importantly, helps create the framework within which economic development strategies are formulated. Industrial research is essential to the realization of a nation's industrialization goals, and, if properly carried out, can help in setting reasonable and feasible goals.

In striving toward these goals, Korea has made substantial gains, through much trial and error, in improving its scientific and technical capabilities, improving administration and support systems, and increasing as well as orienting R&D investment. The total effort was intended to change the economy from a simple labor-intensive to a technology-intensive, and ultimately skill-intensive, structure. In other words, the effort was designed to accelerate the transformation of Korea's science and technology infrastructure from a supporting role in national economic development to a leadership role in creating a technologically self-reliant economy in Korea by 1980.

Transfer of Technology Within Countries: A Relatively Unexplored Frontier

While international technology transfer has been much in the limelight, surprisingly little attention has been given to the crucially important transfers between urban and rural areas, between industry and agriculture, and between business firms of varying sizes. Without a means for active transfer of technology *within* countries, development efforts are futile. The idea is not new, but it probably has not been pursued widely or conscientiously enough. At the macro-level — for instance, in trying to bridge the gap between the urban and rural economies — probably every developing country has tried some type of deliberately planned program of internal technology transfer; Korea's experience parallels some of these efforts in objective and perhaps in approach as well.

Korea's massive program, called "Saemaul Undong," which means new community movement, was undertaken at the national level and involved myriad programs, ranging from digging or improving sewage ditches to applying new farming techniques. The program also aimed at bringing about selective rural industrialization — through the offer of incentives — in the belief that the rural labor force could make a contribution to the development of industry. It became apparent, however, that it would take more than an abundant labor force to make industrialization of rural areas feasible. Many inherent difficulties quickly became obvious, making it necessary to readjust the time schedule for locating industry in rural areas. Upgrading living conditions and introducing means of earning supplementary income was made a major objective. The government channeled support to about 20,000 villages, with the support varying according to the extent of self-help displayed and the nature of the jobs to be done. For the last two consecutive years, rural household income in Korea has slightly surpassed that of urban households, perhaps for the first time in modern history. Many attribute that result to this program.

It is a widely held assumption that a change in rural values and attitudes is a necessary precondition to a self-sustained change in rural economic behavior. But Dr. Vincent Brandt, an American anthropologist who has been studying rural Korea for some years, asserts that rural development gained substantial momentum since the early 1970s for very different reasons. First, there were profound and irreversible modernizing changes in rural attitudes and in the operation of village institutions, particularly after the successful land reforms of the early 1950s. Second, government efforts placed less emphasis on farmers' psychological motivations and more on furnishing essential assistance to agriculture in terms of credit and technical advice and by providing better organizational linkages between the villages and the national economy. Third, improved communications and transportation have played a part in this progress, as have movements of population (e.g., the thousands of people who returned to their villages after military service and others who have moved to urban areas have all established contact points between urban and rural areas). A fourth factor was the transformation of local bureaucracies, which used to be more resistant to innovation than the farmers themselves. This change was due mainly to an unswerving government commitment originating with the chief of state.

In the final analysis, then, the establishment of an infrastructure conducive to innovation should receive highest priority at the national level. The government's role is pivotal in the accomplishment of this task.

Once these changes were under way in Korea, many scientists and professors working in the fields of science and engineering realized that they might have something useful to contribute to rural development as volunteers — even in the little time available to them for such an activity. The Federation of Scientific Societies set up a small secretariat to coordinate such activities, initially with the token participation of about one hundred people. In only two years this has grown into a technical service corps with a network of eight provincial secretariats.

Much to the surprise of the participants, these professionals found many problems for whose solution their expertise was inadequate. At the same time there were many other problems with which they could offer immediate help. Designing a concrete bridge across a creek, for example, was one day's homework for a college-level civil engineering student. An even more important result of these interfaces of scientists and engineers with people at the grassroots level was the two-way learning process that occurred. The rural people learned much from having presented their problems to academicians who, in turn, obtained invaluable insights on how education should prepare people to solve practical problems. It was heartwarming to see how people with such different social and educational backgrounds were able to communicate with each other to solve problems and to witness the close partnerships that developed in the process.

One lesson learned from this experience is that the pool of knowledge and the existing state of the arts can be applied to solve a broad range of rural problems — provided that the agents (not necessarily agencies) are motivated to work with people at the grassroots, even when they have only limited time to devote to such work. Although there is no remuneration for services, the involvement of academics and laymen alike has increased as the program has progressed. Perhaps the most important result of the program is increased awareness of the need for technology transfer within countries—and of the immense economic as well as moral benefits that accrue from it.

Conclusions

Korea's particular experiences suggest several conclusions that can be made about the developmental process in general. First, for countries that suffer from the vicious cycle of economic underdevelopment, it is imperative, initially, to pursue development in some leading sectors with a daring mix of technologies and entrepreneurship. Second, a massive campaign to mobilize in-country talent and bring it to bear on problems at the grassroots level, be they agricultural or industrial, must be undertaken. Third, the developing countries cannot allow themselves to be swayed by the prevalent notion that the generation of technology in developing countries is uneconomical, if not impossible. On the contrary, there appear to be vast possibilities (even an absolute need) in the developing countries for the generation of technologies by those countries themselves.

The development success stories of the last century are few in number. It behooves all of us to be daring and innovative if we are to bridge the gulf that separates the developed and the underdeveloped, the rich and the poor, the skilled and the unskilled, the urban and the rural, industry and agriculture. As Raymond Aron wrote, "Mankind is united by its very conflicts and problems as well as by its technological skills."

Foreign technology has played an important role in Brazilian development, but whether a real transfer of technology has been effected remains an open question. Experience has shown, by and large, that the use of technology supplied from abroad—although allowing at a given stage the manufacturing of any given product—may not be sufficient to create an autonomous structure capable of reaching its own development potential.

Brazilian industrialization relied for many years—and still does to a large extent—on foreign equipment and manufacturing methods, although a significant amount of domestic knowledge has been incorporated into the industrial process through the adaptation and subsequent innovation which normally take place whenever technology is imported. This reliance is easily understandable, since industrial growth is a comparatively recent phenomenon in Brazil. There was hardly any means or reason for the existence of more advanced domestic know-how in the field of manufacturing. It is true that textiles were already being manufactured in Brazil in the late 19th century, and some food processing and other industries existed. But until the 1930s, the country followed the colonial pattern of exporting raw materials and importing most manufactured goods, from toothpicks and shoes to machine tools, cars, and trucks.

The Second World War accelerated industrialization on a large scale, and the installation of the first big steel mill was very significant. Thereafter, trade difficulties caused by the war and the subsequent severe shortage of foreign exchange helped to promote Brazil's infant industry by opening new opportunities for domestic factories to be set up or developed.

What was at the time considered advanced technology was normally sought abroad, inasmuch as it was much simpler, quicker, and safer to purchase it than to spend time and money on risky experiments. Although understandable, this was, of course, a rather myopic viewpoint which nonetheless prevailed for several decades. Very little effort was made to develop domestic technological capability. As a result, a situation of technological dependence was maintained throughout the years, mainly because the purchase of technology was carried on among the affected companies themselves and was thus a

Chapter 9

Foreign Technology and Brazilian Industry

José E. Mindlin

private concern. The purchase of technology was also encouraged by foreign companies interested in establishing agreements to provide technical assistance that assured them a share of the Brazilian market and thus helped to amortize their own R&D expenditures.

Some foreign companies did not set up manufacturing facilities initially; they started their operations with assembly lines, using imported components. In those cases, practically no technology was transferred to Brazil. In addition, many integrated industries were simultaneously or subsequently started by foreign companies, which brought the necessary equipment into the country. The know-how they also brought could only in a small way be deemed a transfer of technology, because it consisted mostly of operating instructions. This know-how should have been part of the investment, but foreign companies normally charged a varying fee for it. Since this fee was a deductible expense under Brazilian law, profits of foreign companies in Brazil were undervalued and were remitted indirectly to the parent companies abroad.

Although there were abuses, this is not to say that the arrangement was necessarily devious or considered unacceptable by either party, Brazilian or foreign. A distinction must be made, however, between supplying know-how to Brazilian companies and supplying it to subsidiaries of foreign companies.

With respect to foreign companies, there is a growing view that their know-how should be part of their investment, inasmuch as Brazil offers them a very significant market. The few existing restrictions to foreign investment in Brazil and to the payment of royalties and fees for technical assistance are still very minor, and some of them were prompted by cases where foreign subsidiaries charged high fees even though no services or new research were involved. Brazilian law currently limits to five years (renewable in some cases for another five years) the period during which payments for technical assistance are tax-deductible and does not allow any payment to foreign companies by their subsidiary companies in Brazil.

In most cases, as far as Brazilian companies were concerned, the pattern of obtaining technology through technical assistance agreements and payment of a fee based on sales worked quite satisfactorily.

Until 1958, the fee was freely negotiated between the parties, but some excessive demands brought about the first restrictive measures. In 1958 the Ministry of Finance limited the amount that could be paid for technical assistance as a tax-deductible expense to 5 per cent of sales. The Ministry also established a scale of limits of from 1 to 5 per cent, according to the essentiality of the products involved. These limits are still in force.

The Competition for World Markets

Another problem arose when Brazil started its export drive in 1964. Many agreements restricted the use of foreign know-how exclusively to the domestic market, a restriction that has since been banned. Brazil no longer accepts agreements containing market restrictions. In those cases where no such restrictions existed and Brazilian companies began to export manufactured goods, they started to compete with their foreign suppliers of know-how. This caused a change of policy on the part of many foreign companies, which became reluctant to provide further expertise to potential competitors. Many foreign companies either decided to establish their own operations in Brazil or insisted on joint ventures that would ensure them participation in the growth of Brazilian companies and markets, as well as some control over Brazilian exports. This, they felt, would help prevent disruption of their worldwide market arrangements.

In this competition for world markets, the problem of know-how gained unprecedented importance. It is a generally accepted notion that the know-how supplied to Brazilian companies was not, as a rule, the most up-to-date; the latest technological developments were kept by supplier companies for their own use. This caused no great inconvenience when production was intended for the domestic market alone, since recently superseded technology still allowed satisfactory performance. But when competition abroad became the issue, knowledge of the latest developments became in most cases indispensable to Brazilian companies.

This was not the only problem, however. Even if the issue of exports had not arisen, the know-how supplied would have been questioned because of qualitative changes within Brazilian industry. Local technicians and engineers, through their efforts in adapting foreign technology, had acquired a new competence and had introduced many innovations. Thus, they could not be satisfied with limitations on information. "Know-why" became more imperative than know-how.

It was then that technology became a national issue. The government, industry, the press, the scientific community, and the general public all became aware that technological research and innovation is a powerful instrument of market control. Although developing countries had the know-how to utilize current production methods, access to innovation was made difficult where it was not denied them altogether. This placed them in a very unfavorable position in comparison with manufacturers of the industrialized world.

It can be argued that this is as it should be, a natural result of the capitalist system and the free action of market forces. Foreign companies naturally contend that technology, as an important asset, should maximize the profits of those fortunate enough to own it. Their argument is that it is not their problem if companies in the developing world are jeopardized by this situation. And from a viewpoint which supposes that no change in existing conditions will occur, they are right. Social tensions, however, lead to very substantial changes that sooner or later must occur, for it is difficult to agree that the present situation — one of the most serious sources of friction between the multinational companies and the governments and business communities of the developing countries — should exist indefinitely.

The Beneficial Effect of Competition

This problem, despite its negative effects in Brazil, also had one beneficial result: it prompted more intense efforts to develop indigenous technological capacity, through public and private investment in domestic research and development. Needless to say, this was an essential step, and it is only regrettable that it was not done earlier. Much more research is now carried on in Brazil, and a good example of favorable results is the nation's improved coffee production. But in general terms, research is not yet sufficiently integrated with production. Governmental efforts to encourage technological research by giving it substantial financial support allow hope that significant progress can be made in the not too distant future. Brazil's intention, however, is not to completely substitute domestic technology for foreign technology, but to enable Brazilian industry to absorb what is being accomplished abroad. It would be totally unreasonable not to explore every possibility of importing technology while developing parallel internal capabilities.

Brazil's entrance into the world's industrial market, and the industrial progress it has already achieved, has brought about a change in the type of technological cooperation needed by the country. Up to very recent times, if not up to now, all technical assistance agreements provided for the supply of know-how. Today, "know-why" is indispensable for the effective absorption of technological knowledge. Foreign companies carry on practically all their R&D abroad, and give Brazilian technicians very limited access to it. When they visit suppliers of technology, under the terms of existing agreements, Brazilian technicians are normally shown only what is already being done on an industrial scale. There may be some exceptions, but on the whole what is being researched or tested is not disclosed. This accounts for the dependence mentioned earlier.

What Brazil needs now is not a scheme of technical assistance but rather a plan of technical cooperation in which much freer access to and exchange of information about innovation should be the pattern adopted by all parties. Foreign companies should carry on part of their research in Brazil and allow the participation of Brazilian technicians. This would certainly be of mutual interest, for much innovation could then appear in Brazil, where technological creativity so far has been stifled.

During the 1950s, and especially after the first Atoms for Peace Conference in Geneva in 1955, a number of less-developed countries instituted research and development activities dealing with atomic energy. The hope was that such activities would not only stimulate the scientific and technological progress of these countries, but also assist their general economic progress and modernization.

An evaluation today would show that these R&D efforts have fallen quite short of expectations in most of the less-developed countries where they have been attempted. Argentina, however, is an exception to that general statement. This paper traces the development of atomic energy in Argentina, a development that has produced useful results ranging from the production of electric power to the use of radiation for medical, agricultural, and industrial purposes. The successful attempt to develop an atomic energy capability in Argentina has also had an important impact on the social, political, and economic development of the nation.

It is important to recognize at the outset of this paper that Argentina's interest in atomic energy was never intended to help the nation develop atomic weapons. Such weapons were not an objective of Argentine policy, either explicitly or implicitly. It should also be noted that much of the development of atomic energy in Argentina has taken place against a background of continuing political and economic crises.

The Main Objectives of Argentina's Atomic Energy Policy

The foremost objective of Argentina's atomic energy policy has been to build up the nation's ability to make autonomous decisions on all matters respecting atomic energy, from monitoring fall-out from weapons tests to accepting or rejecting a nuclear disarmament treaty, from choosing a nuclear power station site to exploring and exploiting uranium ores, and from controlling the disposal of radioactive

Chapter 10

Atomic Energy in Argentina: Toward Technological Autonomy

Jorge A. Sabato

wastes to deciding about radiation in food preservation. Argentina's autonomy as a sovereign nation can only be meaningful if it has the know-how to choose and decide properly.

The second main objective has been to build up the necessary scientific and technological infrastructure required for the optimum social utilization of nuclear energy. Nuclear energy can be an important tool for the development of any nation, provided that society is properly prepared to incorporate it. As with any other new technology, it is essential for the country to be an active participant in its transfer, and not an idle spectator.

The third principal aim of Argentine policy has been to provide a "demonstration effect" showing that R&D is feasible and useful in spite of being carried out in a country immersed in a long and deep socio-political and economic crisis. That may not sound like a very specific objective for an atomic energy policy, but as a matter of fact that was nearly always an objective to all the participants in the process. Some decisions were made for the explicit purpose of building up the confidence of the scientific community.

These three main objectives were not defined explicitly in the 1950s or even in the early 1960s. The policy was built up by trial and error, through failures and successes, until a pattern began to take shape. It was not until the late 1960s that all elements of the policy were finally defined. How this was done will be better understood from an analysis of some of the work performed by Argentina's *Comisión Nacional de Energia Atómica* (CNEA).

The Development of Human Resources

Throughout its history, CNEA has given first priority to the education of scientific and professional personnel: physicists, engineers, chemists, biologists, metallurgists, geologists, mathematicians,

---

•Excerpted in revised form from Jorge A. Sabato, "Atomic Energy in Argentina: A Case Study," *World Development*, 1:8 (1973), 23.

physicians, lawyers, and economists. CNEA has also trained lathe operators, milling machine operators, dye makers, glass blowers, carpenters, technicians, microscopists, surveyors, cartographers, and other technical personnel. Many of these scientific, professional, and technical personnel have also been sent abroad for additional education or training.

The significant feature of this program is that education and training have not been confined to areas of immediate interest for atomic energy (such as nuclear engineering, nuclear physics, nuclear biology, uranium metallurgy, and radio-isotopes) but rather have been broadly based. This approach was based on the assumption that CNEA-trained personnel, if necessary, could eventually be used by the country in fields other than atomic energy. And that, in fact, did happen. At present, hundreds of scientists, technologists, and technicians trained by CNEA are working in universities, industry, other government research institutions, and hospitals.

It was also deemed important to provide the trainees with as wide a background as possible because atomic energy—or any other modern technology, for that matter—is not just a "package of knowledge" but rather a universe in fast evolution. How this program was implemented can be illustrated through the specific cases of metallurgy and physics.

Metallurgy. The development, production, and utilization of nuclear energy requires a vast amount of metallurgical knowledge. A nuclear reactor is an intricate metallurgical "universe." Construction of a reactor therefore requires the resolution of numerous metallurgical problems, ranging from the purity of the uranium dioxide used as fuel to the mechanical properties of the pressure vessel that contains the core, from the many complex stages of fuel element manufacture to the corrosion resistance of the heat-exchange tubes, and from understanding the basic physical properties of the different metals, alloys, and oxides used in the reactor to the techniques used in forging, rolling, extruding, and welding its parts.

CNEA therefore created and organized a metallurgy division in 1955. The purpose of the metallurgy division was not only to give CNEA the metallurgical knowledge it needed in its atomic energy program (particularly in the nuclear fuel area) but also to help the Argentine metallurgical industry improve its quality and efficiency, while at the same time promoting metallurgy as an academic discipline. In order to link itself with the industry, CNEA established SATI (Service of Technical Assistance to Industry) in 1962 in association with the Chamber of Metallurgical Industries. SATI's purpose was to make available to industry the scientific and technical resources available in CNEA's metallurgy division.

Although SATI was set up to study problems raised by the industry, it also was permitted to propose R&D projects that could benefit the industry by improving processes already in use or opening new lines of activity. Routine matters, such as mechanical testing, chemical analysis, metallographic inspection, and the like were not to be performed by SATI, on the assumption that there already were other laboratories in Argentina that could perform those activities quite efficiently. SATI was also to act as a clearinghouse, advising customers where their problems could best be solved.

During the last ten years SATI has studied nearly 500 problems presented to it by industry. Some have been as minor as the study of impurity distribution in aluminum castings, but others have been as ambitious as the complete development of a new copper-zirconium alloy for welding électrodes. Some of the problems dealt with by SATI have been quite divorced from nuclear metallurgy, such as the development of a new process to manufacture tungsten-silver electrodes. Other problems, such as the analysis of cracks in pressure vessels used by the petro-chemical industry, have been directly related to the manufacture of nuclear reactor components.

SATI has also developed other products and processes, including a new type of refractory material to be used in aluminum melting, a new process for the manufacture of aluminum evaporators for refrigerators, a new type of protective atmosphere for bright annealing of copper and its alloys, and a new method to produce tough-pitch copper in small melting furnaces. It has even developed a new type of ball-point pen.

SATI has also engaged in many educational activities. It has organized a number of seminars, conferences, and lectures on specific metallurgical topics of industrial interest, and once or twice a year it has organized special courses for the training of industrial personnel, some at the introductory level, some at a higher level.

Above all, SATI has been (and is) a mechanism for coupling R&D with industry, a sort of window onto reality. SATI has helped to make CNEA aware of the needs of industry and also of its own possibilities and limitations. Thanks to SATI, CNEA has not been an isolated institution but one which understands pretty well the real state of technological development in the Argentine metallurgical industry. CNEA has thus been in a very strategic position to evaluate the actual possibilities of local participation in any big nuclear program. This knowledge proved to be very valuable when development of the Atucha nuclear power station was first discussed.

Physics. It is rather obvious that any atomic energy program requires many good physicists. As of 1955, however, there were only thirty physicists in all of Argentina, and most of these were principally engaged in teaching a rather small number of students. Physics research was being conducted in only three locations, the CNEA laboratories, the Astronomical Observatory of Córdoba, and the Institute of Physics of La Plata University. This situation was partly due to the harassment and political discrimination suffered by the universities during Peron's regime.

It was at that time that CNEA decided to establish a completely new institution, the Institute of Physics at San Carlos de Bariloche. Although financed, administered, and directed by CNEA, the Institute was formally incorporated into the University of Cuyo for the purpose of granting M.Sc. and Ph.D. degrees. The Institute's organization combined U.S. and European models: a full-time staff not only teaching but also doing research; a maximum of twenty students per year living on campus, with fellowships given by CNEA; well-equipped laboratories and workshops; an up-to-date library; and, last but not least, a beautiful location by Lake Nahuel Huapí near Bariloche, some 2,000 kilometers from Buenos Aires.

Since 1958, when the first thirteen students were graduated, the Institute has awarded about 180 M.Sc. degrees in physics. More than half of the recipients of these have also obtained Ph.D. degrees. Less than 100 now work for CNEA, the rest having taken posts at universities and other research centers. As the best school of physics in Argentina, the Institute has won an international reputation.

CNEA's actions with respect to metallurgy and physics illustrate how Argentina was able to create a corps of personnel able to do R&D not only in the specific field of atomic energy but also in many other scientific and technological fields.

CNEA's Decisions on Research Reactors

The nuclear research reactors used in most of the less-developed countries are manufactured in developed countries (mainly in the United States) and then installed by foreign companies. This is the way it has happened in all of the other Latin American countries that have installed research reactors, namely, Brazil, Venezuela, Colombia, Mexico, and Chile.

In Argentina, however, CNEA decided in 1957 that its research reactors would not be purchased abroad and assembled by foreign companies. Instead, they would be manufactured in Argentina and installed by CNEA with the help of Argentine industry. This decision was made on the assumption that not only were reactors important for training and research in the nuclear field, but also that their construction was essential for developing a broad scientific and technological capability. It was reasoned that to manufacture and assemble such complex machines would be an excellent way to develop the indigenous nuclear engineering capabilities that Argentina would need to foster its autonomy. The decision acted as an "ideological cement" to bind together human and material resources into an integrated scientific-technological effort.

CNEA also decided at that time not to import the fuel elements for its research reactors but to manufacture them in Argentina. More than 4,000 of these complex uranium fuel elements have been made, and all have performed without failure. It is also important to point out that technical innovations were introduced in every aspect of the design and manufacture of fuel elements, proving once again that use of an advanced technology by a developing country does not necessarily preclude innovation, provided the right kind of human resources are properly motivated. At the same time, this technological activity led to the publication of several scientific papers related to basic problems in metallurgy, a good demonstration that work as specific as fuel element manufacture can be the source not only of applied but also of basic knowledge.

The Development of Argentina's First Nuclear Power Station

In January 1965 CNEA was ordered by the Argentine government to prepare a feasibility report on the possibilities of installing a nuclear power station. The question was whether Argentina had developed enough technological capability to supervise all stages in the construction of a nuclear power plant, from feasibility studies to final commissioning of the reactor. The hour of truth had arrived for Argentine atomic policy, and for that reason the development of the Atucha power station is worth careful analysis.

Even in 1965, the common practice in Argentina was to contract feasibility reports and pre-investment studies to a foreign consulting firm whenever the project was of an advanced nature or one requiring heavy financial investment from external sources. CNEA decided not to contract the nuclear power station feasibility report but to prepare it under its own direction and responsibility, and with its own scientific and technical personnel. Private consultants, both foreigners and Argentinians, would be hired for specific problems where necessary. Two main reasons lay behind this decision:

(a) to follow a policy consistent with the previous decision not to import research reactors and fuel elements but to continue "learning by doing," and

(b) to provide a demonstration that the usual practice of hiring foreign consultants was unnecessary, since the work could be done perfectly well using indigenous talent.

Buying or selling a nuclear power station is much more than a simple commercial operation, particularly when it is the first. For the buyer, and importer, it means entering the "nuclear age," with all its political, technical, and socio-cultural implications and consequences. For the seller, and exporter, it means the opening of a new market and an increase in political influence upon, and technical and socio-cultural penetration into, the country that is buying. The main consequence is that governments as well as companies must be heavily involved in the negotiations. This explains some of the decisions made by CNEA prior to any request for bids from suppliers of nuclear power plants.

The final decision made by CNEA and supported by the Argentine government was a very pragmatic one: a power plant using natural uranium would not be selected a priori, but bids would be accepted for plants that used either enriched or natural uranium. A choice could then be made after a careful comparison of concrete offers. CNEA thought that in this way it could induce fierce competition among suppliers (and also countries) and would then get better offers. It was the CNEA position at the time that if it was true that natural uranium had important advantages for Argentina, it was very important to quantify these advantages. The only way to do so was through a comparison among different offers.

Another important a priori decision was that financing arrangements ought to be included in every offer, so that once the final choice was made the financing of the project would be automatically secured. Two main reasons lay behind this decision. First, CNEA was convinced that the market was then clearly a buyer's market and competition among potential suppliers would result in very favorable financing conditions. Second, CNEA also was convinced that the usual sources of international finance, such as the World Bank, the Inter-American Bank, and similar institutions, would not give high priority to a nuclear power station for Argentina.

It was clear to CNEA that domestic production of fuel elements for Atucha and any subsequent power stations would be a key element in the program, not only from an economic standpoint (Atucha alone would consume about (U.S.) $2,500,000 yearly in fuel elements) but also because it would guarantee full control of fuel policy. It was then decided that bids from suppliers ought to include explicit references to the manufacture of the fuel elements in Argentina and the conditions under which the corresponding technology would be supplied.

As a matter of policy, CNEA was deeply interested in making Atucha a means for further development of the Argentine nuclear industry. To achieve such a purpose, CNEA specified that bids for the Atucha project ought to contemplate maximum participation by local industry, covering not only such traditional items as civil engineering and ancillary services but also important components of the power reactor's design and construction.

Once these decisions were made, CNEA announced its readiness to listen to offers and at the same time began preliminary negotiations with prospective suppliers and their governments.

Evaluation and Choice

A total of seventeen bids to construct the plant were presented to CNEA by the closing date, and evaluation began at once. This work was performed by the same team that prepared the feasibility report, under the same executive committee, and in consultation with other branches of the government, such as the Secretary of State for Energy, the Ministry of Industry, the National Development Council, the Ministry of Economy, and the National Security Council. A brief description of how the offers were analyzed — each one separately, and then compared among themselves and also with respect to a conventional thermal power station — provide another example of autonomy of decision based upon scientific and technical capability.

Fuel. This was taken as the most important variable of all, but not so much as to become the decisive variable. An offer with the right kind of fuel and nothing else could be outweighed by one with the wrong kind of fuel but with maximum points in all the other variables. (Natural uranium got 100 points and enriched uranium 0 points.) However, the fuel offered by the British company got 30 points in spite of being enriched because the British government guaranteed a fuel supply from other sources besides the United States. The U.S. companies offered fuel from only one source (their own country), as did the German AEG.

Financing. Financing was given very high priority, particularly with respect to the total amount to be financed. One reason for this was the chronic foreign currency shortage in Argentina, but CNEA also wanted to make sure that nothing would stop construction once it began. It was not uncommon in Argentina for public works to be stopped halfway through, due to lack of funds. Consequently, offers that proposed 100 per cent financing obtained the maximum number of points.

Technical data. Every bid was thoroughly analyzed from a technical standpoint, including the nuclear reactor and the turbine generator. With respect to the reactor, points were apportioned according to years of operating experience. That was a more difficult question to answer in 1967 than it would be now. At that time the Calder Hall type of reactor had produced far more kilowatt hours than any other type in the world. The Pressurized Water Reactor (PWR) ranked second, but most of that operating experience was in nuclear submarines. As far as previous experience was concerned, the worst offer was that of Siemens, which had only a 50MW prototype reactor in operation.

Local participation. Much attention was given to this item, a very important and rather difficult one. CNEA did not want a typical "turn-key" contract for a "black box," nor did it want a "white box," that is, a situation where CNEA itself would be the architect-engineer for the project. CNEA simply was not in a position to perform such a task. The solution was to get a sort of "semi-turn-key" contract, corresponding to a semi-open "black box," or what might be called a "grey box." Consequently, points were to be assigned according to how "grey" the box happened to be.

For each of the remaining variables a similar ranking operation was performed and weights assigned. Once the matrix was covered by these numbers, a quasi-quantitative provisional choice was arrived at.

Reaching a New Plateau

The decisionmaking process carried on with respect to the Atucha project was a nodal point in Argentine atomic development. It was then that almost fifteen years of hard work was tested in a very intensive exercise. Although it was a strenuous effort, it was absolutely worthwhile because it showed to what extent Argentina had full command of a field as new and complex as nuclear energy.

Atucha was also a turning point. Until then, CNEA had followed a rather tortuous path trying to find its way. Programs and plans were quite sketchy, and a lot was more implicit than explicit. However, once the contract was signed and actual construction began, CNEA had a very clear path to follow.

CNEA was involved in all matters related to the actual construction of the Atucha plant. Its scientific and technical personnel did work in civil engineering, nuclear engineering, metallurgy, neutron physics, health physics, non-destructive testing, electronics, mathematics, systems analysis, fuel elements, and so on. CNEA also obtained an important degree of participation by Argentine industry, which learned such new technologies as the welding of stainless steel vessels and the manufacture of special tubes for heat exchangers.

Obstacles Which Have Hampered CNEA

The very real accomplishments of CNEA should not obscure the fact that it has had to face up to some major obstacles which have — at times — seriously undermined its effectiveness. Relatively few of the obstacles have been directly political, although the recurrent political and economic crises have had an indirect effect. The principal difficulties have been bureaucratic and administrative, and are common to almost all less-developed countries. They include such factors as rigid limitations on current expenditures, excessive red tape, long delays in the decision-making process, low salaries, and a rigid promotion system. All of these petty frustrations produced an atmosphere which was inimical to creative work. This sometimes led to the emigration of professional scientists, engineers, and other technical personnel.

In addition, the scientists and engineers who remained in Argentina tried to isolate themselves from the rest of society and wrap themselves in a cocoon of "good science." They did not realize that their responsibility was wider in scope and that it included helping to build up the frame of reference within which good work could take place. They were, in fact, assuming that Argentina was a developed country and that science and technology could proceed as smoothly as they usually do in the developed world. The scientists and engineers demanded a coherent policy as an essential prerequisite for them to be able to perform, but that was a very demanding request in a society that was not in a condition to define any policy at all.

Such naivete made them ask for an order, a security, and a continuity that no country in crisis can ever offer. Scientists and technologists were looking for a "strategy for order," while the only possible one was a "strategy for chaos." Like children, they sought a world of dreams instead of facing reality as it was and assuming its corresponding responsibilities. For many of them, emigration was the only answer to finding the necessary peace and security to do R&D. But it was also a way of escaping the most fundamental problem facing any intellectual in a less-developed country—the question of his own contribution to the nation.

Because of these difficulties, CNEA did not use its human resources as efficiently as it should have, basic disciplines were not coupled as efficiently as possible to technology, and administrative and managerial services were not well organized.

Conclusion

The CNEA program has demonstrated how important it is for a less-developed country to build an indigenous capability in R&D. It has shown that the choice is not between dependence and autarky, but rather, that *autonomy* is the most convenient and feasible objective. The question is not one of "imported technology versus native technology," but of an autonomous capability to manage and control all the technology flowing through the country's economic system.

The CNEA experience also demonstrates that a nation's technological policy does not come fully formed. Scholars in general, and scientists in particular, tend to think of science policy as something presented in a well-written document, where everything is logically organized. It is also thought that such a document must precede any action. But reality is, of course, quite different. Policy is often not defined in such a way, and even when it is, the nice document is immediately ignored or changed, either by the very same people who wrote it, or by the next minister in the same government, or by a new government.

A science policy, a technological policy, an atomic policy, will not come from top to bottom, and so to wait for it to happen will be just "to wait for Godot." Those policies must grow from the roots and through the action and work of everybody concerned, primarily the scientists and technologists. CNEA's experience shows that "organic growth" is the answer; "organized growth" is no more than a dream.

T his paper is a distillation of the experiences acquired in setting up a technological center in the state of Minas Gerais in Brazil. The paper highlights the problems of creating a structure which permits a local technological center to participate actively in making autonomous national decisions on the selection, adaptation, improvement, and development of technology to meet local needs.

Traditionally, Minas Gerais has been known for its mineral activities; the state generated great wealth in the 18th century through gold mining. In the 19th century, together with what was then the province of São Paulo, Minas also led agricultural production in Brazil. Its agricultural activity was of major importance in Brazil until the beginning of the present century. From 1930 on, the economic importance of Minas gradually diminished as Rio de Janeiro and São Paulo became industrialized.

The decade of the 1960s found the economy of Minas in a state of relative stagnation. While the GNP growth of Brazil was 32.9 per cent during the period 1965 to 1969, that of Minas was only 25.7 per cent. A detailed study[1] of the Minas economy revealed that development of the state's industrial park had been retarded by geographic factors and by limitations in its physical infrastructure (roads, energy supplies, communications). The atomization and dispersion of the market contained in its territory, coupled with difficulties of access to the key consuming centers of São Paulo and Rio de Janeiro, led to the creation of firms with small production capacities directed almost always toward the regional market. In contrast, the concentration of population and of economic and financial resources in the Rio-São Paulo axis encouraged the establishment of larger-size industries with better economies of scale. The principal characteristics of the Minas agricultural sector were extensive use of land in the producing areas and a low-density consuming market.

Minas Gerais still produces important shares of Brazil's minerals: 99 per cent of the iron ore (close to 100 million tons per year), 95 per cent of the bauxite, 30 per cent of the lime, 99 per cent of the nickel,

Chapter 11

Technological Development in Minas Gerais, Brazil

Juarez Távora Veado and José Israel Vargas

and 100 per cent of the gold and zinc. The state also produces close to 40 per cent of the country's steel, and 60 per cent of the pig iron used in the steel industry is produced in Minas. In order to make charcoal for the steel industry, Minas has become a leader in reforestation in Brazil (800,000 hectares planted in eucalyptus and pines). Minas Gerais also accounts for 20 per cent of the beef, 28 per cent of the pork, 30 per cent of the milk, 65 per cent of the cheese, and 45 per cent of the butter used in Brazil.

In view of the state's economic potential, the government of Minas Gerais decided to make a concentrated development effort through a series of coordinated measures. The First Development Plan (1972-1976)[2] had as its main objectives the diversification of the productive structure of the region, the spatial de-concentration of development, the incorporation into the economy of the neediest regions, support for the interiorization of the development process, and improvements in production.

At that time, Minas Gerais decided to compete with São Paulo and Rio de Janeiro for new industrial investments. A series of measures was passed to support this determination. Among these were fiscal incentives (tax exemptions for the creation of new factories) and, in some cases, purchases of investment stock by the state government.

Among the new agencies created by the state administration to implement this policy were the Industrial Development Institute (INDI), placed in charge of investment opportunity studies and of industrial development, and the Company of Industrial Districts (CDI), given the task of building the infrastructure necessary for new industries in chosen areas. Administrative support for small and medium-size enterprises was provided by the Center of Management Support to Small and Medium Enterprises (CEAG), while the Fundação João Pinheiro (FJP), an agency of the State Secretariat for Planning, opened training opportunities for executives of local firms through its Center for Administrative Development.

As a result of the actions of these state agencies, of the Development Bank of Minas Gerais (BDMG), and of the state electric power company (CEMIG), 384 industrial projects were set up between 1971 and 1977 at a total investment cost of (U.S.) $5 billion. These projects generated more than 100,000 direct jobs. During that period the state experienced a real growth of 99 per cent compared to 68 per cent for the country as a whole.

Creation of the Technological Center

Part of the development effort involved the creation of a technological center to solve the technological problems of the productive system and to provide support services, such as chemical analysis, mechanical tests, documentation and information, industrial design, technical and economic feasibility studies, etc. Although the state already had a center, the Industrial Technology Institute (ITI), its structure was considered inadequate because of intrinsic limitations and lack of flexibility. In 1972 the FJP was put in charge of creating the Centro Tecnologico de Minas Gerais (CETEC), and ITI's activities were discontinued.

Investments for CETEC's initial phase were (U.S.) $3.3 million. The state contributed about 50 per cent, and FINEP, a federal agency in charge of financing studies and projects, contributed the rest. The basic mission of CETEC was to help solve technological, economic, and administrative problems encountered by the productive sector.[3] To accomplish its mission, CETEC was to develop its own technical capacity as well as utilize other research organizations and university facilities through various forms of contracts and agreements.

After choosing the research project as its instrument of management and financial planning, the center began its activities in those areas where Minas Gerais had a natural advantage, such as mining and metallurgical engineering, foods (meat and dairy products), construction technologies, and the support services already mentioned.

Using its own personnel, private consultants, and the universities, CETEC completed a series of projects. Among them were a study of ore dressing that covered almost all the phosphate ores of the country, ore dressing of manganese minerals and zinc ore, and a diagnosis of non-integrated pig iron producers.

At the end of 1975, CETEC's budget showed an uncommon balance among its funding sources: one third of its income came from projects and services purchased by producers, one third came from projects purchased by agencies of the federal government, and one third came from state sources. Certain difficulties became increasingly evident during this first phase, however:

(a) The project system, although intrinsically dynamic, created the problem of providing continuity to the work of the research teams once they finished the specific projects for which they had been set up;

(b) The concentration of effort on individual projects retarded the development of a scientific and technological infrastructure, and the infrastructure is still deficient;

(c) It was difficult to approach complex problems which could only be solved by means of a number of different projects (i.e., a complete program);

(d) Finally, the role of CETEC turned out to be smaller than had been expected; entrepreneurs were insufficiently motivated by longer-term goals and preferred to limit themselves to meeting the demand for technical services needed to achieve more immediate goals.

Science and Technology Planning at the State Level

In 1975 a new state administration, considering science and technology as a pre-investment in economic and social development, decided to introduce a more comprehensive plan for such activities. The role of technology was clearly highlighted by Governor Aureliano Chaves:

> We find ourselves in a country in which the possibilities of technological development, be they through transfer or adaptation, or through the development of indigenous technology, are very broad. Therefore, we must always keep in mind that for our development the following become indispensable:
> — the rational utilization of natural resources;
> — the development of the utilization of non-renewable resources existing in the country, such as coal, niobium, and other minerals;
> — the adaptation of technology to the special characteristics of Brazil and each of its regions;
> — the internal transfer of technology, be it through documentation and information, be it through the education of people, in quantity and quality such that they satisfy the demand.[4]

It was decided at that time to create a system capable of coordinating all the actions of the state in science and technology, inserting them in concrete contexts, and taking care that the actions to be undertaken always had environment and quality of life as explicit variables in planning not only the scientific and technological system but also the planning of government activities at all levels. This system was to be assisted by intense and effective community participation.

Accepting these premises, the government created an Executive Group in FJP to begin those activities. The Executive Group began its work by coordinating a task force collecting basic information on the natural resources of Minas Gerais (geology, soils, limnology, human resources, and other assets). As might have been expected, the work of the task force revealed a lack of basic information on many aspects of the state's economic potential, useless and expensive superimposition of surveys on the same region, and a lack of methodological homogeneity which hampered the use of information coming from different sources.

The integration of science and technology into the development effort was followed by the selection of research and development priorities. Natural resources, energy, environment, and human resources were pointed out as those of greatest interest for the state.

The survey of natural resources began in the northeast part of the state, following the elaboration of Plan Northeast II, an investment and regional occupation plan for the area under the supervision of Ruralminas (the state enterprise for colonization and agrarian development). Financial support was provided by the Inter-American Development Bank and the federal and state governments. The plan is being implemented through the integrated action of state agencies under the leadership and coordination of Ruralminas. The region covered by the study has an area of 117,000 km^2 with 550,000 inhabitants, of whom 400,000 live in rural areas.

The natural resource group had to surmount the methodological and linguistic barriers of various disciplines in order to produce the most practical types of information. This effort was accompanied by certain unexpected economies. For example, the combination of geological maps with geomorphological maps permitted an 80 per cent reduction in the cost of the pedologic survey, thanks to a preliminary soil map based on that information. This loosening of disciplinary boundaries was fundamental for the usefulness of survey work.

The survey indicated which areas were most suitable for the cultivation of various agricultural crops (corn, soybeans, sorghum, cotton, sugarcane, rice, manioc, and castor beans), for forestry, for cattle-raising, and for mineral exploration. Besides that, it indicated areas that should be preserved because of legal exigencies or technical reasons (for example, those subject to accelerated erosion).

In the field of energy, the strategy adopted was to search for alternative sources, particularly those originating from biomass, in an attempt to take advantage of the large amounts of solar radiation available in Brazil and the low population density. The energy of biomass becomes economically viable on a large scale when used in an integrated manner with other regional energy sources, such as hydroelectric power and fossil fuels.

The production of alcohol from biomass can be highlighted. Brazil has in progress a national program to partially substitute alcohol produced from sugarcane and cassava for gasoline. Other ways of producing alcohol are also being studied, such as those based on wood, rice, and babaçu nuts. In these cases the biomass material has multiple uses and it is possible to take practical advantage of the wastes, such as the shell in the case of rice.

In the state of Minas Gerais, wood has long been used to make charcoal, which is necessary for steel production. Brazil has limited reserves of coal (all located in the southern part of the country), and the coal is not suitable for conventional use in steel plants because of its high sulfur and ash content. Almost all the coal used in steel production is therefore imported, imposing severe pressure on the country's balance of payments. The current goal of the National Steel

Plan is to produce 33 million tons in 1988, as compared to 11.2 million in 1977. There is, therefore, great interest in increasing the availability of charcoal. This demands rationalization of all the stages of charcoal production and use—planting seeds, forest management, production of charcoal from trees, utilization of byproducts, and efficient use in furnaces. An extensive research and development program was therefore set up by CETEC with the direct participation of ACESITA (a producer of special steels) and financing from FINEP.

One difficulty in setting up such programs is the lack of confidence in ideas which do not happen to be dominant in the developed countries. To many technical people in public and private entities in the developing countries, new ideas are very suspect if they do not come from advanced countries. The argument that the situation in a tropical country may be completely different from that in a temperate country only partially assuages the doubts in their minds.

Another CETEC program deals with the environment. Planning for the development of unoccupied regions incorporates the environmental variable at the same level of concern as the economic variable, and the establishment of new industries or the expansion of existing ones is preceded, at the request of the financing agencies (such as the development banks), by an analysis of their environmental impact. Basic studies on how to preserve the natural inheritance, such as biological reserves, forest reserves, caverns, etc., are required, and the infrastructure for those studies has to be established rapidly. The recruitment of human resources, the building of laboratories, and the establishment of methodologies all require enormous effort.

A difficulty which called for special attention was the lack of an institutional model more adequate to handle environmental problems. The major obstacles resulted from the lack of experienced personnel, in part because the field had only recently acquired importance and had not been the subject of training and education in the universities and technical schools.

By decision of the state government, the first study undertaken was a report on the environmental situation in the metropolitan region of Belo Horizonte, the capital of Minas Gerais.[5] That eighty-year-old city has had an unusually high rate of population growth in the past decade, and its population now surpasses 1.5 million. The study attempted to collect and analyze all the information on the metropolitan region already available in diverse federal, state, and municipal agencies and to propose goals which came to constitute the essence of the environmental program.

An important group of research efforts also was begun in Rio Doce Park. The park, with an area of 36,000 hectares, is what is left of the Atlantic forest which once covered an extensive part of the state before it disappeared as a result of agricultural and cattle-raising activity. It is a region of scientific interest because of its many mammal fauna, molluscae, birds, fish, and insects, which, together with the park's geology, pedology, and vegetation, are being studied by scientists from universities and research institutes. The role of CETEC is basically that of coordinating the studies, although it also carries out some research itself.

The Commission on Environmental Policy (COPAM) is the forum for the discussion and formulation of environmental policy. It is composed of the subsecretaries of state agencies concerned with the environment, representatives of conservation societies, representatives of the industrial and commercial federations, and representatives of the community. Besides defining policy, fiscalization, and standards, COPAM takes direct action with respect to operations which cause pollution with the objective of improving the environment and the quality of life. As technical support it uses diverse state organs, principally CETEC, as well as private laboratories and consultants.

COPAM was very active during its first eighteen months of existence and won wide public acclaim. In spite of the inadequate legal instruments at its disposal, the commission was able to grapple with the main pollution problems. Starting from the premise that a few firms were responsible for the bulk of the pollution (particularly air pollution), COPAM carried out bilateral negotiations with the enterprises that resulted in agreements for the installation of filters and other devices which would permit the elimination, for example, of 60 per cent of the air-borne sedimentary particles in Belo Horizonte over the following two years.

It is interesting to observe that, despite the eclectic training of its members and of the diversity of the attitudes and interests which they represent, all of COPAM's resolutions have been passed unanimously. Several factors appear to have been responsible for this unanimity, including (a) the creation of the forum itself for open discussion of environmental problems, (b) the focus on environmental problems from a scientific rather than an emotional perspective, and (c) the expression of public opinion through wide coverage by the press.

Another relevant research activity concerns the advantageous use of mineral resources. The major deposits of phosphatic rock are situated in the western part of the state in the region of Patos de Minas. CETEC devised a technological research program involving the direct use of natural phosphate, the utilization of nutrient-rich volcanic soils, and the development of industrialization processes using national inputs, installations, and know-how.

CETEC also works with ferro-alloys, having developed a process for the use of the enormous reserves of manganese ores in the region of Urucum (Mato Grosso) through a research contract with the owner of the deposits. Still other activities deal with the treatment of zinc ores, exploitation of non-metallic minerals, and special alloys.

The Development of Human Resources

Because much of the technology developed in the advanced countries is of limited interest and applicability in a tropical and underdeveloped country, CETEC has taken systematic action to train and educate its own scientists and technicians to carry out independent, indigenous, basic scientific research.

All the activities described have led to a large expansion in the technical personnel of CETEC. Starting with twenty university-trained technicians in 1973, the Center had 240 professionals by the end of 1978.

With support from the National Research Council (CNPq), between fifteen and twenty technicians have been sent annually for training in Europe and North America in the last three years. Upon their return, some of them go to other state organs, which in that way use the management capacity of the Center in their training programs. In addition, close to thirty CETEC technicians are taking advanced courses at Brazilian universities, and ninety university students do on-the-job training at the Center's laboratories on a part-time basis.

Conclusion

CETEC represents a local effort to respond to external demand in a state which is realizing a big leap in development.

The experience is too recent to be comprehensively analyzed. In a period of seven years, CETEC has attempted to accept the challenges posed by the experience of the state and has made the internal changes necessary to adjust to the new situations. Since CETEC is a new institution with a technical staff which is also young, continuous learning has been one of the factors of its dynamism.

The basic goal is to promote the development of technologies appropriate to the physical, cultural, and economic realities of Minas Gerais by utilizing the natural resources of the region, minimizing damage to the environment, and training people in priority areas.

Notes

[1]Banco de Desenvolvimento de Minas Gerais, *Diagnóstico da Economia Mineira,* Belo Horizonte, 1967.

[2]Governo do Estado de Minas Gerais, *Plano Mineiro de Desenvolvimento Econômico e Social,* 1972-1976, Secretaria do Planejamento e Coordenação Geral, Imprensa Oficial, Belo Horizonte, 1971.

[3]CETEC, *Centro Technológico[* (Projeto de Implantação), Belo Horizonte, 1972.

[4]Aureliano Chaves, Desenvolvimento Technológico: Adoção, Adaptação ou Criação, *Fundação J.P.,* Belo Horizonte, 6 (1): 40-44 Jan. 1976.

[5]Governo do Estado De Minas Gerais, *Situação ambiental na Região Metropolitana de Belo Horizonte, Julho de 1976,* Belo Horizonte, 1976.

This analysis, based on observations made during a five-year association with the Science and Technology Policy Instruments (STPI) Project, reviews some of the issues involved in science and technology (S&T) policy formulation and implementation in less-developed countries. The countries that participated in the STPI project were Argentina, Brazil, Colombia, Egypt, India, Mexico, Peru, South Korea, Venezuela, and Yugoslavia (Republic of Macedonia). The STPI project was a recognition that too much effort had been spent on abstract S&T policy formulation, that policy results had been scant, and that too little work had been done to assess policy impact. It also signaled a dissatisfaction with the way in which economic development theory treated technological issues.

The STPI project studies three interconnected aspects of policy design and implementation: the historic and socio-economic background, the characteristics of state intervention, and the nature of technical change in industrial branches. One of the first issues that emerged from STPI research was the importance of directing the design and operation of S&T policies and policy instruments to specific industrial branches. For this purpose, the traditional concept of industrial branch—defined in economic statistics as a collection of similar enterprises — was enlarged to include government agencies, research institutes, consulting firms, financial organizations, and other relevant bodies.

Explicit policy instruments are those intended to affect directly the decisions having to do with the growth of S&T capabilities. Implicit policy instruments are those that, although referring to policies, functions, and activities other than science and technology, have a significant indirect impact on S&T decisionmaking. Of particular importance for the growth of local S&T capabilities are policy instruments related to the process of industrialization, for they influence the pattern of demand for technology, the importation of technology, and the capacity of the industrial sector to assimilate technology. An illustrative list of S&T policy instruments is shown in Table 1.

Chapter 12

National Science and Technology Policies for Development: A Comparative Analysis

Francisco R. Sagasti

The Process of Policy Implementation

It is difficult to characterize S&T policy instruments individually, and in any case, it is more important to examine their interactions. For this reason it is appropriate to characterize the array of policy instruments, both explicit and implicit, as a whole, focusing on a few characteristics that define the style of policy implementation. The findings of the STPI project point to several general characteristics that merit attention; Table 2 of this chapter summarizes these characteristics for seven STPI countries. Some specific features of the policy implementation process are highlighted.

Characteristics of Policy Instruments

Generality. A majority of the policy instruments identified in the STPI project were designed to operate at the level of industry as a whole or of industrial branches, in the sense that their impact was to be felt in decisions regarding overall industrial growth and in inter-branch decisions (e.g., incentives to promote investments, tariff structures to foster the growth of certain branches). Other policy instruments were designed to affect decisions about products within a particular industrial branch (e.g., incentives for specific types of products, tax rebates for certain manufactured exports). Finally, there were a few instances in which policy instruments had been designed to affect technological choices within product lines (e.g., industrial credit tied to the use of a certain technology). Most of the policy instruments were found to apply across the board to all industrial branches and all types of enterprises, regardless of the products they manufactured or the technologies they employed.

Some policy instruments were designed in such a way that discretionary power was vested in the government agencies that were in charge of applying them. In theory, this was supposed to counteract the generality of policy instruments by allowing the agency to discriminate according to the peculiarities of each case. While this has been attempted in a few cases, the lack of well-defined criteria for the use of discretionary power has precluded more selective use of policy instruments.

Heterogeneity. In most STPI countries, a large array of policy instruments of various types were found coexisting together, even though a certain proportion of them were not actually used. These policy instruments were intended to respond to different policy orientations and assumed different forms of rationality among industrial enterprises. This diversity did not alter the generality. Most of them, however different, had rather general effects on technological decisions. This heterogeneity among policy instruments had been a consequence of the temporary presence in government of certain power groups which sought to advance their own interests and designed new policy instruments while leaving the preceding structure of policy implementation virtually unchanged. Thus, in some countries, it was possible to find policy instruments of different vintages, only the latest of which had been put into practice.

Table 1: Policy Instruments

Policy Instruments to Build Up an S&T Infrastructure

> S&T Planning (explicit)
> Financing of S&T Activities (explicit)
> Manpower Training (explicit)

Policy Instruments to Regulate Technology Imports

> Registries of Technology Transfer (explicit)
> Import Controls (implicit)
> Foreign Investment Controls (implicit)
> Joint Ventures (implicit)

Policy Instruments to Define the Pattern of Demand for Technology

> Industrial Programming (implicit)
> Industrial Financing (implicit)
> Price Controls (implicit)
> Fiscal Measures (implicit)
> Incentives (explicit)

Policy Instruments to Promote the Performance of S&T Activities in Enterprises

> Special Credit Lines (explicit)
> Fiscal Incentives (explicit)

Policy Instruments to Support the Performance of S&T Activities

> Consulting and Engineering Design Organizations (explicit)
> Technical Norms and Standards (explicit)
> Technical Information Systems (explicit)

Another reason for heterogeneity among policy instruments derived from power conflicts within the government. Certain policy instruments, and the agencies supposed to implement them, had fallen under the influence of competing groups seeking to use them for their own purposes. The result was a rather mixed set of policy instruments and criteria used to put them into practice. This was most noticeable when policy instruments involved discretionary power, when there was institutional dispersion, or when there was lack of coordination in the application of policy instruments.

Passivity. The majority of the policy instruments identified by the STPI project required the agency in charge to take a passive attitude, with initiative for application of the instrument having to come from the organizations that were to be affected by them. This was closely related to the positive nature of the instruments. Most of them provided incentives to industrial firms, which were supposed to take the necessary steps to obtain the benefits (tax incentives, preferential credits, tariff protection, tax rebates, etc.). In practice, however, the effectiveness of these instruments was limited by lack of knowledge about them among those who were supposed to benefit from them. Relatively few enterprises took advantage of the opportunites offered by the policy instruments, and this led to a relative concentration in their application. A small number of industrial firms had benefitted from several of the instruments. Because most enterprises were unaware of the policy instruments, the result was an effective *marginalization* of the policy instruments. Furthermore, the conditions for application of the instruments were often defined in such a complex way that they became irrelevant to all but a small number of large industrial enterprises with the means to apply for and secure the benefits.

Redundancy. This characteristic was found when there was a rather large number of policy instruments which were supposed to act in the same direction, particularly by conferring benefits on industrial enterprises. For example, many instruments were found which lowered the cost of capital (e.g., various types of special credit lines, tax rebates on interest payments, low tariffs for imported capital goods, special tax exemptions for reinvesting profits, accelerated depreciation rates, special tax credits for investment in certain regions, basic infrastructure services provided by the government, and so on). Even though each may have been designed with a special purpose in mind, their combined effect canceled out the impact that any one of them might have had individually. Practically any industrial firm could benefit from several of these measures, and many firms sought to benefit from most of them. Thus, the fact that there was a large number of different policy instruments oriented in the same direction, that they were rather general and applied to any enterprise, that the initiative rested with the firms that were supposed to benefit from them, and that they were applied by different government agencies, led to a very complex policy implementation structure, and one in which the dispersion of benefits from the various measures made any one of them rather ineffective. This redundancy was closely related to the concentrated benefits of the policy instruments.

Incompleteness. Most of the characteristics mentioned above were pertinent to the positive policy instruments designed to motivate certain behavior on the part of industrial enterprises. Examination of *negative* policy instruments — instruments designed to control the behavior of industrial firms through such means as import restrictions, foreign exchange controls, and registry and approval of licensing agreements — showed that most of them did not cover the whole range of productive units and that government enterprises were particularly prone to circumvent regulations designed to stimulate the growth of local industry and foster the development of indigenous technological capabilities. Prohibitions against equipment and machinery imports, for example, were often ignored or revoked by government agencies. Government agencies also were found to be signing licensing agreements containing restrictive clauses forbidden by existing laws. Thus, negative policy instruments were incomplete and likely to be circumvented through exceptions.

Impact of S&T Policy Instruments

The empirical evidence gathered in the STPI project shows overwhelmingly that explicit S&T policy instruments (with the exception of personnel training) had little impact on technological change, particularly at the early stages of industrialization. The interactions among the three categories are themselves the main determinants of technological change in industry and of the development of industrial S&T capabilities.

It was also found that enterprises often made technological decisions without considering S&T policy instruments. It was only after decisions had been made that firms either took advantage of the benefits or looked for ways of getting around the penalties specified in the instruments.

To date, policy instruments have not exerted much pressure for technological change, but at times they have had a powerful impact on the development of an infrastructure to perform science and technology activities. S&T infrastructures have been successfully developed in some cases, ostensibly for industry, and have been primarily the product of explicit government intervention. However, scientific and technological activities have tended to remain in isolation. The institutions composing the S&T infrastructure have been geared to serving the whole industry or particular branches and have not been able to meet the specific demands of individual firms.

Nevertheless, S&T capabilities are one of the keys to directing industrial development. Less-developed countries that value national autonomy must acquire the ability to evaluate, choose, and absorb imported technology and to generate local technology, transforming it into viable industrial projects. This capabity is dependent on a country's own industrial S&T capabilities.

Furthermore, as development proceeds and a country becomes able to accumulate an economic surplus, it will only be able to invest its surplus internally if it has suitable S&T capabilities, a thriving capital goods industry, and policies that support local technology.

Essential Ingredients in S&T Policymaking

The development of an endogenous scientific and technological base for industry will take very long for most less-developed countries, but this development (whichever political or social form it takes) will not be viable if the potential benefits of modern science and technology are rejected. Science and technology are necessary components of any development strategy in the last third of the 20th century, although the Western style of S&T development is not the only way. There is room for choice, albeit limited, in the sequence of steps and the particular ways science and technology are used.

At present, the West has a disproportionate command of S&T activities, and the possibilities of radically changing the disparities are minimal. However, the margin for maneuver within existing constraints is certainly larger than perceived by most leaders in the less-developed world.

The upheavals of the 1970s among the industrialized economies and the international redistribution of industrial activities may signal new opportunities for the less-developed countries. A country's ability to respond will depend largely on its strategies of industrial S&T development. It must delineate the areas in which indigenous technologies are to be made the basis of productive activities, the areas in which capabilities for choosing, modifying, and absorbing imported technologies must be built up, and the areas in which traditional technologies must be preserved and developed.

The policies of the less-developed countries are bound to fail, regardless of good intentions, unless they are embedded in a context that favors S&T development, unless they are closely articulated with industrial development policies, and unless they acknowledge and incorporate the characteristics of technological change. Thus, they must be designed to fit those situations in which they will be applied.

The only generalization, therefore, that emerges out of STPI research is that S&T policies and policy instruments must be specific. There is a need to avoid sweeping generalizations and the elaboration of "standard" models or frameworks. There are many pitfalls associated with disregarding the specific contexts of underdevelopment or overlooking the full range of factors, both internal and external, that condition the development of indigenous policies.

Finally, it is necessary to avoid simplistic conceptualizations borrowed from one discipline or another in investigating a specific country's S&T development. Various research approaches, disciplinary perspectives, and ideological points of view must be combined if one is to comprehend the interplay of forces that shapes S&T development. There is no substitute for determined local efforts—however modest at the beginning—to understand the particular situation of a country's industry and its S&T capabilities, their possible future development, and the types of government measures likely to be most effective.

Table 2: Characteristics of the Process of Industrial

	Argentina	Brazil
1. Role of the state in orienting the industrialization process	• Provide support for industry on a wide front and in a general way. • Priorities for industry are not clearly defined and left mainly to market forces. • No specific state orientation for industry. • Frequent changes in policy make the role of the state ambiguous and even contradictory.	• Provide support for industry on a wide front and in a general way. • Priorities for industry not clearly defined and left mainly to market forces. • Little specific state orientation of industry, except when the state intervenes as entrepreneur. • Priority awarded recently to the capital goods industries.
2. Reliance on promotion (positive) or control (negative) mechanisms	• Reliance mainly on promotional measures and incentives to support industrialization. • Limited use of control measures, mainly in the form of registration of foreign investment and licensing agreements, and regulation of foreign exchange.	• Reliance mainly on promotional measures and incentives to support industrialization. • Limited use of control measures, mainly in the form of registration of foreign investment and licensing agreements, and regulation of foreign exchange.
3. Mode of state intervention	• Provision of basic services in industry. • State enterprises in charge of key industrial inputs (steel, oil, electricity). • Practically no use of planning mechanisms. • Little regulation of the economy.	• Provision of basic services in industry. • State enterprises in charge of key industrial inputs (steel, oil, electricity), initially as a reluctant entrepreneur but later as an active one. • Limited use of planning mechanisms. • Significant regulation of the economy. • Key importance of state financing for industry.
4. Characterization of the array of policy instruments	• High generality of policy instruments. • Heterogeneity (coexistence of various types and vintages of policy instruments). • Passivity (government agencies do not take initiative). • Marginality (little impact in industry). • Instability (frequent changes). • Impossibility of coherent government action because of conflicts and contradictions.	• Pragmatic design and use of policy instruments, responding to short- and medium-term stimuli. • Increasing sophistication and specificity of policy instruments. • Increasing fragmentation of policy instruments as they become more specific. • Great emphasis on financial mechanisms.
5. Coherence of S&T policy and degree of integration with industrial policies	• Lack of frame of reference or guidelines with continuity to orient development of S&T. • Impossibility of government S&T coordinating bodies to carry out their functions. • Lack of correspondence between industrial and S&T policies.	• Support given to S&T within a pragmatic context of industrial policies. • Government agencies play a key coordinating role for S&T efforts. • S&T policies derived from industrialization policies. • Alternation from an S&T policy response to industrialization, to an S&T policy reorientation of demand for technology towards local sources.
6. Recent changes and trends in government industrial or S&T policy	• Continuation of S&T policy instability and lack of coherence. • Dismantling of key S&T institutions.	• Large increases in allocations for S&T activities in strategic sectors. • Ambitious plan for expansion of S&T infrastructure.

S&T Policy Implementation in STPI Countries

Colombia	Korea
• Provide support for industry on a wide front and in a general way. • Priorities for industry not clearly defined and left mainly to market forces. • No specific state orientation of industry. • Priority awarded recently to industries that can compete in export markets.	• Provide support to selected industries, in a specific but intensive way. • Priorities defined clearly and given to export and strategic industries. • Specific state orientation of industry through several mechanisms (financing, incentives, etc.). • Priority awarded recently to selected "key technology" industries and to energy generation.
• Limited reliance on promotional measures, mainly of credit and fiscal nature, to support industrialization. • Substantial reliance on control measures, primarily foreign exchange controls, regulation of foreign investments, and registering and negotiation of licensing agreements.	• Reliance mainly on promotional measures and incentives within the framework of priorities for selected industries. • Use of control measures centered around import substitution industries. Control of technology transfer is subsidiary to foreign investment control.
• Limited provision of basic services to industry. • State enterprises do not play important role. • Limited use of planning mechanisms. • Little regulation of the economy. • State financing of industry is significant.	• Provision of basic services to industry, and of industrial infrastructure in selected areas. • State enterprises play limited role, and mainly in basic inputs. • Extensive use of planning in close interaction with private sector. • Extensive regulation of the economy. • Key role of state financing of industry.
• Ambiguous use of policy instruments: active in control measures and passive in promotional measures. • Adoption of a restrictive or defensive position with respect to foreign technology. • Lack of selectivity and specificity of policy instruments. • Non-discretionary character of most policy instruments.	• Redundancy of policy instruments to promote export-oriented industries. • Selective use of policy instruments to promote specific industries. • Reliance on government coordinating bodies. • Great emphasis on financial mechanisms.
• Policies of promoting S&T, but without linking them to industrialization policies. • Lack of coordination of S&T activities and of government agencies involved in S&T policy. • Technological considerations not taken into account when setting industrialization policies and evaluating investments. • Lack of correspondence between industrial and S&T policies.	• Technological considerations integrated into industrialization policies. • Heavy reliance on foreign technology for the growth of strategic and basic industries. • Steady support given to expansion of R&D infrastructure in areas of importance for industry. • Government agencies play key coordinating role. • Substantial coherence between S&T and industrial policies.
• Liberalization of trade and the economy. • Relative abundance of foreign exchange reversed for three years prevalent contextual conditions. • Cyclic nature of government action punctuated by elections (1978).	• Substantive expansion of R&D infrastructure. • Key importance of S&T considerations in development planning. • Selection of a number of "strategic technologies" that should be mastered.

(Table 2) Characteristics of the Process of Industria

Mexico

	Mexico
1. Role of the state in orienting the industrialization process	• Provide support for industries on a wide front and in a general way. • Priorities for industry not clearly defined and left mainly to market forces. • No specific state orientation of industry. • Priority awarded recently to the capital goods industries.
2. Reliance on promotion (positive) or control (negative) mechanisms	• Reliance mainly on promotional measures and incentives to support industrialization. • Limited use of control measures, mainly in foreign investment regulation and the registry of licensing agreements.
3. Mode of state intervention	• Provision of basic services, facilities and infrastructure for industry. • State enterprises in charge of key industrial inputs (oil, steel). • Limited use of planning mechanisms. • Little regulation of industry. • Key role of state financing of industry.
4. Characterization of the array of policy instruments	• Redundancy of general promotional measures for industry. • Passivity (government agencies do not take initiative). • Lack of selectivity and of possibility to discriminate in the application of policy instruments. • Discretionary character of a large number of policy instruments. • Few instruments (mainly the control ones) are employed to influence directly the behavior of industry.
5. Coherence of S&T policy and degree of integration with industrial policies	• Policies for S&T oriented towards promotion of R&D. • Limited coordinating role of government bodies. • Technological considerations not taken into account when setting industrialization policies. • Lack of coherence between S&T and industrialization policies.
6. Recent changes and trends in government industrial or S&T policy	• Abandonment of efforts at planning S&T development. • Recent government change (1977) implied a change in S&T policies.

S&T Policy Implementation in STPI Countries

Peru	Venezuela
• Provide selective support to industry based on predefined industrialization model. • Priorities for industry clearly defined by legislation. • Specific state intervention in basic and strategic industries. Regulation of all the rest of industry (little attention paid to private industry). • Recent reduction of state intervention in industry.	• Provide support for industry on a wide front and in a general way. • Priorities for industry not clearly defined and left mainly to market forces. • Little specific state orientation of industry, except through state enterprises in basic industries. • Recent expansion of the role of the state as entrepreneur and financier in industry.
• Reliance mainly on compulsory and control mechanisms to orient industry. • Limited use of promotional measures and within the framework of compulsory laws.	• Reliance mainly on promotional measures and incentives. • Limited use of control measures centered around the registration of foreign investment and licensing agreements.
• Provision of basic services to industry. • Key role of state enterprises in many areas of industry (and limited role of private industry). • Extensive use of planning mechanisms, executed through state agencies and enterprises. • Extensive regulation of the economy. • Key role of state financing in industry.	• Provision of basic services, facilities and infrastructure to industry. • Key role of state enterprises in basic industries. • Recent importance of planning, through massive government investment. • Little regulation of the economy. • Key role of state financing of industry, but facing severe problems, to provide long-term credit.
• Formal character of policy intruments, which have little ability to affect private industry. • Passivity of promotional measures. • Highly discretionary character of policy instruments. • Adoption of a restrictive or defensive position with regard to foreign technology. • Most policy instruments are of a compulsory legal nature.	• Instability of government agencies in charge of using policy instruments. • Lack of selectivity. • High generality. • Existence of gaps in key areas of policy instrumentation. • Reliance mostly on fiscal measures. • Discretionary power involved in a large number of policy instruments.
• Policies for S&T are independent of industrialization policies and relatively more sophisticated and advanced. • Integrated treatment of all aspects of industrial S&T policies in one agency. • Fragmentation of S&T policy efforts, and lack of overall coherence and coordination, particularly with industrialization policies.	• Policies for S&T designed but lacking ways of putting them into practice. S&T objectives not considered in industrial policies. • Lack of coordination of S&T activities. • Emphasis on the massive importation of technology, and little efforts to develop indigenous S&T capabilities. • Lack of correspondence between industrial and S&T policies.
• Relative liberalization of the economy. • Reduction of role of the state in industry. • Financial and economic crisis pushed technological considerations into the background.	• Abundance of financial resources. • Cyclic nature of government actions punctuated by elections (1978).

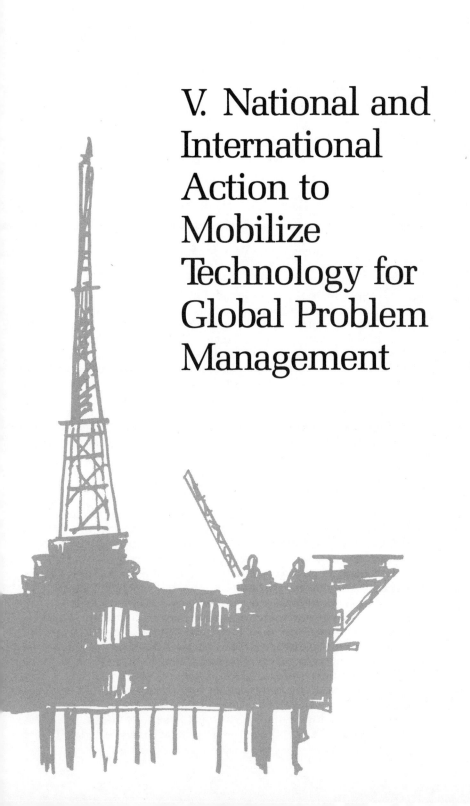

V. National and International Action to Mobilize Technology for Global Problem Management

N atural rubber accounts today for about a third of the world's production of rubber; almost all of the natural rubber comes from Southeast Asia. The technical and economic problems of producing and marketing natural rubber vary somewhat among the producing countries, but the rubber industries of those countries share several characteristics: (1) natural rubber is of immense socio-economic importance to the producing countries; (2) the industry is a substantial source of employment for small landholders, who own up to 95 per cent of the total area under rubber; and (3) the product continues to be sold through a commodity market in which producers have very little control over price.

The basic problems of the natural rubber industry stem from the intensification of competitive market forces that began in the years immediately after the Second World War, resulting in an almost uninterrupted decline in the price of natural rubber. If total natural rubber production had remained static from 1960 to 1970, the loss in export income to the producing countries would have amounted to some $18,000 million (in Malaysian dollars). Because of rising production efficiency, however, the actual loss amounted to $12,000 million (in Malaysian dollars) for all producing countries. The situation has been one of continual erosion of the efforts of the producing countries to increase their income. Unenlightened opinion sometimes ascribes the price decline to overproduction of natural rubber, but this is hardly consistent with the pattern of total consumption of both natural and synthetic rubbers over the past twenty years. Thus, any attempt to restrict production of natural rubber in order to maintain prices would amost certainly lead to further encroachment by synthetic rubber, i.e., a shrinkage in natural rubber's share of the world market. Indeed, the fact that total rubber consumption increased at a considerably faster rate than natural rubber production inevitably led to the displacement of natural rubber from uses for which it remains fully satisfactory in both technical and economic terms. The competitive forces thus called into play have led to a serious market weakness of natural rubber. The synthetic rubber industry, intoxicated as it were

Chapter 13

Malaysian Rubber in the World Market

B. C. Sekhar

with the availability of abundant and cheap petrochemicals from the petroleum industry, miscalculated its long-term capacity. Meanwhile, the natural rubber industry — through lack of confidence and unappreciative of its own strength and uniqueness — lagged behind in its investment policy. While the synthetic rubber industry continued to expand its production capacity, the natural rubber industry exerted only a weak effort.

In its fight for survival, the natural rubber industry was left with no alternative but to implement total modernization programs. These included measures for improving productivity per unit of land area, measures to reduce the overall cost of production so as to produce rubber at economically low prices, and improvements in quality, presentation, and grading. During the past ten years, these programs have brought about substantial improvements with respect to production and productivity. A number of research developments have already ensured a sound economic base for *hevea* cultivation and production. Some of these include:

(a) The development of plants with yield capacities in excess of 2,500 kilograms per hectare, improved agronomic practices to bring plants to maturity within a period of four years, and optimization of yield through selective fertilization;

(b) Horticultural techniques combining the root, trunk, and crown systems to produce the "ideal" trees long dreamt of by rubber plant breeders;

(c) The development of yield stimulation techniques enabling trees already planted and of different ages and varieties to realize their full genetic potential, thereby effecting modernization without resorting to premature replanting.

The fact is that the natural rubber industry has not only withstood the competitive pressures exerted by a powerful oligopolistic industry backed by the massive resources of the multinationals and the industrially advanced countries, but has also successfully and substantially carried out a radical face-lifting modernization. This speaks as nothing else can for the inherent soundness and strength of natural rubber. The industry has not only exploited the slogan "replant or die" but has also assumed the need to "modernize or perish" as the key solution in the last decade.

The Rubber Market

The world is going through what can rightly be termed an industrial and economic crisis. On the industrial front, energy costs and environmental pollution problems are running wild. International currency uncertainties have been aggravated by balance-of-payments problems due to the high cost of imported sources of energy. These factors have impinged in a pronounced manner on rubber. The prices of petroleum-derived monomers have doubled and in some cases trebled. Shortages of certain synthetic elastomers necessitated allocation limits to consumers in some countries during 1973 and 1974. Environmental pollution has attracted the establishment of strong lobbies and intensified research on the health hazards of industrially important petro-chemicals. The hazards of residual vinyl chloride in polyvinyl chloride factories have been shown to be very severe.

Meanwhile, increased acceptance of radial-ply construction of tires has involved greater use of natural rubber and is no doubt contributing to added strength. Improved high-yielding planting materials commercially proven with yield capacities in excess of 2,200 kilograms per hectare, novel yield stimulation methods, modern presentation, technological grading, and effective presentation within Standard Malaysian Rubber (SMR) standards have made natural rubber— Malaysian natural rubber—a high-performance industrial material of great economic attraction. But inflation and the residual effects of rising petroleum prices on fertilizers are tending to negate the achievements of research in reducing costs. Added to this has been a cutback in automobile production arising from economic factors in several consuming countries. Even though signs of increasing automobile production suggest the end of the recession, economic factors may restrict increased use of natural rubber in the near future.

There seems to be an undoubtedly strong and stable future for natural rubber in the long term. In the short term, however, the position of natural rubber is fraught with a number of uncertainties connected with the petroleum industry, currency fluctuations, economic problems caused by balance-of-payments influencing industrial growth, commodity shortages, transient excesses, etc. On balance, the natural rubber industry has every cause for real confidence but no cause for any form of complacency.

Commodity Promotion: The Malaysian Experience

The natural rubber industry plays a major role in the economy of Malaysia. It provides a livelihood for over three million Malaysians, it contributes about 30 per cent of the country's export earnings, and it provides 20 per cent of the gross national product. Although most of the industry is in the hands of the private sector—either as estates or as small holdings — the health of this vital national asset is of prime importance to the government, which must ensure that the industry runs smoothly.

The natural rubber industry today is, to a greater extent than ever before, the "spinal cord" of the Malaysian economy. Almost two million hectares of land are used for rubber production. Export earnings from rubber in 1974 amounted to about 30 per cent of total earnings. Over 60 per cent of the land which produces rubber is occupied by smallholders, who number more than 450,000. Federal and state land schemes are also becoming a significant factor in rubber cultivation. The Second Malaysia Plan called for the development of about half a million hectares, and of this land at least a third was assigned to rubber. This target had almost been achieved at the close of the Second Plan period.

Before World War II, the health of the natural rubber industry depended largely on the confidence and initiative of the private sector, both estates and smallholdings, with whatever support the Rubber Research Institute of Malaysia (RRIM) could give in terms of science and technology. The first organized approach came in 1953, when replanting with improved planting materials became a necessary concept. Pressure from synthetic rubber, as well as expanded research and development activity mounted on behalf of the industry by the Malaysian Rubber Fund Board (MRFB), contributed to significant improvements in the natural rubber industry.

With a third of the population dependent on this commodity, directly or indirectly, Malaysia cannot afford fluctuating rubber prices and oscillating industrial attitudes within or outside the country. The government in recent years has therefore taken a more direct and positive interest in the natural rubber industry. A Ministry of Primary Industries was created, and a number of bills were enacted through Parliament. A number of agencies were set up to streamline marketing: the Malaysian Rubber Exchange and Licensing Board (MRELB) was established to speedily modernize the smallholder sector; the Rubber Industry Smallholders Development Authority (RISDA) was created; the purview of the RRIM was expanded to the whole of Malaysia; and the name of the Malaysian Rubber Fund Board (MRFB) was changed to the Malaysian Rubber Research and Development Board (MRRDB) to emphasize its role as the main policy and planning board for research and development. The basic intention of all these measures was to make Malaysia capable of modifying and even creating a situation conducive to the planned growth of a healthy natural rubber industry instead of simply responding to new developments in the synthetic rubber industry.

The MRRDB has an important and critical role to play in forging strategies and formulating sound long-term plans for the natural rubber industry. The MRRDB can no longer restrict itself to merely financing, coordinating, and administering the organizational units under its wing. The board has become the "eyes, ears, and brain trust" of the government and industry as far as natural rubber is concerned.

The activities of the MRRDB include the planning and formulation of strategies, the formulation of research and development policy, technical advisory services, market research, integrating production with industrialization, and manpower training.

Planning and Formulation of Strategies

Any form of planning to create appropriate strategies requires information and data on every sector of the natural rubber consuming and producing industries and associated industries.

On the consumption side, MRRDB needs to know what the world will require in the way of elastomers, particularly natural rubber, fifteen and twenty years from today. It has to determine the strengths and weaknesses of natural rubber's competitors. It has to establish realistic targets for the proportionate use of natural rubber (a techno-economic norm) the world over. It must continuously keep in touch with developments in associated industries, be they the automotive, plastic, petro-chemical, or synthetic rubber industries.

On the production side, MRRDB needs to devise a forecast (an agro-economic norm) of natural rubber's absolute potential if all scientific and technological innovations are speedily implemented. These production forecasts should then be augmented by forecasts of the requirements for associated facilities, such as acids, fertilizers, equipment, and numerous other infrastructural supports. The planners also need to know which crop is most suited to particular soils and what socio-economic benefits can accrue from correct selection of crops. Rubber trees should not be planted without an assessment of the land's suitability for them.

A comparison between a techno-economic consumption norm for the 1980s and 1990s and an agro-economic production norm for the same period should dictate Malaysia's future investment policy on rubber. Should the industry expand? If so, at what rate and to what extent? These decisions have to be made. When they are made, the full implications must be understood and planned for.

To fulfill this function, the MRRDB has already established a rubber economics and planning unit (REPU). In collaboration with other agencies, REPU has established a data bank, is undertaking research into techno-economic, agro-economic, and socio-economic questions, and is gathering market intelligence through a continuous monitoring system which functions both outside and inside Malaysia. A preliminary study indicates that natural rubber, on the basis of certain techno-economic considerations, could produce 42 per cent of the world's elastomers, as compared to the present 33 per cent.

Formulation of a Research and Development Policy

The industry's research and development philosophy has largely been to defend natural rubber's position in the market from encroachment by synthetics. This defensive posture has become out-dated. A more aggressive policy is now called for, and a number of actions have been taken by MRRDB:

Production research. Although production research has been exceedingly rewarding, there is much more potential. The theoretical limit to hevea yield capacity is about 9,000 kilograms per hectare compared to the current commercial level of about 1,400. Newer and better stimulants are on the horizon. The immaturity period of five to six years has inhibited some potential producers, particularly small-holders, but recent developments promise a reduction of that period to one to two years. The target must be no more than a three-year immaturity period. Highly advanced techniques of tissue culture, horticultural manipulation, more discriminating fertilizer usage, dwarfing, and so on are being vigorously pursued.

Commercial and technological research. Up to now, chemical and technological research has been aimed at protecting the traditional types of rubber use, such as tires. Although marginal efforts have been mounted in selected areas, such as building construction, a new dimension in research is now required. Environmental pollution, high energy costs, and long-term petro-chemical shortages all give new emphasis to photosynthetic conversion of sunlight by plants as a highly efficient and non-polluting means of generating hydrocar-bons. In the case of hevea, the hydrocarbon happens to be a hydrocar-bon polymer having elastic properties, which have been and are still being exploited. What about modifying this hydrocarbon polymer? Very little has been done, but the chemical possibilities are immense. An aggressive approach, such as the one mounted by the plastics industries in the past, is called for. We no longer need to depend on the transportation sector to use two thirds of the natural rubber produced. This change in philosophy in chemical and technological research has been introduced at both the MRPA (Malaysian Rubber Producers Association) and the RRIM.

Much more can also be achieved in rubber processing technology. Reversible powders from latex are no longer considered a pipe dream. More automation is possible in processing factories, and carbon black masterbatching is becoming important in view of pollution and energy costs in consuming countries. Research has merely scratched the surface in these areas.

On the development side, research innovations are being speedily adapted to the smallholder environment through the Smallholders Projects Research Division of the RRIM. RISDA (the Rubber Industry Smallholders Development Authority) will help make these innova-tions available by providing both training and advisory activities.

To give support to the new dynamic approach to research and development, the Coordinating Advisory Committee of the MRRDB has been expanded to include eminent specialists from the United States, England, Italy, France, and Malaysia. This committee meets alternately in Malaysia and London to ensure that the programs for-mulated are consonant with arriving speedily at declared objectives.

Technical Advisory Services and Market Research

Technical Advisory Services (TAS). The MRRDB now has offices in the United States, England, Germany, Italy, Austria, Spain, India, Japan, Australia, New Zealand, Brazil, and the Low Countries to provide technical advisory services. This dispersion of MRRDB offices throughout the world ensures easy contact with all the major consuming and manufacturing areas. It is the intention of the MRRDB to further strengthen this service. Malaysian technologists trained in European languages are being seconded to each of these offices for varying periods of time. For this purpose the MRRDB has approved a substantial expansion of the RRIM Technology Division, and in the near future a new Technology Center will become fully operational in Malaysia at the RRIM Experimental Center near Kuala Lumpur.

In addition, mobile specialist teams from the RRIM and MRPRA (Malaysian Rubber Producers Research Association) will make periodic visits to selected consuming regions. Such teams have visited Eastern Europe and South America recently, and there will be more frequent interactions of this nature.

Market research. All marketing services are centralized in REPU at MRRDB. This service will have the following functions and in certain specific aspects complement those carried out by the MRELB: (a) to market all rubbers from the RRIM; (b) to provide a market service for small producers with regard to Standard Malaysian Rubber (SMR) and special rubbers; (c) to run the MRRDB research stock for promotional purposes; (d) to undertake research on all factors associated with the marketing of natural rubber; and (e) to establish market intelligence and data on raw and manufactured rubber goods.

Integration of Industrialization with Production

Through the efforts of the Federal Industrial Development Authority (FIDA) and the Ministry of Trade and Industry, Malaysian industry is changing rapidly. Natural rubber can play a distinctive role in this transformation. For many years MRRDB has provided technical advisory services the world over, and unique technological expertise has been built up within the MRRDB system. There are a number of compelling reasons for Malaysia to assume leadership in rubber-based industries:

(1) As the world's largest producer of high quality natural rubber, Malaysia is uniquely endowed with raw materials and expertise.

(2) SMR standards and new processing operations have already introduced an element of sophistication. Further integration of natural rubber into manufacture should not create great difficulties.

(3) The MRRDB system can effectively provide technological support. Pilot operations, product testing, trouble-shooting, and training will be part of the services offered by the RRIM Technology Center at Sungei Buloh.

(4) The high costs of energy, labor, and environmental pollution controls offer a distinct incentive to industries to move to producing areas.

The MRRDB is giving priority attention to this last area. In cooperation with FIDA, activities will be mounted to provide relevant techno-economic and market information on rubber-based products. Innovations arising out of MRPRA and RRIM activities will be funnelled into Malaysian industrial activity. Producers, be they smallholders or estates, should be allowed to take advantage of the "value added" concept of manufactured goods. Integration of production and manufacture will have profound effects on the economic stability of the producers.

A committee on rubber-based industries has been set up in the MRRDB, and preliminary discussions with the producing and manufacturing sectors have been held. The TAS has been briefed to play a particular role in providing contacts in consuming areas. While all this is going on, the MRRDB organizations are already equipped to assist producers intending to integrate into manufacturing operations. With the emphasis and assistance that FIDA is giving and the ready support of the MRRDB, the climate for rubber-based industries should be a bright one.

Training and Manpower

Staff development within the MRRDB's units must conform to the new economic policy. For this purpose, the MRRDB is providing scholarships at all educational levels. This policy will enable all MRRDB units to attain balanced growth of skilled manpower in the next three years.

In addition, the training program is being designed to meet the requirements of the new research philosophy and the requirements of the industry as a whole. Scholarships and fellowships in processing, marketing, post-graduate research, and rubber technology are offered. RRIM's training center at Sungei Buloh will continue to provide training in plantation management and rubber technology, and research staff from the RRIM and MRPRA will interact with the trainees. A higher level of training will evolve as a natural development through which latest scientific and technological sophistications will be imparted to industry arising from ongoing research in the biological area for plantation management, and from research in the technological and chemical areas for technologists in the manufacturing sector.

Future Trends

Several world bodies are anticipating shortages of raw materials now and in the long term. Many of the large consumers are concerned about security and adequacy of supplies.

The United States has initiated three steps that are pertinent: a move to increase its natural rubber stockpile to over 530,000 tons, approval of the expenditure of nearly (U.S.) $55 million to research guayule over a period of five years, and the expression of its belief that the international buffer stock should be high as 700,000 tons and that no form of production controls should be instituted. Guayule, which belongs to the botanical species *parthenium argentatum*, grows wild in the arid zones of Mexico. It is an insignificant-looking shrub that contains rubber in its roots. Genetic improvement of guayule will require a long-term program. At best, guayule will provide some elasticity to supplies in times of unusual imbalances in supply and demand. The U.S. approach indicates its serious concern about polyisoprene supplies.

The U.S.S.R. plans to be able to produce one million tons of synthetic cis 1,4 polyisoprene by 1980. Their proportionate consumption of natural rubber is to be reduced to from 8 to 12 per cent. Given the increasingly difficult petroleum situation, the approach taken by the U.S.S.R. must also stem from some concern about the ready availability of polyisoprene supplies.

The European Economic Community (EEC) and Japan have expressed concern regarding the availability of natural rubber supplies but have taken no actions yet.

Under these circumstances, natural rubber producers must adopt a dynamic production policy in which four factors assume major importance:

(1) The need for a measure of price stability in the natural rubber market to ensure that transient imbalances do not disrupt the livelihood of the small farmers who dominate production;

(2) The need to provide fiscal incentives to make natural rubber production attractive in relation to other crops which may not have the same assured long-term market demand but offer greater short-term gains;

(3) The need for financial inducements to ensure the continued role of estates in natural rubber production;

(4) The need for accelerated modernization of smallholder operations, especially the use of advanced planting materials, ethrel stimulation and upward tapping, and the latest agronomic management.

The future scenario for natural rubber is both exciting and challenging, indicating a strong and expanding market demand. With increasing petroleum prices and diminishing non-renewable resources, coupled with environmental and energy considerations, natural rubber may be expected to play a greater role in the spectrum of polymeric requirements. The possibility of modifying natural rubber to provide it with gas impermeability, oil resistance, higher damping with reduced creep, and thermoplastic characteristics has been demonstrated. Its use as a feed stock for polymers cannot be ruled out in the long term.

In all the rubber-producing countries, the natural rubber industry is essentially an industry of the smallholder. The smallholder element is both a strength and a weakness. The resilience of the smallholder through the years has been amply demonstrated, but a number of factors have tended to undermine his confidence and enthusiasm. These include widely fluctuating prices and low returns, uneconomic size of holdings and lack of credits, low yield in the absence of replanting, the migration of rural youth to the urban sector, the continuous declaration of uncertainties created by threats of synthetic rubber substitution, and the accepted thesis that natural rubber's proportionate share of the market is dictated by the extrapolated supply of natural rubber and therefore can be expected to decrease.

Obviously, many of these problems (such as low yields) can be solved by available technologies. Technologies are also available to increase productivity, reduce costs, improve income, and convert natural rubber into a feedstock for alternate polymeric materials. The critical element is that such technologies must become widespread in the producing countries.

The scarce financial resources of those countries, however, are already under strain. Malaysia alone has invested over 1,000 million Malaysian ringgit on replanting, a single operation that is a vital component of modernization. Unless replanting is carried out continuously, the necessary increase in the supply of natural rubber simply will not occur. The world requires an increasing supply of natural rubber with attractive techno-economic features. The producing countries have the technology, the facilities, and the determination to meet this requirement. Implementation will require world support for the producing countries on four counts: first, the introduction of a measure of price stability at equitable levels; secondly, material assistance for replanting and the implementation of available technologies; thirdly, material assistance for research in keeping the industry attuned to the changing techno-economic environment; and finally, cooperation in planning. Further, it will be essential that fiscal policies in the producing countries are oriented to providing adequate incentives for both smallholders and estates.

These are the reasons that have persuaded the producing countries to seek a wider international price stabilization agreement. The interdependence of the world in meeting its resource requirements, both renewable and non-renewable, has hopefully become manifest. A new and cooperative approach is required for planning supplies of essential industrial polymers from biological sources. Natural rubber is a prime candidate for such cooperation.

During the next decade the developed economies may rely increasingly on minerals supplied by the developing economies, and this may make an important contribution to the foreign exchange earnings of the developing economies.[1] Up to now, the large mining companies have provided most of the funds and technical know-how for mineral development, but the situation has been changing because of the recent trend toward greater national autonomy. Some developing countries have already managed to produce a cadre of experts in this field, working through the public and private sectors. Nevertheless, the remaining gaps in skills, financing, and technology will require the continued participation of the large integrated producers in the mining operations of the developing countries. Such participation must be based on cooperative arrangements that are perceived to be fair by both importing and supplying nations if an uninterrupted flow of resources to world markets is to be assured.

In the long run the developing nations may have a greater stake in resource development than the developed countries, since for a number of important minerals technology is providing a broad array of alternatives in the form of man-made materials and processes for extracting minerals from abundant natural substitutes. The advantages of suppliers with rich ore reserves have been further reduced because even low-grade ores can now be made competitive through advanced technology and large-scale extraction. Despite an increased reliance on mineral supplies from the developing countries, by and large, the industrialized nations do not face an immediately critical supply situation. Over the long run, however, developing countries with abundant minerals will be able to gain better leverage over, and larger benefits from, joint exploration and production ventures. Although the position of the industrialized nations may weaken initially, the revolution of expectations and the growing absorptive capacity of the developing countries will intensify the pressure on them to develop their mineral resources. Thus, the interests of the two parties will again interlock, intersect, and interrelate.

Chapter 14

Harnessing Mineral Resources for Development: Some Policy Suggestions

Rex Bosson and Bension Varon

Mineral Sector Development in the Developing Countries

Although the desirability of helping the developing countries improve their knowledge of their mineral resource base is clear, the flow
of exploration funds to many of the developing countries has been
blocked by the hardening of nationalist sentiments over the past
decade. From 1970 to 1973 more than 70 per cent of the exploration
expenditures in the market economies was concentrated in Australia,
Canada, South Africa, and the United States. With the accentuation of
nationalism and the increasingly onerous tax legislation introduced
in Australia, Canada, and Ireland, however, there was a noticeable
drop in exploration expenditure in those countries between 1971 and
1974. The only countries with increased expenditures appear to be
Brazil, the Philippines, and South Africa, and the consensus is that
total exploration expenditure in the non-communist world has dropped since 1970 despite an increased demand for minerals and the near
certainty that additional demand in the next decades can be met only
by substantial new discoveries. A large number of these mineral
discoveries will have to be made in the developing countries, and
these countries — particularly those in which there has been little
development of the mineral sector — will have to participate much
more actively in exploration if they expect to improve their position
in the world mineral markets.

How does a country go about doing this? If it has a well-developed
mineral sector, it can perhaps stimulate exploration by the domestic
private sector through government sharing of the exploration risk,
perhaps through the establishment of a government financed exploration fund which makes funds available to operating companies. Some
countries with well-developed mineral sectors, such as the United
States, Canada, Australia, and Brazil, have already made use of such

*Excerpted and revised from Rex Bosson and Bension Varon, *The Mining Industry
and the Developing Countries*, A World Bank Research Publication, Oxford University
Press, 1977.

funds; so have other countries where the sector is developing rapidly, such as Morocco and the Philippines. Bolivia, Iran, and Thailand have been considering setting up such funds. These national funds have different objectives. Some are designed primarily for the benefit of the small local prospector or company, some conduct exploration for the state, and others facilitate exploration by large domestic and foreign mining companies. The technique has met with varied success but, if carefully planned, it can be a direct and workable vehicle for encouraging exploration in developing and developed countries alike. In addition to spurring interest in exploration by local and foreign companies, a national exploration fund in a developing country can serve to introduce new technology and know-how in exploration and mining operations, familiarize local mining companies with new management techniques, provide some coordination of the exploration effort, and assist in establishing a long-term development philosophy.

One of the more successful efforts to promote exploration is that of the Quebec provincial government. After reviewing the various practices used elsewhere in the world, the government of Quebec established in 1965 the Quebec Mining Exploration Company (Société Québecoise d'Exploration Minière —SOQUEM) as a joint stock company intended to promote mineral exploration and development through direct participation in exploration activities on its own account, for others, and in joint ventures. SOQUEM is a state entity with full autonomy, operating in full competition with and under the same legislation as private mining companies. In the ten years between 1966 and 1975, SOQUEM participated in more than 200 exploration ventures of different types, making four significant discoveries and acquiring three other prospective properties. It should become a self-sufficient, revenue-generating entity by the early or mid-1980s.

A lesson to be learned from this and other experiences is that an aggressive approach to promoting exploration and follow-up development through a fund of this kind may actually be superior to the use of government subsidies. A program that operates jointly and in competition with bonafide mining companies often provides better results than a government monopoly. A major problem, however, is that in a majority of cases the developing country has neither the funds nor the expertise to conduct its own exploration program. It is important to point out that $45 million was allocated by the Canadian government to SOQUEM. Governments should be aware, however, that unless they carry out exploration as efficiently as private entities, their direct participation at this early stage may result in lower returns to the country.

A novel approach now used in Peru and Bolivia for petroleum exploration, and in Indonesia and Iran for mineral exploration, is exploration by private parties (often the large multinationals) under contract to the government. The mining companies have indicated a willingness to do this. One company offered to undertake all the exploration and feasibility work on a mineral deposit at its own expense in return for assurances of a management contract and a portion of the mineral output if mining was begun. More and more concessions are negotiated in two stages: the first pertaining only to exploration, with broad guidelines for the terms of exploitation, the second pertaining to exploitation and negotiated with full knowledge of the mineral deposit as a result of completion, of a detailed feasibility study. This approach is only applicable in countries with a well-established mineral sector or considerable geological information. Countries with little geological data and an undeveloped mineral sector have considerable difficulty in interesting foreign private capital in exploration. In those countries the basic geological mapping (infrastructure geology) and initial exploration will remain the responsibility of the state.

In most of the poorer developing countries and those with little mineral sector development, there has been little or no exploration activity. Because present knowledge of their mineral resources is limited, foreign mining companies will not go in without some indication of the existence of significant deposits. Given the competing demands upon their limited financial resources, however, these countries cannot afford to invest in the risky business of mineral exploration, even though revenues from mineral production might enable some of them to make a quantum jump in economic growth.

In recognition of the limited capability of developing nations to undertake mineral exploration on their own, the United Nations has provided assistance in this area for nearly two decades. The United Nations commenced mineral exploration in 1960 when a project started up in Chile which was financed in part by what was then called the Special Fund—the predecessor of today's United Nations Development Programme (UNDP). Up to June 1967, 184 projects had been completed, were in operation, or had funds earmarked for them. The sums involved amounted to about $260 million, of which 53 per cent was contributed by UNDP.[2] In addition, the United Nations Revolving Fund for Natural Resources Exploration came into being in 1975. The Fund provides a source of financing mineral exploration additional to and separate from the UNDP, although it is administered by the latter. Its principal objective is to spread the very high risk involved in finding new mines, as the Fund is reimbursed according to a complex formula only for those successful projects which reach the production stage.[3]

The Pitfalls of Foreign Aid

Expanded aid programs are clearly required because of the major exploration gap in many developing countries. Although there are many examples of excellent past and ongoing aid programs by multilateral and bilateral agencies, some of the aid currently provided is inefficient and ineffective. Some of it is poorly designed and even more poorly implemented; lack of coordination between the various aid agencies is common, duplication of effort occurs, and costs are often unnecessarily high.

By and large, insufficient care is given to adapting the aid program, particularly the technology, to local conditions. Although the large-scale geological map has often provided the starting point for detailed exploration in the developed countries, such maps are an unaffordable luxury for the poorer nations. Accelerators have to be sought which, though perhaps not as satisfactory technically, can develop sufficient data to attract the needed capital fairly quickly. Similarly, geophysical measurements from airplanes over very large areas are entirely feasible in a developed country with plentiful capital but are less feasible for tropical rainforests. Such surveys burden the government with the expensive task of follow-up work on the ground without which the aerial data cannot be interpreted. Some groups often promote regional geophysical surveys without mentioning the time-consuming and costly follow-up work required.

Vast improvements in aid for mineral sector development can be realized by coordinating the activities of the various parties — the bilateral and multilateral agencies, the multinationals, the national agencies, and the local mining industry. This requires the preparation of a sector development strategy, a conscious determination by the host government to implement this strategy, and good administration. Many developing countries unfortunately do not have the expertise or resources necessary to prepare, implement, or administer such a strategy. One of the other parties, therefore, has to take the lead in a professional, unbiased manner.

The Elements of a National Mineral Policy

Mineral development in any country, whether developed or developing, constitutes only one element of total national development and must therefore be structured to fit into the total economic development plan. The broad objectives of mineral development can be categorized as follows: to ensure optimal use of available mineral resources; to earn or save foreign exchange; to create employment (directly or indirectly), often in remote or depressed areas; to promote backward and forward linkages (service and supply industries and the processing of raw materials) in order to maximize value added within the country to the extent that this is economically sound; to ensure an adequate supply of raw material inputs for industry; and to stimulate regional development, often in remote areas.

As a first step in the formulation of a national mineral policy, the country must decide whether to develop its mineral sector as a private, a public, or a mixed system. The selection should take into account not only political and social considerations but also the exploration, operating, and marketing characteristics of the sector. In practice, political concerns sometimes prevent policymakers from considering anything but political factors, regardless of long-term consequences. This can present an unfortunate obstacle to effective development of the mining sector unless there is scrupulously good management.

The nation can choose to exploit its resources in many different ways between the two absolutes of government monopoly and all-private development. In the case of state development, effectiveness will depend wholly on the ability of the state to plan, provide technical and managerial expertise, commit financial resources, and secure markets. Development under the private sector depends for its success upon a wider range of questions, given its more fragmented situation. These include the following characteristics, many of which also apply where the state holds a monopoly over mineral development:

(1) A clear definition should be provided of the terms and conditions concerning operating practices, employment, training, the environment, safety, fiscal and legal requirements, and land tenure under which a mining company — domestic or foreign, public or private — will be expected to function.

(2) To help assure maximum return to the country from a given mineral resource, the relative advantages of processing the mineral domestically and exporting the raw material should be carefully evaluated.

(3) Although expansion of domestic ownership and control of mineral resource industries is the prerogative of a country, it should take place on a clearly defined and well-publicized basis in order to maximize the country's share of the benefits to be derived from its mineral resources. The rate of such expansion will depend on the need for and extent of reliance on foreign technology, management know-how, capital, and markets.

(4) Mineral policy should include conservation measures to increase ore recovery and minimize waste. Fiscal policy can have an important influence on efficiency and the amount of wasted resources.

(5) Provision should be made for the generation, maintenance, and dissemination of geological and mineral resource data. Such information is expensive; it should be collected carefully and used to prevent the duplication of exploration activity.

(6) Mineral policy should encourage land reclamation and the elimination or control of air and water pollution. Environmental control in mining is of increasing public concern; it is generally accepted that the cost of that control is a part of the operating cost and therefore can be passed on to the consumer. Countries imposing reasonable ecological requirements are not expected to be at a disadvantage over the long term in competing for investment capital and markets.

(7) Mining can often serve as a basis for regional development, and provision may be made for it in mineral policy (through tax allowances as investment incentives, for instance), particularly

in countries with wide regional disparities. But mineral deposits inevitably become exhausted sooner or later, and the facilities and communities which came into existence because of them may cease to have a purpose. This has often led to community pressure to keep submarginal mines in operation. The results include great cost to the country, inefficient use of labor, and a decline in the overall efficiency of the industry. Mineral policy should provide for programs to ease severe dislocations and to facilitate community adjustment to changes resulting from mine closures.

(8) Because they are frequently situated in remote areas, mineral projects often have significant new infrastructure needs, such as housing and community facilities, roads, water supplies, rail lines, and ports. Mineral policy should provide guidelines for determining whether responsibility for creating the infrastructure lies with government, the private sector, or both. The government may wish to supply the infrastructure in order to maintain control over public utilities, freight costs, and social services, and to increase its share of benefits through rents on facilities. Often, however, the responsibility is shared by the private sector and the government. Project evaluation should take account of the costs of the associated infrastructure and of the catalytic effect of such infrastructure on overall regional development.

(9) Mineral policy should ensure that mining provides the host nation with an equitable share of the revenue from such activities. Furthermore, the non-renewable nature of mineral resources makes it essential that government revenues from mineral exploitation be channeled into productive investments in industry, agriculture, and the supporting infrastructure. In many cases, foreign exchange earnings from mineral exports are spent on consumer goods, mineral tax revenues are used to support the government's current budget, and alternative productive capacity or revenue-earning facilities are not created to take over when the mineral reserves are depleted.

(10) Any plan of action for effective mineral sector development requires a factual basis. An inventory of mineral resources is fundamental; hence, knowledge of the country's geology and mineral deposits is a prerequisite. One of the first tasks, therefore, is to prepare a geological map of the entire country. Systematic geological surveys should be carried out and detailed mapping undertaken. Basic documentation of geological and related data should be the responsibility of the state. Documentation of non-geological mining sector data is also required to keep abreast of activities within the country, as are data on worldwide technological trends and developments. Laboratories for the testing and analysis of rock and mineral samples are an early requirement. Research and development facilities are generally a more advanced need.

(11) In the field, in the laboratory, in the administration, and in operations, mineral resource development requires highly specialized personnel. The growth of the industry calls for a continuing flow of geologists; mining, metallurgical, mechanical, and other engineers; and financial and other technical personnel keyed to the industry. Any shortage of trained personnel will compound the difficulties of the industry. Foreign experts may be hired to train local personnel, teach in local universities, and undertake actual field work. Mining, metallurgical, and geological education may be provided in the country, preferably by a shortened university term followed by a period in the field to provide a blend of theory and practice. Scholars may be sent abroad for postgraduate and specialized studies. A technological institute can be established at far less cost than a university or college to produce in a much shorter time a larger number of semi-professionals for positions of secondary responsibility. Education in specialized fields may be provided with the assistance of multilateral and bilateral agencies.

To carry out its mineral policy, the government therefore needs to set up six or seven administrative nodes. First, a policy, planning, and administrative agency is required; this usually means a Ministry of Mines, although mining may be combined with Energy, Transport, or Economic Development. Second, an institute for geological surveys is needed — often set up as an autonomous agency, but under the direction of the Ministry of Mines. Third, educational facilities are a vital requirement. Separate departments need to be established and staffed in the local universities. Fourth, a research and development institute may be required to undertake research and provide technological assistance to the sector. Fifth, in countries where there is a strong desire to develop mining under the administration of the state, government-owned enterprise is the logical arrangement. Sixth, it is often necessary to provide channels for financing the sector. This may entail setting up a separate mining bank, or opening a "new window" at the development bank. Seventh, the government may also wish to centralize marketing functions to strengthen its role as controller and coordinator.

A National Mining Code

After the government has determined its mining policy, the policy has to be translated into a legal framework. This is commonly expressed in a mining code. If a decision has been made to allow private capital to invest in mining, the code must provide the legal framework defining relations between investors and the government. It should cover the preconditions for investment, land tenure, rights and obligations of the operator, as well as investment and tax provisions. Without a code, no legal rights can be established; without rights, who would venture to risk his capital? A bad mining code can be as damaging as no code at all, if not worse. For instance, it may grant rights without corresponding obligations concerning exploration work and at the same time prevent others from doing the work. Conversely, it may be so restrictive and impose such heavy exploration obligations without commensurate rewards as to frighten off sound investment.

Mining legislation will create a feeling of confidence in the investor if the needs and requirements of the government and the rights and obligations of the operator are set out in clear and definite terms. Confidence is not built up when laws and regulations cause needless delays to operators who have made large investments. Procedures must be laid out clearly. It is not enough to formulate and promulgate a mining code; careful preparation of regulations is necessary to eliminate ambiguity and prevent controversy. It is helpful if the investor is required to deal with only one agency, the Ministry of Mines. In one country, obtaining mining exploitation rights requires approval from no less than nine ministries and government agencies. Situations like these are frustrating to investors. If they are foreign investors, they will switch their attention to other countries; if they are domestic investors, they will interest themselves in other sectors.

Dealing with the Multinationals

Even with a well-defined mineral policy and legal code, a country relying upon foreign private capital for development of its mineral sector should pay particular attention to its policies and procedures as they apply to foreign enterprises. Therefore, the precise relationship between the multinational corporation and the host country must be clearly defined, and a mechanism must be established for coordinating and monitoring this relationship. These functions are often widely scattered among various ministries, few of which are even remotely equipped to deal with the whole range of problems that may arise or are in a position to play a central role in developing a consistent set of policies. One solution is to set up a coordinating body which can gradually develop a nucleus of people who are capable of understanding the operations of the multinational corporations and of conducting negotiations with them. Such people are very scarce in the developing countries. In countries where some form of joint participation in the decisionmaking of the multinationals is an objective, this can be done through joint ventures or through majority or minority government ownership. Both sides need to know who they are dealing with on the other side; there should be no ambiguity, and lines of communication should be drawn clearly.

Negotiations between multinationals and host governments often give rise to problems. Most developing countries lack the expertise to conduct negotiations in a way that assures protection of their interests. The results may vary from making excessive concessions (in order to buy the participation of the corporation) to a hard line which frightens away potential investors. Both extremes are equally unsatisfactory. Implementation of good projects has, in many cases, been delayed for years, at great cost to both the host country and the multinational. Negotiators on both sides must consider themselves as entering a partnership which has to be mutually satisfactory. Developing countries should not hesitate to engage experts to assist in such negotiations.

An issue that is often central to conflicts between host countries and foreign investors is the splitting of revenues. The arrangements agreed upon will depend largely on the bargaining strengths of the two parties at the time of establishing the frame of reference for the foreign company's activities. The configuration of the bargaining will vary considerably, depending on the level of development of the mineral sector, the extent to which the existence and economic value of mineral resources is known, the alternative economic opportunities available to the country, and the changing relationship between the foreign investor and the host country.

Technical Assistance: Where, What, and How?

In a majority of the developing countries there is an unquestionable need for substantial technical assistance. Assistance may be needed in such matters as assessing the country's mineral potential, defining the role that the mineral sector should play in the country's economic development, preparing and assisting in the formulation of policy for mineral sector development, preparing and advising on legislation governing the mineral sector, reviewing the administrative set-up and establishing plans for improving it, reorganizing and strengthening the institutions servicing the sector, training and educating nationals, increasing exploration activity, negotiating with multinationals and other foreign private investors, and identifying, promoting, and implementing projects in both the public and private sectors.

Even developing countries with reasonably well-developed mineral sectors can use substantial technical assistance. Many, however, refuse to recognize or accept this fact and persuade themselves that they have sufficient internal capability. Technical assistance is particularly resisted in the formulation of policies and laws, since these involve political decisions. Often, a team or commission of semi-qualified people is set up to prepare new legislation, which then becomes a political football. A better approach would be to seek full technical assistance at the outset, developing policy and legislation on strictly technical grounds and testing them within the political framework. Only then, if the issues are considered politically sensitive, should political adjustments be made.

Individuals and groups capable of providing good technical advice on policy and legal matters are scarce, although a great many claim such qualifications. This expertise can be found in bilateral and multilateral aid agencies, individual consultants, consulting firms, state agencies in the developed countries, universities, and the mining industry itself. Few single individuals are capable of providing a full complement of advice to governments, and a team approach is preferable. One may hear a lawyer, economist, mineral economist, or engineer claim to be an expert in mineral policy or legislation. Some may truly be so, but a country is often better off paying more for a team of specialists. The establishment of a mineral policy requires expertise in such subjects as development strategy and legislation, geology, exploration, mineral economics, public organization and administration, mining and mineral processing, mineral marketing, law, and taxation. Any country contemplating major policy and legislative reform should therefore seek proposals for assistance. These proposals should be scrutinized carefully before selection is made. Ironically, many countries do not even have the expertise to prepare documents inviting proposals or to evaluate those received. Aid agencies could play an important role by providing personnel for those first steps.

Another area requiring a team approach is assistance to governments in evaluating the proposals of, and negotiating concession contracts with, the multinationals. These services are better provided by public and private sector consulting groups than by individual advisors.

More specific expertise is required for strengthening the administrative ability of the government, which may include complete reorganization of the public sector. Many countries have an administrative framework but lack qualified staff and procedures. Duplication of effort and responsibilities is common, and coordination and cooperation between agencies is generally lacking. Teams of experts can sometimes assist in rectifying the problems. Often, however, the administration is too weak to monitor the activities of the sector or implement the experts' recommendations. In such cases, the team may take over some implementation functions and train nationals to carry out those tasks at a later date. Too often, a good technical assistance program is wasted because a proper course of action is not carried through to completion.

Project identification and preparation, including investment planning, is an essential function often inadequately carried out in developing countries. One often comes across situations where projects are justified solely on technical grounds, with financial and economic considerations ignored and the need for an infrastructure overlooked. Consultants and operating companies may prove the best source for assistance in this vital area.

A final word of caution. While it is understood that most expertise resides with reputable firms and agencies, countries seeking assistance would be well advised to question the qualifications of each individual expert assigned to them. For, in practice, it is individuals who provide assistance, not the agency.[4]

Notes

[1]This paper deals with non-fuel minerals only, and thus excludes such sources of energy as petroleum, natural gas, coal, and uranium.

[2]For more detail, see John S. Carman, "United Nations Mineral Exploration Activities," *Natural Resources Forum*, Vol. 1, No. 4, July 1977.

[3]For a description and critique of the fund by John S. Carman, see chapter VI of *Obstacles to Mineral Development: A Pragmatic View*, ed. Bension Varon, Pergamon Press (forthcoming).

[4]For a more detailed examination of some of the issues dealt with above, see Carman, *Obstacles to Mineral Development*, especially the chapters "Dilution of the Value of Foreign Aid with Particular Reference to Mineral Exploration," "Utilization of External Know-How in the Developing Countries," and "Obstacles to Mining Investment in the Developing Countries."

T he relationship between energy and development is straightforward. The process of economic growth is also in large part the history of the substitution of other forms of energy for crude muscle power in every type of productive activity in agriculture, industry, and the home.

Energy is the limiting factor of development. Development means a change from a situation where basic human needs for food, shelter, health, education, and employment go unsatisfied to a state where these needs are met. Any such transformation involves energy, whether it be smelting iron ore to form steel or turning a mal-nourished, impoverished child into a healthy adult capable of achieving full human potential.

If we look at development from this perspective, we see that a large part of development assistance involves the transfer of technologies pertaining to energy. The relation between energy and development becomes very clear if we consider how the use of commercial sources of energy is distributed throughout the world. Of the four billion people on the earth today, one billion, primarily in Europe and North America, use 84 per cent of the energy derived from oil, coal, natural gas, hydropower, and nuclear power. Two billion, living in the more advanced developing countries, such as India, China, Argentina, Brazil, Mexico, and Venezuela, consume about 15 per cent of the world's commercial energy. The final billion, the inhabitants of the rest of the countries of Africa, Asia, and Latin America, consume only 1 per cent.

Instructive as these statistics are, they do not give a complete picture of energy use in the rural areas of the developing countries. Because of the high cost of distributing commercial energy to rural areas, and because potential consumers in those areas are usually too poor to purchase this type of energy, rural needs are largely met through non-commercial energy sources. Firewood, animal dung, and agricultural wastes such as crop stalks, leaves, and chaff are the major resources. Accurate figures on non-commercial energy consumption are difficult to obtain because this type of energy use does

Chapter 15

Energy and Development: Fueling Change

David A. Henry

---

not lend itself to quantification, but it is thought that firewood and other non-commercial sources typically supply about 75 to 80 per cent of rural needs. Consumption varies, of course, depending on the availability of the resource, but it is obvious that rural people in the developing countries are facing an energy crisis more severe than any produced by the petroleum squeeze in the industrialized nations. The increased cost of petroleum products has led those who previously used commercial types of energy to substitute wood, charcoal, and dung. Greater demand has resulted in increased prices for the traditional energy resources available to the poor and a steady reduction in the number of trees available for firewood. The high cost of being poor has thus increased in the developing countries.

Energy policy and research must be reoriented. Energy and development are inextricably linked, and the first concern of both must be to improve the situation of the three-quarters of the world's population who are the rural poor.

Whose Energy Crisis?

"We wish we could enjoy the luxury of the energy crisis of the industrialized countries."

That was the comment of a senior government official in Ouagadougou, the capital city of the Sahelian Africa country of Upper Volta, more than 90 per cent of whose energy is provided by firewood. In Upper Volta the cost of electricity is almost twenty times higher than in Ottawa, the cost of gasoline is four times higher, and 95 per cent of the people spend 20 per cent of their daily income for the wood with which to cook their two meals a day. Of the electricity available in Upper Volta, 90 per cent is used by only 1 per cent of the population.

External aid donors, in their efforts to assist in solving problems like these, may in fact be creating more problems. This is partly because energy programs in the developing nations are designed chiefly by foreign researchers, technicians, and bureaucrats. Input from national researchers is very limited.

In Upper Volta, whose situation is typical of the situation in many developing countries, two factors impede a solution: the lack of a clear definition of the problem that the external donors are trying to solve, and a lack of understanding of the nature of the problem on the part of politicians and planners. Decisionmakers in the developing countries, and their planners and advisors, will have to spend more time deciding how they want to allocate scarce resources for the development of energy technologies and choosing those that are most cost-effective. If the developing countries themselves do not define their priorities, priorities will be established by external forces over which the developing countries have no control. A dependency situation similar to the current petroleum dependency of the industrialized countries is the likely outcome.

Yet despite the fact that non-commercial energy sources account for up to 80 or 90 per cent of total energy consumption in many countries, they are not given the level of importance they warrant. This neglect is due to a number of reasons, chief among them the fact that traditional non-commercial fuels do not appear in national accounts or in balance-of-payments statistics. Furthermore, the people making major energy decisions are not the people who depend on non-commercial fuel.

This "modern-traditional sector gap" is one of the major but less obvious dimensions of the problem in developing more effective renewable energy systems. The gap is not being closed by means of research undertaken in industrialized societies. Relatively few research and development projects have had as their primary objective the creation of technologies which are sustainable within the technical and economic capacities of traditional rural societies, and which can be manufactured with existing national capacity.

China is a notable exception. Chinese success is often attributed to that country's emphasis on local solutions for local problems. These technical solutions, however, were nurtured within a unique and very supportive social and political environment, an environment which does not necessarily exist in other countries. The following figure illustrates the position of traditional societies in the global technology scenario.

Figure 1

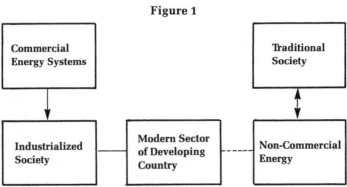

As the figure shows, research and development organizations in the industrialized countries are responsible for producing technology for industrialized societies. These R&D institutions receive an estimated $50 billion per year from public and private sources. Research and development allow the industrialized societies to produce the materials, equipment, and expertise necessary for advanced technologies, some of which have been transferred directly to the modern sector of developing societies. Good examples of these technologies are telecommunication, electric power, and transportation. Some technologies trickle through the modern sector to the higher income groups of traditional societies. The widespread distribution of transistor radios, sewing machines, and bicycles is a typical end result of this process. But traditional societies rely primarily on the empirical knowledge that they have acquired over many centuries, knowing from experience, for example, the specific varieties of wood which are best for wheel bearings on bullock carts. The flow of conventional commercial energy is similar. The average per capita consumption of energy in the OECD countries is estimated to be fifty times that of the developing countries. This means, in turn, that the traditional sector receives a proportionally smaller trickle of energy from the modern sector of the developing countries, as shown in Figure 2.

Figure 2

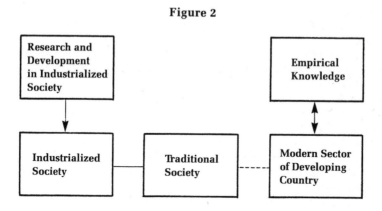

Increasing Access to Energy: The Renewables

What are the possibilities for improving the traditional sector's access to energy? Until recently, it appeared that the possibilities were limited to the gradual expansion of conventional electric and diesel systems. In short, more trickle. However, the OPEC era has begun to produce some encouraging new approaches based on renewable energy sources, such as wind, solar energy, and biomass. Renewables seem to offer the potential to provide a sustainable energy base for the rural sector, supplying energy in a form suitable to the uses made of it at a given time and place, and at a reasonable cost.

The evidence from the pre-petroleum era shows that renewable energy systems were effective on a large scale. In North America, for example, six million windmills were in operation on the farms before farmers began to use energy from fossil-fuel sources. It is estimated that in 1850 those windmills produced an energy output equivalent to the energy contained in 11.4 million tons of coal. Wind energy is now used quite extensively in Argentina and Uruguay for water pumping, and it is estimated that these systems are producing the equivalent of 300 megawatts of electricity in the two countries.

Research on wind energy systems has languished during the last seventy years, and it is only recently that new knowledge in the fields of aerodynamics and materials engineering has been applied to systems for village use. Wind energy conversion systems have been produced in the under-25 kilowatt range with a capital cost of less than $1,000 per kilowatt. This cost is competitive with the cost of conventional hydroelectric generating systems. One major research group in the United States is working on designs for systems ranging from 5 to 25 kilowatts that will cost $500 per kilowatt when mass-produced.

Other machines designed specifically for pumping water are being field-tested and promise to become available at a price well below the $1,000 per kilowatt level. The energy output obviously depends on local wind conditions, but such systems are cost-effective in some regions.

As for direct solar energy, rural and remote applications of photovoltaic cells (originally developed to generate electricity for space satellites) hold considerable promise. The technical aspects of this energy source are already well-defined, and the major task now is to reduce the price. Reputable groups in both the public and private sectors predict that the price of photovoltaic cells can be reduced to $500 per kilowatt by the end of the 1980s. This technology would be ideal for widespread application in small units of one horsepower or less. It lends itself particularly well to pumping water for irrigation by small farmers.

The "sleeping giant" in the energy arena is biomass, in the form of wood, cow dung, and other organic matter. Biomass is still labelled by most experts as non-commercial fuel and given a relatively low priority, despite the fact that it keeps fires burning in the hearths of most of the people in the developing countries. It is neglected for three main reasons. First, it is difficult for any private group to see how it can profit by research and development work on biomass energy. Second, governments and development agencies are stocked with experts and administrators who have difficulty relating to biomass energy technology. Third, there is very limited biomass research capacity in both the developed and the developing countries. This should not be taken as a justification for doing nothing. It should be taken as a clear indication that a much greater commitment of people and money must be made to exploring biomass as an energy source.

Making More From Less: Two Cases for Conservation

In addition to making greater use of renewables, the traditional sector needs to make better use of available energy. Because the largest energy-consuming activities in developing-country villages are domestic uses — primarily cooking — followed by agricultural uses, improvements in the use of energy in these activities would lead to substantial savings in energy budgets. Two simple examples illustrate the point.

In the developing countries, wood is customarily burned in open cooking fires at the extremely low conversion efficiency of 5 to 10 per cent. A number of observers of the fuelwood dilemma in the Sahelian countries and elsewhere have suggested that some simple improvements in stove construction could greatly improve efficiency, thereby reducing fuel consumption by up to one half. The results would be enhanced preservation of forest resources and reductions in the amount of household income spent on fuel. The pressures to implement some such conservation measures are increasing. A recent study in Kenya, for example, predicts that by the mid-1990s the demand for fuelwood will be from one to two and a half times the sustainable production.

The second largest energy-consuming activity in the developing countries is agriculture. About 82 per cent of the farms are smaller than eleven acres. Human and animal labor account for almost the entire energy input on these smaller farms, and the handtools and equipment used on most of them are woefully inefficient. A study in India, for example, estimated that about one third of the draft energy of bullocks is lost to friction through poor design of carts and plows.

Although the savings that could be obtained by more efficient use of human and animal energy could be substantial and would have an immediate impact, little research has been directed toward these areas.

Tapping Human Resources

One of the challenges that confronts those concerned with the energy crisis in the traditional sector is the lack of knowledge about the local social and economic dimensions of the problem. This calls for some well-defined research by developing country researchers which, in addition to producing a clearer understanding of the problem, would develop an indigenous capacity for planning and implementing research programs in the developing countries.

One example of a research program in which such an approach has proven worthwhile is the Southeast Asia Program for Research Awards in Population (SEAPRAP). This program provides funds to graduate students in six Asian countries to enable them to do field research in a rural area of their own country.

The SEAPRAP program was designed to ensure that the students had good institutional support and that potential users of the information (as well as potential employers, primarily government agencies) were brought into the dialogue. Students found a receptive audience when they completed their research, and the program had a number of additional advantages. It was low in cost, simple to administer, and attracted some of the brightest students. It put student researchers in direct contact with the traditional society of the country and at the same time linked them with fellow researchers in other countries, thus providing a very useful opportunity to compare notes on experience and research results.

Serious consideration should be given to applying such a model to the study of renewable energy sources. A review of the existing documentation reveals that the countries with the most serious energy problems now have to rely on information and research produced by foreign scientists, some of which is of questionable value.

Strengthening the capacity of the developing countries to direct energy research and choose their own technologies could also counter the field's heavy domination by the scientists, engineers, and technicians who design energy systems. These "hardware" people have a substantial head start on the "software" people—economists, sociologists, and agronomists. Until the latter assume a much more dynamic role, the interests of the scientists and technologists will continue to dictate the future. One of the obstacles that social scientists must overcome is their reluctance to get involved in some of the hard technical issues.

Technology is a complex blend of technical, social, economic, and political issues. If social scientists expect to take an active role in shaping future energy systems, they will have to get involved in the energy technology marketplace by taking the risks involved in determining the allocation of future energy resources. If they do not, they will find themselves confined to a lesser role: deskbound chroniclers of what went wrong!

Some of the major political decisions in both developed and developing countries in the next two decades will focus on the allocation of resources for the acquisition of energy technology systems. Some major errors will be made, no doubt, but those errors can be minimized if there is the capacity and the will to undertake a rigorous analysis of future policy options.

Research Strategies Powered by People

If research on renewable energy sources for developing countries is going to produce results that are useful to people in the traditional sector, great care will have to be taken to ensure the active participation of those people in the research. At the present time the people in traditional societies are the unheard voices of the world. They are, however, the people most affected by decisions taken in their name.

The development and application of new energy technologies will demand careful attention to non-technical issues, which often tend to get overlooked in the rush to get on with the job. Elementary as this fact may seem, there is already growing evidence in some regions that a particular technological solution may have negative effects that completely cancel out the desired benefits.

The proliferation of small diesel irrigation pumps in the developing countries, for example, is creating a serious imbalance in groundwater systems. Farmers are pumping water faster than it is recharged by rainfall. Wells have to be constantly deepened, and in many instances the water level has already fallen below the reach of smaller farmers who irrigate with manually powered systems. Meanwhile, the larger farmers buy more land and bigger engines and dig deeper wells. As a result, smaller farmers become landless laborers.

At some point in the discussion of energy sources the issue of "appropriate technology" is bound to arise. This term produces some fairly strong negative reactions from people in both developed and developing countries. The most effective method of dealing with this issue is to ask, on a case-by-case basis, if the energy technology matches the particular need. Does the technology dictate use, or serve it? Appropriateness will also, in the final analysis, depend on whether the technology can survive in the national or local economy on its own merits, without continuing external support.

If any significant progress is to be made in improving the use of renewable sources of energy, a concept of manageable increments will have to be applied. Given the tendency of people to fear the unknown, it will be necessary to create a climate of confidence in new technologies. This can only be done by proving — with empirical evidence — that there is a better system, technique, or machine.

A more effective system for supporting local industries and entrepreneurs will be required to enable the hardware of many of the renewable energy technologies to reach the rural marketplace. There are already some encouraging initiatives in industrial cooperation, but much more must be done to reinforce the capacity of infant industries to move into this new field.

To meet the needs of traditional societies it will also be necessary to develop researchers with a broader range of skills which will enable them to bridge the gap between the modern and the traditional sectors. These researchers will have to be aware that the results of their research will be judged primarily by the people it is designed to serve. It is unlikely that this level of awareness will be developed by removing people from the developing countries to pursue research in the industrialized countries.

Energy research for development will require the establishment of a number of new linkages that can draw upon knowledge and skills from a number of sectors. It will also require a commitment from bilateral and multilateral donors to a reorientation of their policies and priorities. Without this commitment, it is illusory to speak of development. Technology is the application of science. Whether a new generation of technology will be used to improve the lives of the people in the developing countries will depend largely on the ability of politicians and scientists to establish effective mechanisms. Politicians are the link between people and their problems, and the scientific community. The rate of application of new technology in the energy field will be determined by their initiative and leadership.

everal worldwide issues involving food and nutrition urgently require greater attention from natural and social scientists in all countries if there is to be adequate progress in global development during the last two decades of this century.

One major problem is getting the international economic order, of which food trade is such a major component, working well again — this time with the objective of global efficiency, so that it also effectively enhances the development of the poorer countries. The international systems that worked so well for the industrial countries in the 1950s and 1960s have been faltering and breaking down on many fronts in the 1970s, as evidenced by periodic crises in food and energy supply and distribution, economic inflation, recession and stagflation, and environmental concerns. Continuation of the present world systems could mean a loss of trillions of dollars annually in global output by the end of this century. Building a new, more efficient, world economic order is the only alternative to continuing stagflation in the developed countries of the Northern hemisphere and ever-increasing deprivation in the poorer countries of the South.

Another central issue relates to the contribution that science and technology can make to hastening the elimination of absolute poverty and its manifestations, hunger and malnutrition, before the end of this century in the context of advancing self-reliant economic growth. If in the immediate future most developing countries were to apply policies such as those which have already succeeded in poor countries such as Sri Lanka and South Korea, and to some extent in China, then by the year 2000, there could be at least 10 million fewer deaths each year than are currently projected by the United Nations, and an even larger number of births could be avoided.

There is a tendency to think of the objective of "mobilizing science and technology for development" as relating primarily to increasing *production* and to regard it as a primary preserve of the natural sciences and their technical application. It is now becoming clear, however, that major input from the *social* sciences is equally neces-

An International Challenge: Science and Technology for Managing the World Food Problem

James P. Grant

sary. If the world's food supply were to increase even by 50 per cent over the next five years, this increase alone would not greatly affect the existing patterns of human deprivation. What is also needed are changes in modes of production and patterns of distribution. World hunger in our times is less a problem of production than a consequence of the lack of purchasing power among the growing numbers of unemployed and underemployed in the developing countries. This is amply illustrated today as India, the European Economic Community, and the United States wrestle with the problem of large food surpluses while the number of hungry and malnourished—some 500 million people — remains virtually the same, if it has not in fact increased. We are learning, furthermore, that some methods of increasing food production, such as large-scale mechanization of farms, can exacerbate the conditions that foster poverty by increasing the numbers of the underemployed and the landless.

A working world food system requires more than significant increases in production. It also requires the development of a world food reserve system to prevent a repetition of the experience of the early 1970s, when a 3 per cent drop in food grain production led to a 250 per cent increase in price. According to a U.S. Federal Reserve study, rising food prices in 1973-74 were as responsible for global inflation as were rising oil costs. The skyrocketing costs of food, fuel, and fertilizer at that time graphically illustrated the vulnerability of the poorer developing countries, and poor people everywhere, to external disruptions of their food supplies.

The events of those years forced a major reassessment of more than twenty years of experience in international development cooperation. The result of this reassessment is growing recognition that only a rural development strategy — a strategy based on labor-intensive agriculture and involving entire rural populations in productive work — can hope to meet the food needs and development aspirations of most of the developing countries while holding down food costs in the developed nations.

The importance of such a strategy was reinforced by the findings of the two-year study of the world food and nutrition situation conducted under the auspices of the U.S. National Academy of Sciences (NAS) and published in 1977. A principal conclusion of the study is that there must be far greater international cooperation on agricultural research, development, and investment to increase food production in developing countries if the future food needs of those populations are to be met and if food producers and consumers in the developed countries are to avoid sharply rising food production costs which would contribute significantly to inflationary pressures. Given the necessary political will in the industrial democracies and in the developing countries, it should be possible to double food production and per capita incomes in the developing countries *by the end of this century*, thus overcoming the worst aspects of hunger and malnutrition as manifested in high infant mortality rates and low life expectancy.

Problems in the World Food System

The Inflationary Impact of Rising Agricultural Production Costs in Developed Countries

Over the past quarter century, a growing imbalance has emerged in food production and consumption. The developing countries, which in 1950 were virtually self-sufficient in food production, were by 1970 importing between 15 and 20 million tons of grain, half of it in the form of food aid. By 1975 the grain imports of those countries had reached 45 million tons. The International Food Policy Research Institute projects a tripling of grain imports to between 120 and 145 million tons or more per year by 1990 unless there is fundamental improvement in the capacity of the chronic food-deficit countries to produce more food.

Projections of this magnitude have many adverse implications for the developing countries. Rising imports will require increasing amounts of scarce foreign exchange and will mean more unemployment and underemployment in rural areas at a time when those are already serious problems in most developing countries. Meanwhile, as the NAS study noted, it will become increasingly difficult for the United States and other developed countries to play as important a role in world food production as they have in the past. Although the NAS study cites no specific figures, increases in production costs could range from 50 to 100 per cent or more within a decade if current production patterns continue. A comparable cost increase could occur in the 1990s. The inflationary potential of such increases would be substantial. The adverse consequences of rising food production costs are particularly serious at a time when the weight of the evidence indicates that inflationary pressures will serve as the principal impediment to OECD growth policies in the 1980s and beyond.

There are two major reasons why production costs can be expected to rise precipitously. First, per hectare yields of major crops have dropped in the United States since 1973-74. This contradicted the expectations of most observers, who had assumed that the pattern of ever-increasing yields that had prevailed since World War II would continue. Until there is another generation of basic research to draw on—which is at least a decade or more in the future—rising yields per hectare in the United States and most other developed countries will only be possible through more intensive production efforts, such as greater use of marginal agricultural land and increased applications of fertilizers. These efforts will inevitably drive production costs upward. The NAS study indicated that fertilizer costs will increase sharply in the years ahead because of at least three factors: the rising cost of raw materials from which to make fertilizer as natural gas and oil become scarcer and the difficulty of mining phosphate rock increases, sharp rises in the price of facilities for producing nitrogen and phosphate fertilizers, and rapidly rising costs for transporting and distributing fertilizer. The cost of producing urea fertilizer in the industrial countries, for example, will probably at least double by 1990 from a base cost of about $115 a ton in 1978 (in constant 1978 dollars).[2]

The second factor pushing grain production costs upward is the rising demand in the industrialized countries. Demand for grains in the developed countries is expected to reach 846 million tons in 1990, an increase of more than 200 million tons over 1970. The projected increase is nearly equivalent to all current grain production in the United States. Meanwhile, total grain demand in the developing countries in 1990 is expected to be more than it was in 1970. As indicated earlier, 100 million tons or more of this increase will have to be imported from the developed countries, principally the United States, if past trend lines prevail. (This change in yield and cost trends for grain in the developed countries is occurring at the same time that the yield trends for food production from the seas and fresh water sources have flattened out. No major relief in food prices can be expected from this front.)

The current under-production in the developing areas, therefore, is serious not only for them but also for the developed countries, for reasons that most developed country consumers do not yet comprehend — namely, that developed country production is already running into trouble on the cost front.

The Food Production Potential of the Developing Countries

By now it is generally agreed that the answer to the need for increased food production lies primarily in increasing production within the food-deficit developing countries if substantially higher world food prices are to be avoided in the late 1980s. South Asia, in particular, could double or even triple its food production at current international price levels if the financial, organizational, and applied research obstacles to greater use of its grossly underutilized water, labor, and other resources could be overcome.

Yields per acre in India, for example, are approximately 1,000 pounds, compared to 3,000-4,000 pounds in the more advanced countries. India has about the same overall quality of natural environment — land, water resources, temperature, etc. — as the United States; it also has roughly the same arable acreage. Twenty per cent of its land is already under irrigation (in comparison to 10 per cent in the United States), and this could easily be doubled in the 1980s—at a time when worldwide additions to irrigated acreage are expected to slow sharply as compared to the past twenty-five years. India, therefore, could be producing at least three times more grain per acre than it is now doing, *at present cost levels*, if it could overcome certain problems of organization, finance, and applied research. This would increase its total output from the current level of 120 million tons of grain to more than 300 million tons (compared to a present U.S. level of 250-260 million tons). Such an increased level of output at current cost levels would have a profound effect on world prices—and fertilizer demand — ten to twenty years hence.

Some other regions in Asia already have made remarkable progress. South Korea and Taiwan, for example, now produce as much grain per acre as the United States.

In short, the comparative advantage in terms of dollars and cents for increasing agricultural production in the 1980s and 1990s clearly rests with the developing countries. It would be to the advantage of the developed as well as the developing countries if by the year 2000 the developing countries were growing 120 to 140 million tons more grain each year than is likely under current conditions. To do so, however, will require major institutional and structural changes as well as major capital investments and increased research.

Overcoming Mass Hunger and Absolute Poverty While Promoting Self-Reliant Growth

In 1974 at the World Food Conference in Rome, the U.S. Secretary of State proposed that the world adopt the objective that within a decade no one would go to bed hungry. The Conference adopted that objective, but without a set time frame. It is now clear that achievement of that objective, even by the end of this century, is an ambitious goal and attainable only through major strides in science and technology as well as through greater political will. The principal concern should be how to combine equity and growth, preferably in such a way that equity accelerates growth. Key issues to be addressed include the following:

1. *Directing basic research toward the poor majority.* Many of the research advances of recent years, such as new grain strains and pesticides, have tended to favor the relatively more affluent farmer. The poor farmer has difficulty in securing the capital, the land, and the knowledge—and taking the risks—required to benefit from these

scientific advances. This explains the claim sometimes heard that "the green revolution is running red" in certain areas. New grain strains have promoted social discontent as larger farmers, who are in a better position to take advantage of new technology, squeeze out tenants and small farmers. Research in the future should concentrate far more on meeting the needs of the small producer. If scientists, for example, were able to develop grain strains that were nitrogen-fixing —as are soybeans and alfalfa—the need for costly chemical means of restoring the soil's fertility would be reduced. This, in turn, would lessen the capital needs and risks that present such difficulties for small farmers. Similarly, as pest-resistant strains of grain are developed, the small farmer will have less need to buy pesticides. It will also reduce the small farmer's need to secure the cooperation of the 50 to 100 farmers around him as a precondition to effective use of pesticides. (This cooperation must be obtained at the present time because of pest migrations.)

Very little—probably less than 1 per cent—of the world's research budget is now spent on needs like these, despite their importance to the smallholders who till most of the acreage of the developing countries and who represent so large a percentage of humanity. Scores of examples analogous to the above can be cited. Much of India's energy, for example, comes from traditional agricultural sources, notably firewood and dung, which are relatively accessible to the 80 per cent of the population living in rural areas. Only insignificant amounts of research have been devoted to increasing the output from these traditional renewable sources—even though it is now apparent that such sources have great promise.

The same situation has prevailed in health. One hundred times more research has been devoted to diseases that are prevalent in the rich industrial nations (such as cancer and heart disease) than to greatly neglected, environment-related diseases of the developing countries. Schistosomiasis, malaria, river blindness, and diarrhea afflict thousands of the poor in the developing countries, greatly diminishing their contribution to production for their own as well as general consumption needs.

Clearly, future research in health and agriculture must be heavily weighted toward solving the problems besetting poorer populations. Involvement of social scientists is also needed to determine how the benefits of advanced research might be extended more effectively to the poor. Improved credit mechanisms, for example, could make high-yielding grain varieties more accessible to poor farmers.

2. *Accelerating the development and acceptance of appropriate technology.* Belatedly, we have learned that in the people-plentiful and land- and capital-scarce developing countries, many small farms —if effectively assisted with appropriate technology, credit, low-cost health care, and educational systems — can be far more labor-intensive, productive and cost-effective, as well as far more conducive to maintaining lower birth rates, than large farms or agribusinesses. The criteria for choosing technology should be whether it re-

sponds directly to the fulfillment of basic needs, enhances local values, and increases self-reliance by using local materials and people.

A major challenge is bringing more energy to villages and farms in Asia, Africa, and Latin America. Extending electrical grids to cover most developing countries will take a very long time and will be extremely costly. Such grids—if based on oil or gas—would become obsolete shortly after the turn of the century, if not before. Under what circumstances, therefore, is it possible to convert local renewable sources of energy—sun, wind, and agricultural waste—into electrical or mechanical energy that can help perform time-consuming tasks, such as cooking foods and pumping water? Can greater advantage be taken of the fact that most of the developing countries are in warmer climates and receive more hours of sunlight? For the answers to what is already technically possible and what further technology is required, more serious and extensive study is needed. Such technology, far from being "second-class," as some allege, would constitute the first application of new energy solutions upon which we must all one day rely. They also could affect significantly the price of oil for all countries in the 1990s.

Related to this is the question of the most effective mechanisms of international cooperation for devising approaches to low-cost energy systems. There are some indications that small, non-governmental organizations have a comparative advantage in developing innovative techniques. More effective means need to be found to support their pioneering work.

3. *Conducting comparative studies of development experience.* Many different approaches to economic development in the developing countries have been advanced in the post-World War II era. There is a major need for comparative studies evaluating the successes and failures of different countries and regions in rural development. The opportunity to learn from comparative studies and transfer that knowledge into practice has rarely been utilized. What can be learned from the Chinese experience, which seems to have combined increased production with the meeting of basic material needs? How is it that Sri Lanka, with a per capita income similar to that of India and lower than China's can have a Physical Quality of Life Index (PQLI)[1] of 83 — better than that of China (PQLI 71), vastly better than India's (PQLI 42), and comparable to that of the United States in 1940 (PQLI 83)? How is it that South Korea in the 1960s and 1970s has simultaneously managed to achieve domestic growth rates of 9-10 per cent annually, to meet basic human needs effectively (PQLI 82), and to narrow dramatically its regional income disparities?

4. *Designing better international mechanisms for mutual cooperation for improving food production and nutrition.* Reasonably effective mechanisms of international cooperation now exist with respect to agricultural technology. The internationally supported research centers (such as the International Rice Research Institute and the Consultative Group on International Agricultural Research) and

the overarching international food organizations (the World Food Council and the U.N. Food and Agricultural Organization) provide an impressive international cooperative research network for increasing food production. As yet, however, similar international institutions do not exist to deal with international research and development needs relating to the distribution of food, energy, or health. Improved cooperative mechanisms are necessary in all these areas to reach worldwide goals by the year 2000.

Conclusion

As the world community moves forward in supporting increased use of science and technology for development, far greater emphasis needs to be given to designing and implementing approaches and strategies that give priority to enhancing the condition of those people and countries experiencing the greatest need. Evidence is growing that such strategies can be applied so as to lower the rate of inflation in both North and South and accelerate progress for all.

Notes

[1]This figure is based on data from E. A. Harre, Owen W. Livingston, and John T. Shields, World Fertilizer Market Review and Outlook (Muscle Shoals, Alabama: National Fertilizer Development Center, Tennessee Valley Authority, 1974), p. 27.

[2]The PQLI index, developed by the Overseas Development Council, summarizes many aspects of well-being. It is a composite index that combines three indicators — infant mortality, life expectancy at age one, and literacy. Each of the three component indicators is indexed on a scale of 0 to 100; the PQLI index is calculated by averaging the three indices giving equal weight to each. See Morris D. Morris, Measuring the Condition of the World's Poor: The Physical Quality of Life Index (Pergamon Press for the Overseas Development Council, June 1979).

T he prolonged drought which afflicted the Sahelian countries of West Africa from 1968 to 1973 called worldwide attention to the precarious situation in that region. During that period, cereal harvests fell by one-third of their normal level and the number of herd cattle declined in some areas by as much as one-half or more. The drought sparked an awareness of the following: (a) such ecological problems as diminishing soil fertility, overgrazing, desert encroachment, and deforestation; (b) the economic imbalance resulting from a decline in the earnings of the peasant population, widening the already substantial income differential between the rural and urban populations; (c) the need for a fresh development policy taking account of the positive features of the Sahel as well as its fragility; (d) the need for a high degree of consistency between the activities undertaken and the need to make full allowance for all the ecological, economic, and social effects of the projects contemplated; and (e) the need to strengthen international aid to the Sahel and, above all, to improve its implementation in a consistent and uninterrupted manner over a long period of time.

The Purpose of the Club du Sahel

In 1973 the Sahelian countries affected by the drought — Mauritania, Senegal, Mali, Upper Volta, Niger, and Chad—saw that their problems were identical and that they had to combine their efforts in order to contend with the difficulties they were facing. Accordingly, they set up the Permanent Interstate Committee for Drought Control in the Sahel (CILSS). They were subsequently joined by the Cape Verde Islands and Gambia.

In 1976 the governments of industrialized countries and official development agencies interested in the Sahel joined with the CILSS member countries in forming the Club du Sahel, a flexible association enjoying the support and administrative backing of the Organization for Economic Cooperation and Development (OECD). The purpose of

Chapter 17

Scientific and Technological Cooperation: The Experience of the Club du Sahel

Jacques Giri

the Club is to create the conditions for cooperation among all of its members in order to spare the population of the Sahel from the disastrous consequences of another prolonged drought and enable it to emerge from its current state of underdevelopment and dependence. The working approach is a novel one, however, and there are several good reasons for taking a closer look at it:

(a) The programming involves close collaboration among Sahelian, European, and North American experts. The idea of a concerted approach is not so common that it does not warrant reemphasis. Solutions arrived at jointly have much more chance of being accepted and applied by the parties concerned than solutions presented as prescriptions.

(b) The programming is being done in the light of limited but precisely defined objectives, selected with the aim of meeting essential human needs and approved by the political authorities of the Sahel. Particular attention has been paid to ensuring the food self-sufficiency of the Sahelian countries. This general objective has been broken down into specific targets for the amounts of cereals, meat, fish, and other foodstuffs to be produced by the years 1990 and 2000. The next step is to define a series of actions which will allow those targets to be achieved.

(c) The programming has also been done with due regard to a number of self-imposed constraints, such as the need for a stable ecosystem, a more equitable income distribution between rural and urban populations, and the maintenance of a high rate of employment in rural areas.

(d) Particular importance has been attached to the need for consistency between the activities recommended. For this purpose, nine interlocking teams were set up. Four of these were so-called "vertical" teams covering the main production sectors, i.e., rain-fed crops, irri-

*Revised version of a paper presented at an OECD workshop on Scientific and Technological Cooperation with Developing Countries, April 1978. Reprinted with the permission of the Club du Sahel.

gated crops, livestock, and fisheries. The other five were so-called "horizontal" teams covering human resources, the adaptation of technology, ecology and environment, policy on prices, marketing, and storage, and transport and infrastructure. The task of the vertical teams was to draw up production programs, which were — then examined — or are still in the process of being examined — by the horizontal teams. Each project has, therefore, been examined from several different points of view so that a coherent program can be built up by successive approximations. In addition, a synthesis group has monitored the consistency of the work done by the various teams.

Development of the Sahel: The Need for Fundamental Change

One of the essential points of the strategy drawn up by the Club du Sahel is the need to bring about, before the end of the century, a far-reaching change in the system of plant and animal production. This new system of production will have to comply with a number of conditions.

While increasing land productivity, it will have to safeguard the often fragile soil. Fertility can no longer be maintained solely by the traditional method of leaving the land fallow for long periods. The use of natural or artificial fertilizers will become an essential requirement throughout the entire region.

At the same time that land productivity is increased, a high level of employment in rural areas will have to be maintained. Industry is in its infancy all over the Sahel and, regardless of the rate at which the Sahelian countries are industrialized, it will probably still be on a modest scale by the end of the century. Thus, the bulk of the population will still have to find employment in agriculture or stockraising. This will preclude any widespread use of capital-intensive techniques that employ a limited labor force in a system of mechanized farming. Increased productivity must be obtained by greater use of animal traction and improved farming with hand tools.

The new system of food production will have to supply, in both quantity and quality, not only enough food to feed the population better but also a sufficient volume of exportable products to enable the Sahelian countries to pay for such imports as fuel oil, fertilizer, manufactured goods, and so forth.

The new system of food production will also have to be made less vulnerable to drought by increasing the proportion of irrigated farming land and by adopting such methods as the dissemination of cereal varieties that are capable of ripening quickly in the course of a short rainy season.

It is difficult to imagine that this new system of production can replace the old one without changes in other aspects of society. Past experience seems to point to the fact that rural development schemes restricted to changes in production techniques may not be very successful and may even be complete failures. Production techniques are closely intertwined with other aspects of the traditional socio-cultural system. These social-cultural elements must also evolve if the population of the Sahel is to be able to increase food production while at the same time enjoying improved living standards.

Acquiring a Better Knowledge of the Sahel's Potential Productivity

Despite the considerable work done in the past, especially by such French institutions as the Office de la Recherche Scientifique et Technique Outre-Mer (ORSTROM) and the Bureau de Recherches Geologiques et Minieres (BRGM), the potential productive capability of the Sahel is still insufficiently known. In the case of those areas in which the ecosystem is particularly precarious, such as the nomadic area of the sub-Sahara, it is necessary to know what the limits of the land's capability are so as not to over-exploit them and thereby create an irremediable imbalance.

A better understanding of the Sahel's capabilities will require:

(a) *A better knowledge of soils.* This is needed to determine which lands are best suited for farming and grazing, the conditions for maintaining fertility in cultivated areas, and the possibilities for re-newing the natural vegetation in uncultivated areas.

(b) A *better knowledge of water resources.* Despite the plentiful data already collected on aquifers, better knowledge is required of their potential use for watering cattle, for meeting human needs, and for irrigating crops. Likewise, the major river basins are not yet known well enough. For example, there is no overall model combining all the data available on the River Niger so as to make full use of its possibilities for irrigation, navigation, and energy production.

(c) A *better knowledge of weather forecasting.* It is clear that better weather forecasting could be particularly useful in the Sahel. Basic data on meteorology would be very useful in helping the region to adapt to new sources of energy.

(d) A *better knowledge of the fishery potential.* The Club's studies have shown the importance of sea and inland fisheries in the Sahel. It is not yet known, however, whether these resources could supply the population with as much protein as livestock farming and also yield large exportable surpluses.

(e) A *better knowledge of mining resources.* West Africa is rich in natural phosphates, which could play an important part in maintaining soil fertility.

Acquiring a Better Knowledge of Demands and Constraints

Attempts to develop the Sahel continue to be hampered by the lack of basic data on such matters as current production, population, consumption of food, and elasticity of demand. However, it is also important to obtain a better knowledge of the existing socio-cultural systems. One must have this knowledge in order to contract integrated development projects which take into account all the technical, economic, social, and cultural factors.

Developing and Implementing New Production Systems

Developing new production systems is clearly the key to future progress in the Sahel. But certain problems are bound to arise, depending on the region.

In the least watered part of the Sahel, which borders the Sahara and has traditionally been used for stockraising, a new ecological balance must be found. This will mean combining measures for preserving or restoring fragile areas. There is a need to restore surface vegetation by reforestation, temporarily banning controlled brush fires, erecting wind-breaks and fire-breaks, and so on. Farming methods which use natural manure and which work the soil without causing erosion must be developed. And techniques must be devised which suit the local potential for livestock production, including the breeding and rearing of animals in the better watered areas.

In the areas further to the south, where a larger amount of annual rainfall makes the land more conducive to agriculture, a combination of crop farming and stockraising is required. This has not existed before, but it would make possible more intensive livestock farming by providing animals with fodder crops or edible residues of crops to add to their consumption of natural fodder. It would also make possible more intensive agriculture by providing animal traction for working the soil and by improving soil fertility through the use of organic manure and the growing of pulses for fodder. The latter are nitrogen-fixing plants.

In the areas not now farmed, i.e., the "new lands" deserted either because of endemic diseases now being eradicated or for historical reasons, advantage should be taken of the current movement of people to these areas by introducing production systems suited to their potentials.

In each of these areas of the Sahel it will be necessary to select the combination of techniques, tools, and vegetable or animal varieties that will increase the productivity of the land and yet be acceptable to the populace. What is required, therefore, is multidisciplinary research that closely combines technology, economics, and sociology. A number of research studies and experiments have already been completed, including those undertaken by the Institut de Recherches Agronomiques Tropicales et des Cultures Vivrieres (IRAT). Until now, however, most of the research and experimentation was concentrated more on cash crops than on food crops. As the drought showed, further research activities must concentrate above all on food crops.

Reducing Vulnerability to Drought

Reducing the Sahel's vulnerability to drought can be done by spreading the use of new plant varieties with short growing cycles which are less sensitive to erratic rainfall, by finding a new balance between rain-fed crops and irrigated crops, and by developing grain storage methods that are more efficient and cheaper than the traditional ones.

Protecting Plants, Animals, and Harvests

It will be of no avail to intensify food production in the Sahel unless crops, herds and harvests are safeguarded at the same time. Measures for protecting them will prove to be all the more valuable because programs for intensified farming will almost inevitably lead to increased attacks by birds, rodents, insects, and plant diseases.

It will, therefore, be necessary to make a more thorough study of the factors which govern bird, rodent, and insect life and plant diseases in various ecological conditions and to make arrangements at the regional level for observing and controlling them. Arrangements for safeguarding the health of the herds and for finding the most suitable methods of storing harvests are also a vital necessity.

Improving Living Conditions

It is not sufficient, however, simply to increase food production. One must also improve the living conditions of the populations of the Sahel. The technology team has explored two matters of particular interest.

The first of these concerns forms of energy. In rural areas, firewood supplies most of the heat and energy. This has led to increasing deforestation. It is therefore very desirable to replace the existing system for producing energy with a more suitable one that would save wood and thereby assist reforestation while making it possible to satisfy heavier and more varied demands for energy, e.g., for lighting, pumping water, and refrigeration.

Energy requirements in the rural areas of the Sahel have special (and little known) peculiarities. The conventional sources of energy, such as gas and oil, are prohibitively expensive. Thus, it would be most appropriate to develop a system largely based on the use of "new" sources of energy which can be found locally, such as solar energy, wind power, and vegetable wastes. This calls for much more research and a bigger effort to adapt appropriate technology.

The second matter relating to living conditions is the processing and handling of food products. Today, these operations utilize considerable manpower that could be used for more productive tasks. The development of better techniques for saving time and labor and for preserving food (e.g., stabilization of millet flour) would certainly have an important impact on village life in the Sahel.

Interdependence in Sahelian Development

The preceding list of all the factors that should be combined to develop a new production system in the Sahel does not, of course, claim to be exhaustive, nor should it be regarded as a group of factors which operate independently. All these factors are closely interlocking. Crop-growing techniques, for example, cannot be studied independently of livestock farming requirements, and the latter, in turn, are connected with the utilization of animal waste, either as manure, for producing energy, or for other purposes.

Furthermore, the question of whether one should straightway apply highly sophisticated techniques to the development of the Sahel or use less developed and intermediate techniques instead is irrelevant. The need is for an optimum mix of technologies. The use of advanced techniques, such as remote sensing and its refinements (use of multispectral scanners), can be of outstanding service by tracing changes in land fertility and land use. Additionally, photovoltaic batteries may prove to be especially well-suited to the Sahel's requirements because of the area's abundant solar energy.

At the same time, improvements of a much simpler nature also are important. The use of hearths instead of open fires for cooking could save large quantities of firewood. Likewise, improvements in manual farming techniques or the introduction of animal traction could be made without advanced technological means. Generally speaking, the traditional techniques born of long experience should not all be given up. Some can be kept or improved upon or otherwise combined in some manner with newer techniques. The point is to succeed in developing a new body of techniques. The key then is to establish a better balance between man and nature in the Sahel. To this end all means might be regarded as justified.

The Role of the Sahelians

It is, of course, for those mainly concerned—the Sahelians themselves —to assume responsibility for choosing this new production system and to play a large part in developing it. Accordingly, the Club's program provides for a number of projects for increasing the ability of the Sahel countries to collect data, conduct research, and carry out necessary experiments. These projects could take the form of:

(a) *Setting up national cells for improving knowledge of the Sahel's potential*, including a knowledge of the ecology of the pastoral areas, the fishery potential, the possibilities of new lands, etc. In this connection it is planned to build up data bases.

(b) *Improving programming ability*. The lack of properly worked out projects and of programming ability in the Sahel has been stressed by all the Club's teams, both vertical and horizontal. For example, reforestation is held up by lack of enough projects, and what can be done in the next few years will not suffice to stop deforestation but only to slow it down. Deforestation, with all its damaging consequences, will continue for ten or fifteen years. An increased capacity for planning and programming new projects is essential if the proposed change in the production system is to be made effective by the end of the century.

(c) *Pilot projects for trying out new production systems in a number of sectors* — projects combining crop farming, forestry, and animal husbandry in parts of the Sahel now inhabited by nomads; projects combining crop farming and livestock farming; and projects for farming new land. After exchanges of views between Sahelian and non-Sahelian specialists, these projects should become the laboratories for developing the Sahel of tomorrow.

(d) *Training schemes*. All this research, experimentation, and information work can only be done if there are trained Sahelians to do it. They will be required at all levels, from researchers and remote sensing specialists to pioneers who will gradually introduce the new techniques into the main agricultural communities.

Although there are a number of research centers in the Sahel which are already working on most of the main problems, they vary widely in their effectiveness. Some lack resources or staff. Most of them are too isolated and have little or no connection with each other and with the corresponding main research centers in the industrialized countries or in other developing countries. In the case of solar energy, for example, there are four research centers working on this subject in the Sahel, often with interesting results despite their very modest resources, but without coordination between them and with little connection with world research.

A priority requirement is to improve their effectiveness, but to do this one must begin by strengthening their connections with one another and with the outside world. Accordingly, the member countries of the CILSS are now setting up an Institute of the Sahel, mainly as an instrument for coordinating research and training in the countries concerned.

The initial program for the Institute includes setting up a network of scientific and technical documentation so as to circulate information and break down the isolation of the Sahelian research centers. The Institute also will set up a planning and forecasting unit covering the social sciences, sociology, economics, and demography to collect data and carry out research of interest to all of the Sahel.

The Role of the International Donor Community

While the Sahelians should take in hand and develop their research work, it is also clear that this work will bear little fruit, at least in the short and medium term, unless it is well-supported by the international donor community. What can the latter do?

(a) It can participate in financing the vast amount of research, development, experimentation, and extension work so required. The economies of the Sahelian countries are as a whole much too fragile to enable them to allocate the large resources, especially in foreign exchange, needed for financing such an effort. This situation may well continue for a number of years to come.

(b) It can provide research workers, experimenters, and experts who would cooperate with their Sahelian colleagues in making this effort successful. Despite the rapid development of higher education and technology in the last decade, the number of well-trained Sahelian experts is still insufficient to undertake much additional research work. Thus external assistance is necessary, at least in the short and medium term.

(c) It can participate in giving theoretical and practical training to Sahelian research workers and experts in the universities and laboratories, and also in the field.

(d) It can circulate information to enable the scientific and technical advances which can be used in developing the new Sahelian production system to be applied quickly and on terms acceptable to the Sahel States (problem of patents and licenses).

(e) It can draw the attention of scientific and technical circles in the developed countries, including universities, research centers, and industry, to the special conditions of the Sahel in order to arouse interest in applying new techniques or adapting existing techniques for solving the Sahel's problems. It is estimated that 98 per cent of the R&D in the world has been done in the industrialized countries for their own sake. A slight reorientation of this mass of research work could have a considerable impact on solving the Sahel's problems.

The First Practical Achievements

After the Sahelian authorities adopted the so-called "first generation" program in Ottawa in May-June 1977, the secretariats of the Club and the CILSS turned their attention to the actual implementation of this program. Several meetings with financing institutions were arranged in the second half of 1977 to deal with specific problems. The first meetings dealt with crop and harvest protection, the rehabilitation and development of irrigated perimeters, and reforestation. As a result of these meetings, donor commitments were made with respect to several programs and projects. Each of the programs includes a number of operations, or parts thereof, which involve scientific and technical research. For example, the regional project for rehabilitating irrigated perimeters includes not only restoring or improving existing irrigation systems, but also working out pilot irrigation projects which will help in developing a new production system. Likewise, the reforestation program includes a number of studies on wooded and grazing areas for improving soil knowledge.

It may be interesting to dwell a little longer on the crop and harvest protection program, which is an important item in the strategy proposed by the Club. Any scheme of protection must include planning and implementation activities at the regional level. The enemies of crops and harvests cannot be controlled in one country if they are left uncontrolled in neighboring countries. Control would soon become very difficult if not totally ineffective.

One of the first meetings with the financing institutions was devoted to this problem. The meeting adopted a program of action which is both multibeneficiary, since it involves all the Sahelian countries, and multidonor, since it involves several OECD countries, namely, the United States, Canada, France, the Federal Republic of Germany, and the United Kingdom, as well as such international organizations as the FAO and the United Nations Development Programme (UNDP).

The new integrated pest control program will include all methods of control: chemical control, crop-farming techniques, development of immune varieties, biological control, etc. In the first stage, chemical control methods will be the only methods used for protecting crops. Chemical control is the only technique that is operational in the short term, although implementing it is bound to have some adverse effects on the environment despite all precautions. But the program will also include considerable research on diversifying the methods of protection, making them more effective at lower cost, and reducing their harmful effects. Special attention will be given to the development of techniques for biological control over the long term.

Here, then, is a practical example of undertaking scientific research for a definite purpose, with the assistance of various disciplines, such as entomology and plant pathology, and applying the knowledge internationally to benefit the Sahel with the participation of the Sahelians themselves.

Humanity increasingly will have to depend on renewable resources derived from the biosphere it shares with plants, animals, and microbes. While the exploitation of domesticated plants and animals has been successfully practiced since time immemorial, it was only one hundred years ago that we started to learn how to exploit beneficial microbes and how to defend ourselves against pathogenic microbes.

The "domestication" of microbes requires more skill than the domestication of plants and animals, but its benefits are no less. At the moment these are reaped chiefly by the developed countries of the world. Most developing countries have not yet reached the stage where they can take full advantage of this important biological research. Out of the 100,000 microbiologists now living, only a small percentage are found in the Third World. This is particularly tragic because applied microbiology is eminently suited to making important contributions to the fulfillment of basic human needs in developing countries.

The UNESCO/UNEP/ICRO Program

UNESCO, the United Nations Environment Programme (UNEP), and the International Cell Research Organization (ICRO) — a non-governmental organization — have recognized how useful applied microbiology could be in the developing countries. This recognition has led them to forge a joint program whose aims are to help advance the growth of applied microbiology in the scientific infrastructure of the developing countries and to promote development-oriented research activities in the technically advanced countries.

The UNESCO/UNEP/ICRO microbiology program seems an appropriate practical model to study in the context of mobilizing technology for world development because:

(a) It involves the initiation and development of technologies ranging in scale from household to industrial, with emphasis on low-cost, low-energy technologies that are within the economic and technological capabilities of the developing countries. It makes a special effort to stimulate rural self-reliance;

Chapter 18

Microbiological Science for Development: A Global Technological Opportunity

Carl-Göran Héden

(b) The guidelines followed by the program, developed from practical experience in the field, are in harmony with the principles formulated in the New International Economic Order (NIEO);

(c) The program directly impinges on both scientific and technological infrastructures in a wide range of disciplines as a consequence of the strong interdisciplinary character of microbiology;

(d) The program's subject matter is restricted to a well-defined area of applied biology in which an obvious backlog exists in developing countries.

The Rationale of the Program

Bacteria, fungi, protozoa, algae, and viruses are all microbes, that is, microorganisms a few thousandths of a millimeter in size. Yet their total biomass is estimated to be of the same order of magnitude as that of plants and animals. Much of the activity of microbes is essential or beneficial to human life, but some of it is detrimental. Microbes are the oldest living organisms on earth and may be considered the ancestors of all other forms of life. Because of their special qualities, microbes play an important role in shaping the biosphere and man's place in it. Microbes are the main "pumps" in the cycles of carbon, nitrogen, oxygen, and sulfur, and are thus responsible for the steady-state composition of the atmosphere. For instance, 30 to 50 per cent of all carbon dioxide converted into organic matter is consumed by photosynthetic microbes (in plankton) in the oceans, and some 90 per cent of the carbon dioxide brought into the atmosphere is produced by microbes during the degradation of organic matter. If the latter process ever came to a standstill, the carbon dioxide content of the atmosphere would drop to zero within a century and plants would no longer be able to grow. Thus, microbes are at the root of marine productivity and, at the same time, the main agents responsible for the

*Excerpted in revised form from "The UNEP/UNESCO/ICRO Programme on Applied Microbiology: A Case Study in Transfer of Science and Technology." Contributed to the U.N. Conference on Science and Technology for Development by the UNEP/UNESCO/ICRO Panel on Microbiology, submitted by the International Cell Research Organization, October 1978.

natural decomposition of wastes. The technology of waste treatment, in fact, is essentially based on an intensification of this natural process by technical means; sewage treatment is the largest microbiological industry in the world. Another example is found in the symbiotic and non-symbiotic microbial fixation of atmospheric nitrogen, which is counterbalanced by microbial denitrification leading to the loss of fixed nitrogen from soil and water to the atmosphere. These parts of the nitrogen cycle are of primary importance for soil fertility.

Beneficial microbes have been used unknowingly for centuries in many traditional processes in which food is preserved or altered in quality by judicious, semi-controlled microbial action, as in the making of wine, vinegar, sauerkraut, cheese, and acid milk products. Many of these processes have been rationalized by the use of pure cultures or mixtures of selected strains, resulting in the production of an essential part of human food intake, which varies in different regions of the world. Microbes even play an important role in the production of meat, since herbivores depend on microbial activity in the rumen for the conversion of cellulose into essential nutrients. In the developing countries in particular, however, many traditional fermentation processes are still being practiced without the benefit of full scientific control and hence are still subject to becoming health hazards and causing unnecessary losses in nutritional value.

The importance of microbes in food production has gradually become dwarfed by the rapid growth of the so-called fermentation industry, which over the past five years has successfully embarked on the production of such diverse products as alcohols, organic acids and ketones, amino acids, vitamins, drugs, antibiotics, vaccines, enzymes, and fodder protein (single cell protein). In Japan, for instance, this industry is now responsible for 6 per cent of the nation's income. An important characteristic of the industry is that it consumes agricultural by-products which, if unused, would qualify as waste materials. The rising prices of non-microbial protein and of oil are now making the industry even more important. Meanwhile, we have also learned that microbes can be used in the control of disease in man, plants, or animals. Generally, mass-produced microbial pathogens for the parasite or the disease vector are introduced at strategic points. The environmental advantages of biological over chemical pest control are well known.

One of the major factors limiting food production, and often the chief factor, is the absence of nitrogen. In developing countries where the water supply is adequate, it is often the amount of nitrogen available to higher plants that determines the amount of food that can be produced. In many of the arid regions, lack of nitrogen is second only to lack of water as the main reason why crop yields are low. This deficiency of nitrogen is evident in all major food and feed crops of the globe, except for legumes.

In the technologically advanced countries, much of the plant need for nitrogen is supplied by fertilizers. Fertilizer nitrogen is synthesized by the chemical industry, and the relative cost of the fertilizer is low in comparison with the value of the food to the human population. In most of the developing countries, on the other hand, the relative cost of fertilizers is quite high, making it too expensive for small farmers. In many regions fertilizer is totally unavailable or the roads are inadequate for transporting it.

Microorganisms have a unique role in the nitrogen nutrition of plants. The reason is that some of these organisms carry out essentially the same function as the chemical industry, namely, taking nitrogen from the atmosphere (where it is unavailable to higher plants) and converting it to a usable form. This the microorganisms of soils do at no cost to the farmer and with very little need for environmental manipulation.

In some instances, the addition of selected strains of the nitrogen-fixing genus *Rhizobium* to soils or seeds can replace industrially produced nitrogenous fertilizer. Promoting the growth of nitrogen-fixing algae can achieve similar ends in rice fields. Actions like these provide important savings in energy and industrial investment and at the same time reduce the pollution of water with nitrogen compounds that contribute to eutrophication and disease.

Microorganisms are gaining increased recognition as alternatives to chemical pesticides. Most pest species have natural enemies within the microbial world, and it is known that the activities of microbial pathogens, parasites, and predators can be directed against agricultural pests and thus increase the production of both food and fiber. Microbial agents of biological control are a welcome addition to the arsenal of weapons in our war against pests, and they are used increasingly in integrated programs of control to alleviate disease and hunger in the world.

Although waste treatment is now essentially protective in character, the more positive approach of recycling wastes is receiving increased attention. Especially in the developing countries, existing processes like sewage farming and fish culture in waste ponds should be optimized and made hygienically safe. The use of wastes in the aquaculture of desirable algae or plants is being explored and exploited, and the following list of waste treatment processes which employ microorganisms to yield products of potential value is far from exhaustive: the production of fodder yeast on spent liquor from paper manufacture by the sulfite-pulping process; the production of "wheast," a nutritious food substance formed when lactose-utilizing microorganisms are grown on whey, a waste resulting from cheese manufacture; mushroom production on rice straw or compost; methane fuel formed by anaerobic digestion of animal manure or plant residues; and microbiological processing of cellulosic and starch wastes to enhance their nitrogen content and hence their value as human and animal feed.

The versatility of microbes is clearly demonstrated by their applicability in the mining of ores of several metals. Mineral deposits and slag that cannot be economically exploited by conventional mining and chemical methods can sometimes be profitably extracted by microbial treatment. Acid production by specific types of microorganisms has facilitated the mining of low-grade ores of copper, zinc, and uranium, and microorganisms have assisted in the reclamation of oil from shale. Yeast has been used to remove undesired wastes from petroleum by a process which not only increases the commercial value of the fuel but also produces single-cell protein for animal feed.

In the present context, no justice can be done to the vital role microbes play in the development of biochemistry, molecular biology, and genetics. Their small size and rapid multiplication, coupled with the fact that the entire living world possesses a basic unity, has made microbes rewarding tools for research in these areas. It is conceivable that microbes will also turn out to be useful organisms for laboratory studies of fundamental ecology.

The current public concern with limitations on the world supply of fossil fuels poses challenging possibilities for the creation of renewable sources of non-polluting energy by microbiological methods. The capacity of microorganisms to produce bio-gas, hydrogen, and methane has attracted particular attention, and several procedures have been developed for the formation of these substances from waste materials. Sewage grown on "energy farms" can produce ethanol obtained from sugar by fermentation.

It should be added that the various uses of beneficial organisms are far from exhausted. Many new developments can be expected in the next decade as a result of genetic strain improvement by the use of immobilized enzyme technology and other imminent scientific and technological breakthroughs.

Harmful microbes manifest themselves most clearly in infectious human diseases. Protective action has been most successful where an understanding of the principles of infection is prevalent in the population and is combined with curative and preventive medical treatment. Many diseases under control in the advanced countries are still rampant in the developing regions of the world. This was strikingly illustrated at the 22nd World Health Organization Assembly, where the delegate of one Asian government stated that waterborne diseases accounted for 60 per cent of all morbidity and 40 per cent of all mortality in his country. He estimated that 90 per cent of the rural population (and 72 per cent of the total population) suffered from intestinal parasitic infections and that less than 10 per cent of the total population had access to piped water supplies.

Microbial diseases in plants and animals have called forth defensive management in agricultural and animal farming, the outcome of which has a great impact on the precarious food situation in many parts of the world. Certain foods may contain pathogenic microbes or toxins of microbial origin even though their nutritional value has remained unimpaired. Salmonellae in meat or fish meal, and aflatoxins in peanuts, are examples. Developing countries that lack the microbiological expertise to prevent such contamination therefore cannot export such foods, since they do not meet health standards.

Besides pathogenic microbes, many other microbes can spoil foods and other valuable materials, ranging from wood to stone monuments. Food spoilage deprives the world's population of a large percentage of the world's harvest, and microbial corrosion and other forms of biodegradation cause annual losses in the millions of dollars.

Knowledge of spoilage mechanisms and preventive action by canning, refrigeration, and other forms of preservation, as well as chemical protection, has reached a high degree of effectiveness in the developed world, however.

In short, the microbial segment of the biosphere is of vital significance for human survival. This state of affairs calls for a variety of responses: (a) protective action to safeguard the proper global functioning of the biogeochemical cycles; (b) defensive action to combat harmful microbes; and (c) intensive exploitation of microbial resources for food and fodder production, energy, waste recycling, biological nitrogen fixation, and other purposes.

The domestication of the microbe has developed relatively recently and is far from complete, even in the developed countries. In contrast to the domestication of plants and animals, that of microbes requires some basic general education combined with specialized skills not readily transferred by the social mechanisms found in agricultural tradition. Successful handling of microbial strains, or even recognizing them for what they are, requires much more knowledge than growing a crop or raising cattle.

It is therefore not surprising that the developing nations of the world thus far have not fully profited from the microbial resources at their disposal. Through lack of basic education, expertise, and appropriate microbial strains, they are foregoing benefits that are available to the developed world while they remain exposed to the environmental hazards of harmful microbes, which, for their people, are still as mystifying, erratic, and deadly as they were for the whole world a hundred years ago. Since microbiological problems and the expertise to solve them are unevenly distributed around the world, developing countries can derive great benefits from the transfer and application of existing knowledge. Developed as well as developing countries may expect to gain much from future developments in basic and applied microbiology. It is, therefore, imperative that mechanisms be created to provide developing countries with locally useful strains of microorganisms and with adequate training and research facilities for using them.

Areas of Activity

The UNESCO/UNEP/ICRO program addresses itself to the following main subject areas:

(a) Registration and preservation of the microbial genetic resources of the world and making them available to developing countries.

(b) The application of microbiological nitrogen fixation (Rhizobium, blue-green algae) so as to reduce the requirements for chemical nitrogenous fertilizers. The use of commercial fertilizer promotes eutrophication, and their manufacture requires large amounts of energy. Many countries have to import fertilizers, which requires increasing amounts of foreign currency.

(c) Microbiological methods for the production of food and fodder, including single cell protein as well as indigenous fermented foods.

Food preservation and methods to counteract postharvest microbiological food spoilage.

(d) Use of microbes in management of the environment. Water and
waste-water purification. Waste utilization and recycling, including
bio-gas production and upgrading of cellulose waste by protein en-
richment for use as fodder.

(e) Microbiological aspects of health problems in man, plants, and
animals occurring as a corollary to microbial waste utilization and
food production and the microbiological control of pests and vectors.

(f) The use of bio-technology for the full exploitation of available
renewable resources at appropriate scales, ranging from the household and village levels to the industrial level and geared to the
promotion of self-reliance in the areas of food, fodder, fuel, and fertilizer, especially in rural areas. Application of appropriate technology and simple diagnostic and measuring equipment (field kits).

(g) Training of manpower and strengthening of infrastructures for
research and for dissemination of applicable results on a national and
regional basis. Promotion of microbiological societies and two-way
interaction with international non-governmental organizations.
Stimulation of the interest of decisionmakers and the public at large.

(h) Promotion of the participation of developing countries in international programs focused on global environmental problems in
which microbes play an important role, such as the safeguarding of
the biogeochemical cycles; for such programs, data from developing
countries are required. Due recognition is given to the different
priorities that developed and developing countries can give to such
projects.

(i) Creation of an awareness of the positive and negative impacts
that can be anticipated from scientific breakthroughs in microbiology
(e.g., enzyme engineering, genetic engineering).

Methods of the Program

While UNESCO and UNEP provide the program official status,
organizational expertise, administrative facilities, and basic funding,
the ICRO provides scientific guidance–through a Microbiology Panel
whose members are selected for scientific competence and willingness to cooperate actively without remuneration. Rotation ensures
both continuity and "rejuvenation," and an increasing number of the
panel's members are being drawn from the developing countries. The
most important instruments used in the execution of the program are
surveys, conferences, training courses, Microbiological Resources
Centers (MIRCENs), and coordination activities.

Surveys are conducted to provide an insight into the status of
applied microbiology in different geographical regions and also serve
to identify persons and organizations capable of serving as focal
points for program activities. The Panel now possesses a useful data
base for future policies as well as the means to obtain more specific
information when required.

Conferences on Global Impacts of Applied Microbiology (GIAM) have an important function in the program. Participants from developed countries (a minority) join their colleagues from the developing countries in discussing a broad spectrum of topics of direct interest to the region in plenary and specialized sessions. Satellite events range from travelling seminars to training courses, and special symposiums dealing in depth with topics of regional significance (e.g., nitrogen fixation, indigenous fermented foods) often are added to the program. In many cases, microbiologists from a specific region meet one another for the first time during a GIAM conference, thus promoting future cooperation on relevant regional needs.

About thirty training courses involving over 500 trainees have been held in Asia, Africa, and Latin America on subjects involving the major areas of activity. The teaching faculty consists of a few foreign experts who assist in the preparatory work and as many local and regional experts as possible. The study program includes lectures, bench work in the laboratory, evening seminars, and field trips. Additional activities now under consideration are special refresher courses, technician training, and expansion of the existing small fellowship program in conjunction with the MIRCENs.

In 1976-1977 a pilot project was started involving two MIRCENs specializing in nitrogen fixation (Porto Alegre; Nairobi), two MIR-CENs specializing in the collection, preservation, and maintenance of cultures (Bangkok; Cairo), and two auxiliary MIRCENs (Stockholm; Brisbane). These institutes were selected because they were both capable and willing to expand their activities to fulfill an additional regional function with regard to training, research, preservation of cultures of economic importance and, most important, dissemination of cultures and information on how to use them. Some of these MIRCENs have become operational and have engaged in preparing regional catalogues of cultures, directories of institutes, and newsletters. They will become focal points for future training activities of the program.

The Brisbane MIRCEN comprises the World Data Center on Microbial Genetic Resources and has special centralized functions, both receiving and disseminating data on all available microbial cultures in the world and assisting in the identification of new isolates. The Stockholm MIRCEN, housed in the Karolinska Institute, provides training support and technical assistance, specializing in the design of simple diagnostic equipment that can be made in the developing countries.

The program has helped promote the formation of regional networks for cooperative research by bringing together scientists who were previously unaware of each other's activities. In addition, numerous personal ties have been forged between scientists from developing and from developed countries, to the benefit of both. The program is expected to make the universities and governments of the developing countries more aware of the importance of applied microbiology which, especially in developing countries, does not receive the priority its potential benefits warrant.

IIED   About the International Institute for Environment and Development

The International Institute for Environment and Development (IIED) is a non-profit corporation, with offices in London and Washington, which works with the United Nations and other international institutions as well as national governments and non-governmental organizations. Currently, IIED is especially concerned with the worldwide issues of energy, shelter, and water; the resources and environment of Antarctica; the environmental consequences of major aid programs; and the use of science and technology for development. Robert Anderson and Sir John Foster are Co-Chairmen of the Board of Directors and Barbara Ward (Lady Jackson) the President of IIED.

IIED's Energy Program is a two-year study designed to assess how vigorous promotion of energy conservation and the use of renewable resources can affect an industrial nation's future needs for fossil fuels. Although the program has tended to concentrate on the energy policies of the developed countries, especially the United Kingdom, IIED has also initiated a study of the role of international institutions and bilateral aid programs in encouraging research and development of renewable energy resources in the Third World.

The objectives of IIED's Marine Program are to research and promote resource management regimes for the Atlantic continent and the Southern Oceans and to serve as an NGO information center in London monitoring the work of the Inter-Governmental Maritime Consultative Organization (IMCO).

The work of the IIED Assessment Program team is intended to assist both the United Nations Environment Programme (UNEP) and member governments in evaluating progress toward the objective of improved environmental monitoring in the course of development. The information gathered also provides international development financing agencies with an external, comparative view of their environmental efforts.

In addition, IIED operates a media information unit called *Earthscan* to increase public awareness of global environment/development issues through an editorially independent information program aimed at reaching leading media around the world.

The convening of symposia to help clearly define issues and identify priorities for major United Nations conferences on global issues has been an important IIED activity since 1974. In addition to the Jamaica Symposium on Mobilizing Technology for Development held in January 1979 as a contribution to the U.N. Conference on Science and Technology for Development (UNCSTD), IIED also organized such meetings prior to the U.N. Water Conference (1976), the U.N. Conference on Human

Settlements (1976), and the World Food Conference (1974). The results of these symposia have made important substantive contributions and have served as a useful bellwether for the world conferences whose objectives they were designed to support.

IIED Board of Directors

Co-Chairman: Robert O. Anderson
Co-Chairman: Sir John Foster

Abdlatif Y. Al-Hamad
Henrik Beer
Antonio Carrillo Flores
Barbara Ward (Lady Jackson)
Aklilu Lemma
Ian MacGregor

E. M. Nicholson
Saburo Okita
Aurelio Peccei
Enrique Peñalosa
Otto Soemarwoto
Maurice F. Strong

Council

Harrison Brown
Gerardo Budowski
Carlos Chagas
Khun Pradisth Cheosakul
Rajeshwar Dayal
Robert K. A. Gardiner
Christian Halby
Felipe Herrera
Roy Jenkins
Robert S. McNamara
Arvid Pardo

Raúl Prebisch
Jack Raymond
Benito F. Reyes
Chung Hyun Ro
Walter Orr Roberts
James Rouse
Joseph E. Slater
Soedjatmoko
Victor L. Urquidi
Lord Zuckerman

IIED North American Office
Suite 501, 1302 Eighteenth St., N.W.
Washington, D.C. 20036
(202) 462-0900

IIED European Office
10 Percy Street
London W1P 0DR
01-580 7656-7

About the Overseas Development Council

The Overseas Development Council is an independent, non-profit organization established in 1969 to increase American understanding of the economic and social problems confronting the developing countries, and of the importance of these countries to the United States in an increasingly interdependent world. The ODC seeks to promote consideration of development issues by the American public, policymakers, specialists, educators, and the media through its research, conferences, publications, and liaison with U.S. mass membership organizations interested in U.S. relations with the developing world. The ODC's program is funded by foundations, corporations, and private individuals; its policies are determined by its Board of Directors. Theodore M. Hesburgh, C.S.C., is Chairman of the Board, and Edward J. Schlegel is its Vice Chairman. The Council's President is James P. Grant.

Prominent emphases in the Council's current work program include: (a) analysis of the implications of the increasing *interdependence* of economic growth (or stagnation) in the industrialized and developing countries; (b) assessment of the costs and benefits for all countries of the major proposals for a New International Economic Order being debated in the North-South dialogue; (c) identification of improved ways to achieve Third World population and health goals, including analysis of how development can affect health and fertility; (d) continued study of alternative development strategies that seek to combine economic growth and meeting basic needs while also emphasizing local values, initiatives, and participation; (e) refinement of the Council's new measurement tools—the Physical Quality of Life Index (PQLI) and the Disparity Reduction Rate (DRR)—to complement the use of GNP growth and other indicators in measuring development achievement; and (f) analysis of relations between the United States and Mexico as a concrete example of how emerging forms of global interdependence affect traditional bilateral economic and political issues.

Three aspects of the ODC's recent and ongoing program of work relate closely to the objective of "mobilizing technology for development":

In a recent ODC book, *The Uncertain Promise: Value Conflicts in Technology Transfer*, Denis Goulet demonstrates, with case-study illustrations, how confusion over basic values and social priorities often leads to the uncritical purchase of technologies that may ultimately prove inappropriate and even *counter* to genuine development. The study shows, however, how developing countries *can* manage technology well—and in a few cases are beginning to do so—by constructing a "vital nexus" linking their basic value options, their development strategies, and their technology policy.

ODC's work in the area of "energy for development" began five years ago with its publication, in its annual assessment of U.S.-Third World relations, of an analysis of the impact of the 1973-74 oil price rise on the developing countries. ODC's work on energy and the developing countries presently includes six ongoing activities: (1) exploration of U.S.-Third World mutual interests in energy R&D and in improvements in the organization of the international community to deal with the global energy problem; (2) analysis of U.S. objectives in the field of energy as they relate to the Third World, and of how the achievement of those objectives interacts with the achievement of Third World development; (3) encouragement of dialogue between experts and policymakers in the South and North on Third World energy problems and views; (4) analysis of the potential of small-scale renewable energy for the rural areas and urban slums of Third World nations (including setting up a method for testing the most promising equipment in village sites); (5) policy analysis of specific Third World energy problems (usually at the request of policymakers in the U.S. Government, the World Bank, or other public bodies); and (6) generation of basic data about energy in the Third World, with particular emphasis on energy use, needs, and sources in rural areas.

In the area of food policy issues, ODC's work emphasizes the need for cooperative international approaches to managing the world food problem. ODC's studies and other activities in this area seek to focus government and public attention on the causes of hunger; on linkages between U.S. and foreign food production; and on the needs for international cooperation to increase food production in the developing countries, for more effective and equitable food distribution, for a global food reserve, and for a better food aid program.

A more detailed description of the Council's program and a list of its publications are available on request.

Overseas Development Council
1717 Massachusetts Avenue, N.W.
Washington, D.C. 20036
(202) 234-8701

ODC Board of Directors

Chairman: Theodore M. Hesburgh, C.S.C.
Vice Chairman: Edward J. Schlegel
Chairman, Administrative Committee: Davidson Sommers

Robert O. Anderson
William Attwood
* Marguerite Ross Barnett
Edward G. Biester, Jr.
Eugene R. Black
Harrison Brown
Lester R. Brown
Ronald B. Brown
Robert S. Browne
* Carleton D. Burtt
Wallace Campbell
Thomas P. Carney
Lisle C. Carter, Jr.
Kathryn Christopherson
Harlan Cleveland
Frank M. Coffin
Owen Cooper
Richard H. Demuth
Charles S. Dennison
John Diebold
* Thomas L. Farmer
Clarence Ferguson, Jr.
* Roger Fisher
* Albert Fishlow
Luther H. Foster
* J. Wayne Fredericks
* Orville L. Freeman
* Lester E. Gordon
* Lincoln Gordon
** James P. Grant
* Edward K. Hamilton
Arnold C. Harberger
* Susan Herter
** Theodore M. Hesburgh, C.S.C.
* Ruth J. Hinerfeld
Vernon E. Jordan
Nicholas deB. Katzenbach

Tom Killefer
* J. Burke Knapp
Peter F. Krogh
* Anne O. Krueger
* William J. Lawless
Walter J. Levy
David E. Lilienthal
* C. Payne Lucas
Harald B. Malmgren
Edwin M. Martin
Edward S. Mason
C. Peter McColough
* Lawrence C. McQuade
John Mellor
* Alfred F. Miossi
Thomas A. Murphy
* Randolph Nugent
William S. Ogden
F. Taylor Ostrander
Daniel S. Parker
James A. Perkins
John Petty
Samuel D. Proctor
* Charles W. Robinson
* William D. Rogers
Bruce W. Rohrbacher
Janeth R. Rosenblum
** Edward J. Schlegel
David H. Shepard
Eugene Skolnikoff
* Davidson Sommers
* Stephen Stamas
* C. M. van Vlierden
Clifton R. Wharton, Jr.
Charles W. Yost
* Barry Zorthian

*Member of Executive Committee
**Ex Officio Member of Executive Committee